Penguin Handbooks

The Pauper's Homemaking Boo

Jocasta Innes was born in Nanking, China, and by the age of twelve had visited every continent in the world. She was chiefly educated at Bedford High School and at Girton College, Cambridge. For some years she worked as a feature writer on the *Evening Standard*. Now married to novelist Joe Potts, she lives in Swanage, Dorset, and has three children, two by a previous marriage. She has always taken a greedy interest in food, and learned to cook in a hit-or-miss fashion from books, starting with the tricky stuff and working backwards to the point where sensible people begin. She reckons that she graduated to serious or creative cooking in the last five years, and finds being hard-up a genuine stimulus and challenge where cooking is concerned: more work, perhaps, but infinitely greater satisfaction. Her previous literary work mainly consists of translations from French and Spanish and *The Pauper's Cookbook* (Penguin, 1971). Her other interests are painting, swimming and collecting junk.

JOCASTA INNES

The Pauper's Homemaking Book

Illustrated by Rosemary Grimble
Photographs by Mike Wall

PENGUIN BOOKS

Penguin Books Ltd,
Harmondsworth, Middlesex, England
Penguin Books,
625 Madison Avenue, New York, New York 10022, U.S.A.
Penguin Books Australia Ltd,
Ringwood, Victoria, Australia
Penguin Books Canada Ltd,
2801 John Street, Markham, Ontario, Canada L3R 1B4
Penguin Books (N.Z.) Ltd,
182–190 Wairau Road, Auckland 10, New Zealand

Published in Penguin Books 1976
Reprinted 1977, 1978

Made and printed in Great Britain by
Cox & Wyman Ltd, London, Reading and Fakenham
Set in Monotype Bembo

Contents

6 CONTENTS

Acknowledgements

Looking back on the preparation of this book I marvel at the forbearance shown by so many kind people – family, friends, total strangers – who came within range of my D.I.Y. zealotry. They answered questions, gave advice, made suggestions and, most helpful of all, listened endlessly.

First, I would particularly like to thank Lesley Wright, whose resourcefulness, enthusiasm and grasp of detail made her an invaluable assistant. How many assistants would cross-stitch two yards of rug canvas in the last stages of pregnancy? For the sheer plod of this achievement, no less than her lucid drawings and painstaking research, Lesley gets my special citation. So, too, does Rosemary Grimble, who had the long and taxing job of converting my rough scribbles into her clear and elegant illustrations. Not to mention Jill Norman, whose editorial pencil slices through muddle and trims off twaddle with such exhilarating accuracy one forgets to scream till it's all over.

My sister, Judy Astor, was immensely generous with suggestions and information and I am very grateful to her, as I am to my mother and the many friends – Bronwen Cunningham, Betty Toker, Betty Bolton, Sarah Letts, Sal Wilkinson, Christine Goodwin – who allowed me to pick their brains. Special thanks to Joe who sat it out like a man and managed to look interested most of the time. And finally, my apologies to any painters I may have offended by ranting on about their frames to the extent of forgetting to mention their pictures.

Introduction

I had a lot of trouble thinking up a title for this book. The pauper bit went without saying because doing things on the cheap, or oeconomy, as Samuel Johnson called it, is something I know about. In this book I wanted to pursue that theme out of the kitchen and into the rest of the house. But I needed another word which would convey, simultaneously, the notions of usefulness and enjoyment. Oddly, considering what a nation of craftsmen we once were and that the pleasure of making something useful is at the root of craftsmanship, no such word seems to exist in the language. It is as though practical undertakings must be grim, and pleasurable ones quite useless. Then someone suggested 'homemaking'. In the end I settled for that, although the admen have squeezed most of the life out of it, because it does come closest to suggesting what this book is chiefly about – the pleasure to be found in creating, with the cheapest of materials and tools, that necessary, comforting ambience we call 'home'.

When you think about it, what makes a house – or bedsit, or garret, or modern semi-, or flint cottage – a home is not so obvious. Comfort and prettiness aren't all of it, although they certainly help. Money alone can't do it, in fact it often gets in the way. I've been into moneyed houses, filled with beautiful pictures and furniture, and decorated with great care and taste by the best decorators, which lacked nothing but this one quality of homeliness to bring them alive. They were like stage sets waiting, beautiful and static, for the play to begin. What makes you know you have entered a home, I think, is a sense of relatedness between the actual place and the objects in it and the person, or people, who live there and put them there. In an artist's home – almost all painters' homes are fascinating for this reason – it is the evidence of a strongly idiosyncratic taste that hits you. In a pauperish home – some of the homeliest places I know belong to people with the least money – it is perhaps the resourcefulness of it all. You know, without being told, that things have their story. A pair of beautiful eighteenth-century chairs a rich couple acquire as wedding presents are beautiful, but just chairs. But the chair discovered on a rubbish dump, carried home in triumph, stripped, mended, painted and re-covered, perhaps finding an old letter or coin down the back of the seat, is not just a chair, or a thing, it's a character with a history, part of the owner's private mythology. It is this, much more than Magistretti chairs and buttoned leather Chesterfields, that makes a home, and a hard-up couple who have to scour junkyards for their furniture, sit up half the night making curtains, and do every blessed thing in the place themselves, are well placed to find it.

My readers, as I see them, have passed the stage of flitting from pad to pad. They are setting up house in earnest. They want to create an environment for themselves that is cheerful, comfortable and a bit different. They have lots of ideas and energy, and – after paying out mortgage or rent, and gas, electricity and phone bills – almost no cash. Almost *no* cash, I repeat, because most books purporting to give advice on how to set up house from scratch (written by well-paid journalists) seem to forget what this means in real terms. It means sleeping on a mattress on bare boards because all your savings have gone on making one room presentable to show your friends and relations into. Or agonizing about whether you can afford to hire trestles after you have paid for the paint and brushes. If you are in this position, as I know, it is infuriating to read, in a supposedly budget-minded book, that hessian wall covering is the best choice for the hall and staircase because it doesn't show fingermarks. Perhaps not, but it costs the earth. And while it is useful to know that curtain lining material makes cheap, pretty curtains, one is not grateful for a photograph showing a pair clearly run up by an interior decorating firm, with elaborate scalloped pelmets, printed floral borders and forty yards of material, as an example of what an enterprising girl can do. What you do want to know is the *most*, not the least, that can be done with limited resources – limited as to tools, equipment and space as well as cash; the *most*, because you already know all about the uplift value of scatter cushions, posters and white emulsion and want to experiment with something more exciting, like dragged paint, antiquing or stencils.

In planning the book, I've tried to anticipate – leaning on my own experience – the urgent needs as well as exciting possibilities facing the hard-up homemaker. How to get hold of cheap dining-chairs, odd tables, how to revamp old sofas, make curtains, what to do about the stairs, how to re-lay secondhand carpet. Basic stuff like this comes at the start of the book in that section called Getting it Together. I have explained any technical points in some detail, not because I think my readers are morons but because nothing is simple till you have done it a few times, and it is unfair to suggest that interlining curtains, or piping seat cushions, is plain sailing from beginning to end. Any ideas on the carpentry side, incidentally, are deliberately simple, even elementary, because my readers probably haven't got power tools or a workbench, or the experience necessary for dovetailing, pegging and the other tricky techniques that go into building a solid piece of furniture. Except for the carved toys, the carpentry ideas are ones I can cope with myself, with no experience of anything more complicated in that line than putting up a shelf.

Having, I hope, helped with the pressing needs, we move on, in the section called Putting on the Style, to the more stimulating possibilities of colour and paint in transforming junk furniture, lamps, and picture frames. Paint is cheap stuff but it can be used in very classy ways. Going by my own experience, I thought readers would like to know about relatively esoteric uses like dragging, glazing, bambooing, marbling. There is a whole section, with illustrations of motifs to start you off, on folk-art decorating as well as the more formal style of furniture-painting derived from eighteenth-century designers like Robert Adam. An attractively painted, bamboo-decorated bedroom chair would cost at least £40–£50 from an interior decorator. But you can find a pretty chair, with the caning gone, for £2, re-cane it for 60p, and paint and bamboo it yourself for, at most, another 60p. The invisible factor in comparing these costs, of course, is your time, which is free and you must be prepared to give generously. Invariably, where you can't spend much cash, you have to spend more time – looking for things, planning how to do them, doing them. But don't imagine that time plods by, every minute begrudged. At worst, making and doing things is satisfying in a monotonous sort of way, at best it's a little creative explosion, involving mind, hand and eye so closely and excitingly you can scarcely tear yourself away to eat, or sleep.

There is a whole, long section on wood finishing – from the basic stripping down of the old finish to various ways of beautifying the piece which turned out to be dreary beech, not figured pine. Bleaching, pickling, dyeing, driftwooding, even gilding – experimenting with these techniques is fun and useful, whether you are trying to put a good finish on blockboard cupboard doors, or revamping a hideous, but solidly made, oak office desk. Even if you settle for polyurethane sealer, it's useful to know that wire-wooling it between coats, and finishing with wax, gets rid of that tacky shine and makes the seal last twice as long.

The day will come when your place is more or less the way you want it – usually less than more, but that's how it should be, a home should evolve with you – and there is time to spare for making pretty things, for yourself, for the house, to give away as presents, even to sell if you are well organized and stumble on a marketable idea. The last section of the book, called Pretty Things, is given over to suggestions for pleasantly improving the shining hour; some on the practical side, like advice on remodelling old fur coats or sewing leather; some pure, self-indulgent pottering about, like punching tin or making silhouette pictures of yourselves and your friends. All the materials are cheap, but the things can be as beautiful as your taste and skill can make them. Half the pretty knick-knacks dealers chase after and eager tourists pay through the nose for, were made in leisure moments a century or so ago by people like us. As machines take over from men in the production of almost everything we consume and use, there is a keen and understandable nostalgia for the hand-made thing, with all the little irregularities and imperfections of something shaped, painted or stitched by those non-precision tools, the human hands. Unlike most factory-made articles which begin to die a little the moment you use them – think of cosmetic containers – a hand-made thing improves with time and handling. True, colours fade, finishes wear off slowly, stitches break, but in some mysterious way this only adds to their charm. As D. H. Lawrence said, in one of his poems, things men have made with wakened hands, and put soft life into . . . go on glowing for long years.

You will make some mistakes, bound to, but they won't cost much. One's first attempts, whether it's painting roses on a blanket box or making a silk tassel, usually look clumsy in retrospect, but at the time they fill one with astonishment – did *I* do that? And all the time you are *learning* – about colour, texture, design, learning to respect the skills of the craftsman so unerring he made it look easy, learning about yourself too, testing out abilities and skills you may not know you possessed. Learning by doing is the best way there is. Everyone is a maker in some degree, look at small children, pounding plasticine, splashing colours about. The pity is so many people cork up the discoverer and maker in themselves about the time they grow out of model gliders and dolls. Maybe the world didn't lose a Cellini or a William Morris, but surely they lose touch with one of life's essential pleasures.

TOOLS AND EQUIPMENT

In writing this book I have had in mind people like myself, who cannot afford the gleaming panoply of tools most do-it-yourself manuals seem to think necessary, or the space to store them. So, no work bench, no power drill or sander and no question, often, of the right tool for the job. However, a skeleton range of tools is necessary and I shall mention here the ones I have found most useful and versatile while working on this book. Buy them as you need them. Don't neglect sources of secondhand tools – salerooms, junk shops – which are often of better quality than cheap replacements. I bought an old tool-box in a very miscellaneous lot at an auction, which paid for itself several times over in pliers, hammers, assorted paint brushes, jars of brass screws, even a bag full of tubes of artists' oil colours.

SEWING MACHINE. Mainstay of any pauper's equipment. If some rich aunt gave you a bang up-to-date swing needle model as a wedding present, you are laughing. Otherwise get a secondhand one. Singer and Jones are reliable makes, but there are many others. Mine is an ancient Jones, a heavy and very strong piece of machinery designed for use in schools. I am devoted to it. Despite its clumsy appearance, and Heath Robinson conversion to electricity – yards of flex and an iron pedal – it tackles the thickest cloth, even leather, as gallantly as an old mule, never breaks down and sews a good plain even stitch. You should be able to get a hand-operated machine in good working order for around £5–£7. Electrified models cost a bit more. Try a machine out before parting with your cash. Check the wiring on electrified models – frayed flex should be replaced, especially with small children crawling about. If you can afford it, have the machine re-serviced, or get hold of a do-it-yourself book which explains how sewing machines work, and clean and oil the parts yourself. For spare parts, make friends with someone who deals in secondhand sewing machines and may have a stock of bits and pieces from old models. If you live in London, there is a shop in Camden Passage, Islington, which specializes in old sewing machine parts. N.B.:

it may sound a detail, but buy the best sewing thread you can afford: the cheaper makes are maddeningly fragile.

STANLEY KNIFE. The all-round tool par excellence. I can't think how I ever managed without mine. I use it for cutting mounts, carpets, leather and fur, and for re-upholstering. Keep a good supply of spare blades handy, especially when cutting cardboard which blunts an edge quicker than anything. There is a saw-tooth blade attachment too, for fiddly wood-cutting.

LEATHER PUNCH. Another stand-by. Use it for punching holes for belts, for decoration on leather, for fitting eyelets (the usual eyelet punch is useless on anything thick), for making neat professional holes through cardboard, stencil board, etc. The adjustable variety, obtainable from most craft shops, is best.

HAMMER, TACK HAMMER. You need a medium-weight hammer for carpentry, and a tack hammer for upholstery and delicate little jobs like tacking in brads round a picture frame.

ASSORTED CARPENTRY TOOLS. You should have at least two screw-drivers, one large strong one which can double as a chisel or lever, and a small one. Also pliers, and a small bradawl. A Surform plane is a useful tool for rounding off pieces of wood or planing the surface layer off rough deal – its action is something between a plane and coarse sand-paper. Some kind of hand drill is essential, with a good assortment of bits. You need different bits for drilling wood and drilling masonry. Buy a good-quality drill; the cheapest models are too light to be very useful, and don't grip the bits really securely. Two saws are a help – one panel kind, with a long flexible blade for sawing large sections of timber roughly to size, and a rigid tenon saw for finer detailed cutting and shaping. A hacksaw blade on its own is handy for taking old bits of furniture apart as you can slip it through a crack to cut through old screws or dowel pegs. It can also be used to cut really fine detail on things like the wooden toys in this book. Or, more traditionally, use a good strong penknife, and lots of sandpaper. Abrasive papers come in all sorts of textures and finishes, from the coarsest kind, which will rub a splintery surface smooth, to finest glass paper and cabinet papers which are used to dull gloss paints or put a satin finish on bare wood. Wet and dry paper is useful for rubbing down large areas of paintwork, as wetting the paper lubricates it and speeds the job up as well as preventing the abrasive 'cutting' the paint too drastically. Keep a good selection of abrasive papers. Also wire wool, medium and fine grade. The coarser kind is useful with paint strippers, or a rust remover like Jenolite. The fine grade is invaluable for delicate rubbing of paints, varnish, shellac and bare wood.

WALLART. I find this an excellent rough-and-ready filler for patching up damaged composition picture- or mirror-frames, and for small, not too elaborate modelling. It sticks to any surface, dries rapidly and can be sanded smooth, though not poreless. For a superfine finish on frames, coat with two layers of gesso, and sand down. Art shops for both.

PLASTIC WOOD. Another invaluable filler for restoring wood, composition frames, even pottery intended for decoration rather than use. It is easy to handle, not being sticky, and dries fast if you build the area up a layer at a time. It needs patience to get a perfectly smooth surface, and much careful sanding down with medium then fine abrasive paper (see restoring wood). It comes in various colours – walnut is best for restoring antique mahogany, dark oak and, of course, walnut, plus a little stain to tone the colour up or down. Natural – the easiest to get hold of – is good for pale woods.

ADHESIVES. Araldite is the toughest adhesive for mending broken china and glass, and sticking most substances together. Mixed with kaolin or titanium dioxide or Polyfilla (see china repairs) it can be used to rebuild missing bits of china, or for remodelling missing bits of frames, figures, etc. A little difficult to handle, because it is so sticky – keep some meths handy to wipe tools and fingers on. For glueing wood, the experts recommend old-fashioned Scotch glue or fish glue, but these can be hard to get hold of. Evostick wood adhesive answers very well for sticking down veneer or mending breaks or re-glueing chair legs, drawer corners etc. For glueing fabrics, carpet, etc. use Bostik or Copydex. Copydex is flexible, while Bostik dries invisibly so it doesn't matter if you smear the right side slightly. Ordinary flour-and-water paste, with a little alum added, is as good as anything for mending torn prints, or sticking down paper. For jobs like decalcomania (*see* lamps) or any sticking job with paper where splashes will show, use Polycell wallpaper paste. Ordinary glue size is useful for stiffening and sticking substances simultaneously – string for winding round lamp bases, canvas for lining belts.

PAINT BRUSHES. For decorating jobs, you need at least three brushes – one ½-inch brush for small detailed work like window frames, a 2- or 2½-inch brush for paintwork and a large brush for painting walls with emulsion, distemper or glazes. The large brush can double for pasting wallpaper. Get the best brushes you can afford (cheaper at decorators' merchants) and clean them carefully after each job. For decorative painting you need an assortment of brushes, a fine sable pencil for lines and fine detail, one or two medium-sized pointed camel brushes for petals or shading, and a soft, fat, sable or camel-hair brush for folk-art motifs. Watercolour brushes can be used instead of oil brushes – they are a little cheaper and the shorter handles make them easier to use on furniture decoration. Buy three brushes to begin with, and add to your collection as your needs arise.

PAINTS. Watercolour or gouache colours are useful for painting cardboard, toys, washing in backgrounds to silhouettes, painting lines on picture mounts. Gouache gives more intensity of colour than water colours. Use it also to colour water-based wall paints. Artists' oils are used for some of the decorative painting in the book. They can also be used to colour commercial oil-based paints. Mixing your own colours means you can get precisely the shade you want. Acrylic paints are full of interesting possibilities in the decorative line. For painting boxes, chests, stencils, murals, panels, etc., they have immense advantages: rapid drying, first and foremost, which means you can finish a painted box in an evening instead of waiting a week for all the stages to dry hard, and versatility, meaning that they can be used thick or watered down for a transparent effect. These paints are expensive, in pauper terms. Buy a skeleton range to start with – primary colours plus raw umber, black and white – and add small tubes of new colours as you can afford them. Use real turps for mixing artists oil colours. This is cheapest bought in large quantities from a chemist or good ironmongers.

An assortment of varnishes are useful for finishing painted wood furniture, picture frames, etc. Polyurethane varnishes are tough, fast drying and easily obtainable. The natural colour is most versatile. Colourless, water white, varnishes are not easy to find. I often use artists' picture varnish for small objects which won't get much wear. Shellac is another specialized finish, rapid drying, used to give a very thin coat of shine, which sinks into the surface rather than lying on the top of it. It is excellent too, after priming, for giving a satin finish to a high-class painting job (*see* decorative painting).

I think this covers most of the needs you will meet in this book, though there may be one or two more specialized tools mentioned. (For small, fiddly jobs I often use an icepick.) Everything should be easily come by even in a small town. But if you find yourself stumped for something – how often one hears the excuse 'There just isn't any call for it these days' – go to your classified phone directory. A little intelligent ringing round and questioning will nearly always find whatever it is you want.

Finally, for almost any homemaking enterprise, you will need stacks of jam jars, old tins, rags, boxes and so forth. You may long to chuck them all away, as they accumulate in drawers and cupboards, but you will regret it if you do. The alternative is to have every available saucer covered with drying oil paint, milk jugs full of stripper, tools lying about in drawers, tea towels impregnated with linseed oil. This is not only wasteful and squalid, but potentially dangerous. Professional craftsmen, I now realize, are methodical and tidy because in the end it saves them time, effort and money. Five minutes spent cleaning brushes properly shows respect for your tools and in the long run saves money. I am basically a disorganized and untidy person, but I've bludgeoned myself into cleaning up, and putting things away, from sheer necessity.

Section 1

Getting it Together

There it is, your own place, empty rooms, blank walls and bare boards. Where, with your few sticks and tiny hoard of cash, to begin? There's so much you need, so much that must be done, and it's all so expensive, your head reels. Well, assuming you have the bare necessities (bed, cooker) I would start, prosaically, with the kitchen because eating in saves money and that's what you need most. An old deal kitchen table is cheap, and a lasting investment. Buy two chairs or stools to be getting on with, and a secondhand kitchen cabinet with a drop leaf (storage and extra working surface). Anything with doors and shelves – metal shoe lockers, old office equipment, bookcases – can be used for storage. Clean and paint them if they are worth it, otherwise use them till you can afford better things. Such things as fridges, if you think them vital – I would get a sewing machine before a fridge – can be found in salerooms, but there's usually no guarantee they work. The best place for bargains is cards in tobacconist windows – people ask less for a quick sale, and you can usually check whether it works. Always look in unobvious places – and leap in with your best smile and a small gratuity whenever you see builders chucking things on to a bonfire. Many is the dresser, ripped untimely off the wall, I have watched burning with a mild sense of outrage in my heart. Buildings up for demolition yield splendid trophies (old doors, handles, shelves, junk in the attic) but please do it through what they call the proper channels (foreman, owner), or you might find yourself up on a charge of breaking and entering.

Having provided for the inner man, your next requirement, unless you are very advanced, may be privacy, or curtains. Street-market stalls, junk shops and salerooms (soft furnishings like curtains seem to go cheap in sales) may yield curtains decent enough to hang as they are, or solid enough to quilt a prettier material on to, by machine (*see* curtains). Bare boards everywhere can be perishing cold, especially in the country, so I would be inclined to buy some sort of carpet next, the cheapest you can find in reasonable shape. It doesn't matter how ugly it is, because you will use it eventually as underlay for something better. Now, at last, permit yourself some comfort in the way of chairs and a sofa. For these, haunt salerooms on viewing days and leave bids for pieces you fancy. Better a well-upholstered piece with the cover in tatters (re-cover it) than a trim looking suite padded in straw and fibre that hits back at you when you sit down. Even if the well-upholstered piece has broken springs and webbing, it will be worth your while to get a friendly upholsterer (certainly, if you live in a country district where their charges tend to be lower) to re-seat it for you, leaving you to do the close covering. Alternatively, get hold of one of the many books on basic upholstering and do the job yourself. I must warn you though that it's a slow process for a beginner, as there are several techniques like tying springs and stitching a hard edge which have to be mastered as you go along.

The minute a place begins to look half civilized you notice the lack of such things as occasional tables, bookshelves, cupboards to tidy away the usual domestic overspill. I have included some ideas for tables to make, cheaply, but keep your eyes open for the odd windfall, which may not necessarily look like a table. My sister cottoned on to the plate glass and chrome thing long before it became trendy and snapped up a sweet display stand from a shop going out of business, with four adjustable glass shelves on a central chrome pillar. It takes everything from a phone to a cat basket and looks light and handsome. Adjustable bedside tables, with a wooden top on a cast-iron stand, turn up in junk yards for a few pence and look smartly functional if you replace the ugly stained wood tops with a slab of plain deal an inch thick and clean up the iron base. You can have them sandblasted professionally to a dull steely grey colour, or get off the old stove enamel finish yourself with Nitromors (stronger than Polystrippa) and coarse wire wool, and burnish with fine abrasive papers. Those heavily carved octagonal tables from India or the Middle East, with a loose top resting on a folding stand, can be bought in junk shops for a few pounds and look pretty if you strip off the heavy varnish stain with caustic, and bleach them to a light buff colour. Deal planks resting on bricks are still the quickest, easiest solution to the problem of what to do with books. More permanently, there is a wide choice of wall bracket arrangements which are not expensive or difficult to put up unless your solid wall turns out to be plasterboard. Cupboards are always a problem unless you are handy enough to build them as and where the need arises. I have suggested some cheap possibilities in the section on salerooms, and the section on painting wood contains ideas on making the ugliest cupboard inconspicuous, if not beautiful. Cut the legs off a hideous cupboard, paint it to merge into the decorating scheme and shove it tight into a corner and it won't be half so noticeable. If your place is big enough to absorb large pieces without strain, look for old mahogany linen presses in the salerooms. They often go cheap (dealers buy them for the wood) because the trend is away from monumental furniture, but they are usually solidly made, well-proportioned and take an amazing amount of stuff – blankets, linen, lengths of material, winter or summer clothes.

AUCTIONS AND SALEROOMS

I go to a good few auction sales, especially country ones, and I've often noticed that the saleroom crowd is a predominantly middle-aged one – any youngish couples usually turn out to be dealers. Either young couples haven't cottoned on to the advantages of furnishing a home via the saleroom or they find the whole procedure of competitive bidding intimidating. This is a pity, because a sale is still the cheapest source of almost anything in the household furnishing line from beds to bibelots (why else would dealers frequent them?) and any shyness that one feels about piping up during the bidding wears off very quickly once one has got used to the scene, and the scenery, and the dealers' trick of signalling their bids by waggling a little finger surreptitiously while staring hard in the opposite direction. Dealers are not, I must admit, the most genial and candid crowd of people, at least not while they are about their business. They tend to look and behave rather like bit-players in a gangster movie, stomping about in squashed hats and flapping raincoats, eyeing their surroundings with hard-eyed disfavour and generally trying to give the impression that they are tougher and meaner than the next guy. But you soon realize that all this is a put-on to intimidate and bamboozle their professional rivals and need not concern you in the least. Incidentally, don't be afraid to enter the bidding against dealers. I know there has been a lot of talk about the Ring, and suchlike sinister conspiracies, but even if such malpractices occur they are unlikely to operate at such small-time affairs as those conducted in the local saleroom. Every man for himself is the rule here, and if you bid against the dealers, the chances are you may still get the thing cheaper than you would if you bought it from an antique shop. This is for the simple reason that a dealer usually has a shrewd idea what he can get for something, and he also wants his profit – which seems to be around 30 per cent in most cases – so if the bidding goes over what he reckons to be his profit margin he may well back out.

Another common misapprehension is that some involuntary gesture, like rubbing your ear, will be mistaken for a bid on your part and land you with something you don't want and can't afford. But according to my friend, a local auctioneer (who runs one of the liveliest provincial salerooms I have visited), auctioneers develop a sixth sense about these things – they know when you are just rubbing your ear and when you are doing it with intent. And if any doubt arises, they stop to make sure before going on with the show.

If you are quite new to the saleroom scene it is a good idea to get into the habit of dropping in on viewing day (usually held the day before the sale proper – your local paper should give details) and again during the sale if you can spare the time. This will give you an idea of the sort of prices things fetch, and generally give you the feel of the place and people. Prices do vary quite a bit from one part of the country to another, and again between town and country salerooms. In my experience, country salerooms produce rather more bargains, but this isn't a hard and fast rule by any means. A small, unsigned but attractive oil painting which might go quite cheaply in a London saleroom where it may be surrounded by much finer work, will sometimes fetch a high figure in a country saleroom where there may be several local dealers who want something decorative to stick in the window. On the other hand, things which are on the verge of becoming fashionable in the antiquaries of London and the big cities – bamboo furniture, to quote one instance – will often go cheap in country sales because there is a definite time-lag between town and country where fads and fashions are concerned.

Come the day when you see something you want and decide to bid for it. You can do this in person at the sale (the attendant will tell you what time to turn up) or leave a bid with the saleroom staff. If you are interested in a whole bunch of items, you would do best to attend the sale and be ready to pounce if the bidding goes right for you. Sales are unpredictable affairs, and something you dearly covet may go for a song, while another thing may fetch twice what you would have expected. If you are after just one or two lots, leaving a bid isn't a bad move because you can decide how much you can afford to pay beforehand and there won't be any danger of being tempted to overspend in the heat of the moment. Check with the attendant though as to how much he thinks the lot will fetch – no point bidding way below the average figure. The bid you leave should be a delicate adjustment between how much you think the lot is actually worth, how much it is worth to you, and how many other people you think may also be after it. If it is something that turns up all the time at sales – what some auctioneers call cooking furniture – i.e. fridges, beds, bedroom chairs – keep your bid low because if you don't get it cheap this time you will another. If it is something uniquely appealing to you for some reason, best leave as high a bid as you dare. If it goes for less you will get it for less, and if you don't get it at least you won't be kicking yourself for leaving a quite unrealistic bid when you could have gone higher. Be prepared for many disappointments. If you are going to play the salerooms successfully, patience and perseverance are essential. You can go to four, five, six sales in a row and not find a thing you want, or you find things you want but get squeezed out of the bidding. But the day will come when flu, foul weather and other favourable circumstances keep the competition away, and all your bids come romping gloriously home. The feeling of triumph which this induces – not to mention the hard cash saved, make up for many disappointments.

Another point worth remembering if you are after the outstanding bargains, is that sales tend to be organized with the best stuff round about the middle of proceedings, so that dealers have time to get there for the battle royal and away again afterwards. A few plums will be offered earlier and later too, of course, to tempt people to stick around as long as possible, but on the whole the end of any sale – this goes for Christie's, Sotheby's and country house sales too – is where the lots go cheapest. Everyone is tired and fed up by then, and it's often all the auctioneer can do to whip up a bit of interest in his raggle-taggle audience. Knowing this, the salerooms tend to keep the grottiest lots to the end. But if you keep your eyes open and your wits about you you will sometimes spot a good buy among the junk. Look hard, because its charms may not leap out at you – it wouldn't be there if they did. I bought a pretty Regency hall-table for 50p not long ago because it had been effectively camouflaged with three coats of dark green paint and a piece of lino tacked over the top. What caught my eye was the slender tapering legs, brass drawer handles and castors. A glance inside the drawers revealed that the wood was pine, and the piece well made – smoothly sliding drawers are a good sign. Altogether it was obvious that it wasn't a kitchen piece. I also bought a large oval framed mirror for £3, with the intention of stripping off the many coats of hideous paint and doing it up myself. It proved a real bargain when I uncovered the original gold leaf, in pretty good condition. So look closely at anything shapely smothered in old paint. It might also be worth your while to bid for lots that need a bit of work doing on them – cane-seated chairs with the caning gone, steel andirons coated with rust, pine dressers with the shelf part missing, glass-fronted bookcases with the glass broken, easy chairs with first-class upholstering but the covers torn and dilapidated. Dealers often pass over things like these, however attractive, because it takes up valuable time getting them restored and mended. If you are good with your hands, you can do all the repair work yourself – this book should help you there.

Lastly, as I have already suggested, there still are a few things knocking around cheap at salerooms which haven't yet been reinstated by 'the trade'. I bought two unusually quaint and attractive bamboo pieces for £15 each a year ago – both built on bureau lines with cupboards above and below, and inset mirrors and panels imitating Chinese lacquer. I bought them because they were cheap and I liked them – always the best reason for buying anything – and needed somewhere to store books. Possibly I had a subconscious inkling that bamboo was about to make a comeback – certainly I have since seen inferior pieces in chi-chi London antique shops for prices of £60 and upwards. Other items which are going up, but still can be found cheaply, are those intricately carved and pierced wood Eastern pieces – chairs, octagonal tables, even sofas. Like-wise all that fancy wooden stuff inlaid with mother of pearl, Middle Eastern this time. Cleaned up, and in the case of the carved gear, stripped and bleached or painted off-white, all these objects – the tourist tat of half a century ago – look exotic and pretty and pleasantly hand-made. One last tip – old trunks are still cheap. Look for those Victorian portman-teaux with domed lids, a wicker frame covered with waterproofed canvas, and lined with ruched cotton. They often have sturdy leather handles and trimmings and brass fittings and locks. With the canvas part repainted in some suitably antiqued shade (see antiquing) they look at-tractive, and make useful storage places for blankets, toys, or scraps.

WINDOWS

Stately-home curtains

Even today, the 'best' curtains, which are also the most expensive, are sewn almost entirely by hand. This includes not only the usual hems, side seams, curtain tapes and hooks, but a great deal more internal stitchery which is not visible from the outside, but which serves to weld the three thicknesses of curtain fabric, interlining, and lining together so they 'handle' as one. Laborious it may seem – and indeed is (I made three pairs once for windows 11 feet high) – but like many slow, traditional methods of making it gives results which short cuts cannot equal. Curtains made to these perfectionist standards hang beautifully, falling into rich folds, keep out draughts (one reason why they are *de rigeur* in stately homes), hold together till the actual fabric is in tatters and look wonderfully luxurious. Initial cost, if you were to order some from one of the top interior decorators, is staggering – £200–£300 a pair – and running costs, or cleaner's bills, are in proportion.

If you want some really handsome window dressing for a favourite room there is no reason why you shouldn't make your own and enjoy delusions of grandeur for the cost of the materials. The making is not difficult, though slow. One absolute essential is a table long and wide enough to take the bulk of the curtain spread out flat. It's not the sort of job which can be done successfully on the sitting-room floor. Apart from housemaid's knee and sweatshop elbow, you might well suffer a slipped disc. As well as the table, you need a sewing machine (to join the fabric widths together), miles of cotton thread and the usual sewing tools.

Stately homes favour glazed chintzes, velvets, and silks for their curtains, but much humbler materials look very well given this sort of treatment. Choose something solid, with body to it – no flimsy dressmaking cottons or synthetics which will begin to look tatty after a couple of cleanings. Curtains like these are *forever*, nearly. Ticking, washed first to remove some of the dressing, cotton sheeting, twill, or denim would all be suitable, and to relieve the plainness you could add a border of cotton rug fringe, plain or dyed, or webbing. Or you could add a coloured border or band in contrasting material.

How much fabric? This depends on what system of gathering or pleating you are thinking of using. With curtains as heavy as these I think one can have too much fullness, especially if your windows are only standard height – say 8 feet. I cut down some stately-home cast-offs to fit 8-foot-high windows and by the time all the worn and faded bits were removed they were barely $1\frac{1}{2}$ times the width of the windows. I used ordinary Rufflette standard tape with dozens of hooks to gather them up and they certainly don't look skimpy. Always allow plenty of hooks and rings with heavy curtains – one every 3 inches is not too much. The original curtains, I noticed, were tightly cartridge-pleated and sewn by hand to an extra wide curtain tape, as were all the giant hooks.

Unless your windows are very lofty, or you definitely want a triple-pleated heading, $1\frac{1}{2}$ times to twice the window width should give ample fullness. For a triple-pleated heading (figure 1), using Rufflette Deep Pleat tape, you will need $2\frac{1}{2}$ times the width as a 48-inch-wide fabric pleats down to $22\frac{1}{2}$ inches. For length, measure the height of the window from curtain track to floor level, and add 8 inches per curtain for hem and heading.

You will need the same amount of lining and interlining. Curtain interlining or 'bump' is a thick, fluffy material like loosely woven cotton blanketing, and comes in various weights. Any large store – John Lewis and its subsidiaries are particularly good on this sort of thing – should be able to show you a selection. You should not economize on the interlining because it is this which gives curtains like these their handsome, heavy look. You could cheat on the linings on the other hand by using old, but not threadbare, sheets.

Making

Cut fabric and lining to the previously measured length. The interlining can be a few inches shorter as you don't want a bulky turnback at the hem or heading. Any lengths of fabric which need to be joined to make up the necessary curtain width should be machined together. Make sure the tension is just right; if it is too tight the seam will pucker when hung vertically and spoil your curtain. Iron seams open and flat. Now lay the curtain fabric on the table, right side down and lay the interlining on top, making sure both are lying smooth and flat. What you have to do now is loosely catch both fabrics together, using a large herringbone stitch, down the length of the curtain. How many lines of this invisible bonding

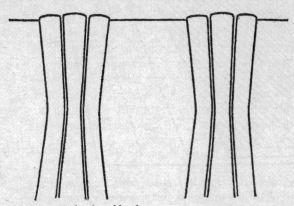

Figure 1. *Triple-pleated heading*

the curtains will need depends on their width and the weight of all the materials used. One about every 8 inches is usual. When you have worked out how many you need – the first comes 8 inches in from the side hems, as these are efficient bonding in their own right – it is a help to mark the lines out on the back of the curtain fabric, using coloured chalk and a long ruler. They should be as straight as possible. Do the centre line of stitching first because this will make the bulk of material more wieldy. Pin fabric and interlining together alongside the first chalk line, then fold back the interlining down its length half-way across (figure 2). Start at the top and work downwards when stitching. Your herringbone stitches (figure 3) should be quite long, 3 inches or so, but the actual stitch which catches up the curtain fabric should be tiny, taking up a few threads only so that it will not show on the right side. Don't pull any of the stitches tight, for the same reason – they should lie a little slack. When you have come to the bottom of the interlining, end off with a few stitches caught securely in the interlining. Now spread the curtain and interlining flat over the table again, and fold back the interlining above the next chalked guideline. Sew as before. Repeat till you have finished that half of the curtain. The other half is done the same way except that you will have to sew in the opposite direction unless you are ambidextrous, i.e. from bottom to top. When curtain fabric and interlining are stitched together you can trim the sides, heading and bottom of the interlining (leave 1 inch to fold back) to the correct width and length of the curtain. Fold the curtain sides, hem and heading back over the interlining. Smooth to

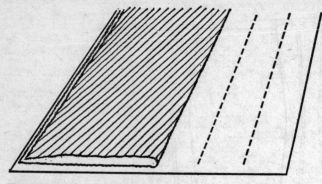

Figure 2. *Interlining folded back for stitching to curtain fabric. For easier handling stitch centre lines first – dotted lines represent chalked guidelines for further stitching*

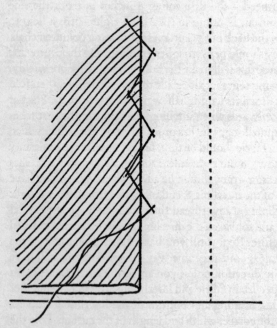

Figure 3. *Giant herringbone stitch used to catch interlining invisibly to curtain*

make sure that they are lying perfectly flat, then pin to hold the thicknesses together while you tack the folded-back edges to the interlining with large stitches (figure 4).

Now for the lining. This is invisibly stitched to the interlining in the same way. Now that the bulk of the curtain is stitched together and manoeuvreable, it is simpler to sew all the lines of herringboning from top to bottom. To reach the outermost chalk mark, fold the curtain in half before laying the lining out on top. Fold back the lining and sew as before, catching in the interlining only. Take the lines of herringbone to within 3 or 4 inches of the top and bottom of the curtain. When the herringboning is completed lay the curtain out flat, and fold under the sides, hem and heading on the lining. Hems on the lining should be set about 1 inch in from the edges of the curtain all round, except at the top where they should be nearly up to the edge. Pin at intervals. Then hem the lining down all round, taking large hemming stitches (figure 5) arranged so that the stitches are largely hidden underneath. Stitches 1-inch long are about right, but do not pull the thread too tight.

The real perfectionist will sew the curtain tape on by hand too so that there are no rows of machining visible to mar the smooth flow of the curtains on the right side. You may find you have to handsew them on because some machines balk at stitching through so many thicknesses. Rufflette tape should be sewn 2 or 3 inches down from the top, to give a bit of a heading unless you are having a pelmet. Deep pleat tape is sewn flush with the top. Handsewing is a nuisance because you have to catch in all three thicknesses of fabric every inch or so, if not with every stitch, otherwise the lining will be taking the whole weight of the curtains when hung. Use small, close stitches, for strength, and stab right through the curtain every inch or so, taking a tiny backstitch to make sure the sewing doesn't slip. Sew down both sides of the tape.

To sew on fringe or webbing, first pin the fringe or webbing on at intervals on the right side and then stitch in place using fairly large stitches inside and little ones on the surface – ordinary running stitch with a back stitch now and then. Webbing has to be sewn on along both sides, and the corners should be neatly mitred (figure 6).

Contrasting borders or bands

These look very attractive, though they are a good bit more trouble to

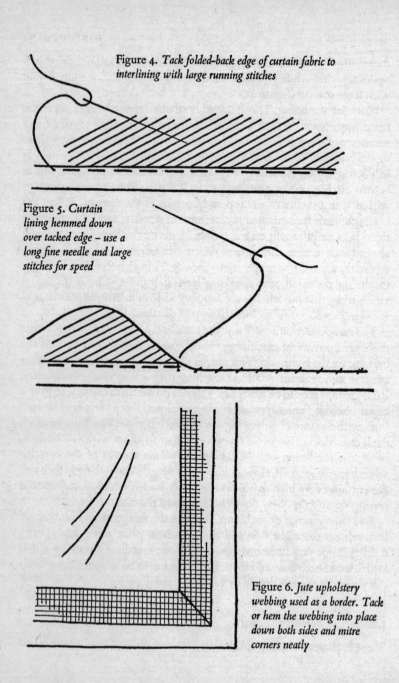

Figure 4. *Tack folded-back edge of curtain fabric to interlining with large running stitches*

Figure 5. *Curtain lining hemmed down over tacked edge – use a long fine needle and large stitches for speed*

Figure 6. *Jute upholstery webbing used as a border. Tack or hem the webbing into place down both sides and mitre corners neatly*

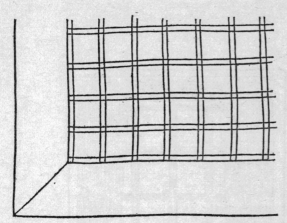

Figure 7. *A wide contrasting border should be machined into place before making up. Remember to subtract border width when cutting out curtains. Press machined seam open*

do. A wide border should be machined in place round the edge of the main fabric before interlining and lining are sewn into place (figure 7). A contrasting band set some way in from the curtain edges as with webbing can be hemmed in place along both sides after the curtain is completed.

Quilted curtains

If your windows are elegantly proportioned, high and slender as in many old houses, it seems a pity to smother them with voluminous curtains. The eighteenth-century treatment for windows like these seems often to have been narrow curtains of stiff material with just enough fullness to give a little gathering when drawn. The prettiest modern equivalent I have seen were made of the cheapest cotton available (curtain lining) quilted over old curtains which had been cut down to the right size. (Two thicknesses of fabric in these are best, i.e. fabric and lining. If the old curtains are too bulky, the new ones will look like eiderdowns.) All the quilting was done by machine, a swing-needle model with zigzagging and various fancy stitches, so parallel bands of plain stitching were varied with fancy ones. A fair labour, it must be said, but the quilting gives just the 'body' narrow curtains need if they are not to look meagre and droopy. These were finished with narrow fringe

Figure 8. *Narrow machine-quilted curtains dress a nicely proportioned window without smothering it*

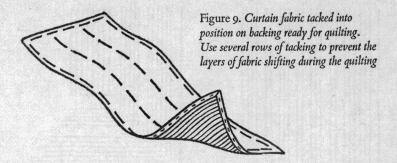

Figure 9. *Curtain fabric tacked into position on backing ready for quilting. Use several rows of tacking to prevent the layers of fabric shifting during the quilting*

and little tie-backs looping them to the window-frames, and looked quaint and charming.

Though there is a lot of machining involved, these quilted curtains are very easy to make. Measure length and width of windows. The curtains should be a couple of inches longer than floor level because quilting shortens them, and allow 2 inches or so as a heading above the curtain rail. They should be $1\frac{1}{4}$–$1\frac{1}{2}$ times the width of the windows, depending how wide these are – narrower if the window is very narrow, wider if the window is broad. Cut fabric and lining of a pair of old curtains to the size of the finished curtain, plus 2 inches either way, then cut the fabric to cover these with $1\frac{1}{2}$–2 inches turn-back all round. Lay fabric over the backing materials, making sure they lie squarely and smoothly over each other, pin here and there to hold them securely, and then run a few lines of large tacking stitches through all the thicknesses to hold them together while you are machining. Fold the hem allowance on the curtain fabric back over the linings all round and tack down (figure 9).

Choose a sturdy sewing cotton in a matching colour, or one of the extra strong synthetics (bearing in mind that your biggest outlay will be on thread, so don't fly too high). It's not fatal if the thread breaks but it wastes time. Now decide how you want your quilting lines to run. If you don't have a swing-needle machine, you can vary the effect by bands of stitching very close together alternating with more widely separated ones, or bands of plain fabric. But the more closely you quilt your curtain the better it will look – large unquilted areas tend to sag after a while. If you have a really up-to-date machine, you can work out any combination of plain and fancy stitching that appeals to you. You can either machine straight up and down the curtain, or follow the curtain rec-

 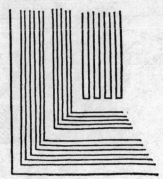

Figure 10. *Alternative ways of machine-quilting curtains*
(a) *Straight up and down*
(b) *Following curtain outline*

tangle and fill in the oblong centrepiece with any arrangement you like (figure 10).

Try to keep your lines of machining reasonably straight if not mathematically parallel – a little irregularity looks attractive. You can run your first lines of machining near enough to the edges to take in the hems, or hem them by hand later. Use a rufflette tape, machined on, to hang them by and plenty of hooks to prevent drooping. Tie backs can be made with narrow strips of the curtain fabric quilted to match and looped through rings attached to the frames, or hooks. A narrow fringed edging – about 1½ inches – looks pretty. Or you could make a narrow frill of the same or contrasting fabric and machine that round the edges. A pleated frill (professionally done) looks even nicer but puts the price up.

Roller blinds

Roller blinds in your own fabric are quite easy to make and much cheaper than any you could order. The most important thing is to choose a suitable material – it should be a close-woven cotton with plenty of body to it, otherwise the blind will look sadly floppy in a very short time. Most commercial blinds are made of holland with a permanently glazed finish, which can be wiped down. The grander custom-made blinds are waxed to give body and a smooth finish which can be dusted. The nearest a do-it-yourself job can get to these finishes is to pick a suitable material, and give it one of the new, semi-permanent spray finishes to stiffen it. If you particularly want to use a softer material, perhaps a light printed cotton which matches the curtains or bed cover, you can greatly improve the wear and look of the blind by backing it with natural coloured holland or waxed cambric. John Lewis, Oxford Street, stock fabrics like holland, and the waxed cambric can be ordered from The Russell Trading Co. (Suppliers' Index). If you are lining your blind the fabric and lining should be cut and sewn as one. The only snag with linings is that they cut down on the light.

Another point when choosing blind material is that it must be wide enough to cover the window area, with 3 inches over for hems each side – a seam down the middle ruins the look of a blind. If the window is very wide make two or three small blinds instead.

Before deciding on a material hold it up to the light so you get some idea of the effect it will give screening a window. A bold print may look colourful in the hand but gloomy with the light behind it, especially if the ground colour is a dark one. Natural coloured fabric – cream, off-white, etc. – gives the softest light and the plainness can be relieved by stencilling patterns on the blind or adding a fringe at the bottom. It rather depends whether you want the blinds to be drawn most of the time (to shut out an ugly view) or just at night.

You can buy kits to make up your own blinds from Whiteleys, John Lewis and branches, and the Army and Navy Stores. Some large department stores and do-it-yourself shops up and down the country also stock them. You need a spring roller the width of the window frame (unless you have windows which open inwards, blinds are best hung inside the window recess), two window brackets, a metal end and pin, a wooden batten the width of the blind, and a cord and acorn fitting with the plate and screws to fix it on with. Your blind fabric should be 3 inches wider than the roller and 9 inches deeper than the window.

To make

Spread the blind fabric out on a table and make sharp creases at each end exactly along the cross weave (weft) of the material. It is essential that the fabric hangs quite straight. Trim the fabric along the creases. Cut 2 inches off one end to make a pocket for the batten. Trim the selvedges off both sides of the fabric – they are often more tightly woven than the rest of the fabric and could cause puckering. Fold back $1\frac{1}{4}$ or $1\frac{1}{2}$ inches (check with roller width) each side and crease sharply. If you have a machine which does zigzag stitch you can machine up these hems catching in the raw edge. Otherwise, turn under a $\frac{1}{4}$ of an inch and then machine down each hem.

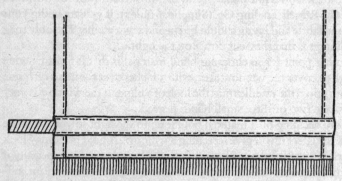

Figure 11. *Back view of blind showing wooden batten and batten pocket*

POCKET. Turn in $1\frac{3}{4}$ inches at each end of your strip, and a $\frac{1}{4}$ inch along both sides, and press carefully. On the wrong side of the blind Sellotape (pins leave holes) both ends of the pocket to the sides of the blind about $2\frac{1}{2}$–3 inches up from the bottom edge (*see* figure 11). Machine both long sides of the pocket down carefully. If necessary stick more Sellotape across the strip here and there to keep it slipping about as you machine.

If you are trimming the bottom of the blind with fringe turn a $\frac{1}{2}$ inch of fabric up on the right side of the blind and tack down. Then tack the fringe in place, covering the raw edge and machine or handsew. For an ordinary hem turn $1\frac{1}{2}$ inches under on the wrong side, turn raw edge under and machine down flat. (Set the batten pocket correspondingly higher in this case if you want a pelmet effect when the blind is up.) Cut the batten about an inch narrower than the blind and slip it into the pocket, narrow edge upwards. Mark the centre of the batten and screw the cord and acorn fitting in place. Press the blind.

ROLLER. Fix the brackets in place either side of the window, and cut the roller to fit between them. Fix the metal cap over the cut end (the other end has the spring attachment) and hammer the metal pin home. Now attach the top of the blind to the roller. Most commercial kits sell a grooved roller to which the blind is attached with metal clips. In the old days the top of the blind was simply tacked along the roller using $\frac{1}{2}$-inch tacks. Now roll the blind up and slot into brackets. Side, top or end brackets are available to suit your type of window.

BRASS ROD FINISH. Another swank looking way of finishing off the bottom of the blind, which also improves the hang of it, is to sew wide loops of the blind fabric (figure 12) at regularly spaced intervals along the bottom of the hem, which should come 1 inch or so below the batten pocket. Four loops to the average width blind are enough. Machine-hem the sides of each loop before machining into place. Insert a brass rod into the loops with a brass knob finish at each end. Your brass rod should be 1–$1\frac{1}{4}$ inches in diameter, and should fit loosely in the loops. To measure the length of the loops add about 2 inches to the circumference of the rod. Brass looks particularly rich with a dark-coloured blind, or a brightly patterned one, but a plain or painted wood pole (you can buy this by the foot in most do-it-yourself shops) would be just as attractive with pale colours or delicate prints, and much cheaper. Finish with screw-in wood or china knobs each end. Or use a pair of small old brass door knobs.

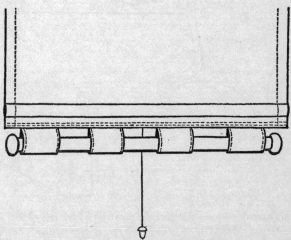

Figure 12. *A brass or wood rod passed through self fabric loops makes a handsome finish to a blind and helps it hang tautly*

Figure 13. *Decorative wooden pelmet shown here with a fabric roller blind. Inset (a) shows side view of pelmet. Use screw hooks and eyes or mirror plates to attach pelmet to windowframe or wall*

DECORATED BLINDS. Trendies are having their plain holland blinds decorated with pastoral scenes and fairy castles, hard to copy unless you know about batik dyeing. But you could try stencilling (*see* stencils) a simple pattern in a contrasting colour right round the blind, or in stripes lengthways. Use paint-on dyes available from art shops. Practice first on a spare piece of material till you can manage a clear-cut print. Or, for the adventurous, paint a free-hand design – Tree of Life, Grecian urn, peacock, or what you will – right up the middle, using Sellotape to mark out the pattern areas.

Small windows

Figure 13 shows a neat and pretty way of finishing off a small window from an Early American interior. The blinds here were old-fashioned wooden slats held together with cords, and slats and wooden box pelmet were painted a soft greeny blue, but a fabric blind would do just as well. The pelmet is exactly the same as the conventional shaped box pelmet except that the fancy cut-out is at the top. As well as dressing up the window it hides the blind fixings. I should make it of ply or deal; hardboard is easier to cut but looks flimsy. Paint it to match something in the room. If the walls are plain, you could decorate it with a swag of roses and leaves.

Festoon blinds

Festoon blinds these days seem always to be made of nylon net and relegated to bedrooms, which is a pity because in the right material and the right setting they look extraordinarily pretty. Surprisingly, though the fixings are a bit fiddly to work out, the blinds themselves are not difficult to make. One great advantage of these blinds is that they can be taken down and washed easily; a strong point if you live in a sooty town.

They look their best in long narrow Georgian windows, but any long window would do. The most attractive I have seen were made up in crisp, paper thin silk, light as cirrus clouds. Not cheap of course, unless it means you can dispense with curtains. You can use cotton lawn or voile or muslin instead. Nylon net is useful for lining baby's cradles but it casts

Figure 14. *A festoon blind trimmed with fringe and tassels veils and softens an early Victorian window, making curtains unnecessary*

a deathly pallor over windows. White or cream are the best colours to choose, unless you are very sure of what you are doing and want a particular effect. Hold any material up to the light before deciding – a shade which looks innocuous in the hand may be hectically bright with the full light of a large window behind it.

MEASURING UP. The blinds should be $1\frac{1}{4}$–$1\frac{1}{2}$ times the length of the window, and as wide as the window recess. Most cotton materials like lawn and voile come in 36-inch widths, which means one join to make up the necessary width for an average sized window. The join *must* come at one of the lines of gathering where it won't show. When working out

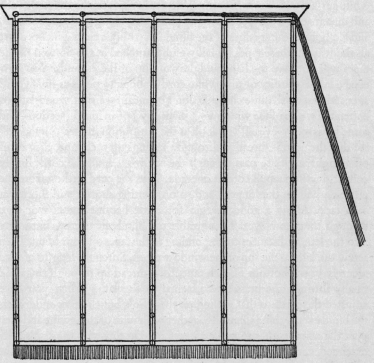

Figure 15. *Back view of blind and batten ready for fixing. Thin cord is threaded through split rings inserted into curtain tapes, then through eyelet screws in batten. In some cases the eyelets can be screwed direct into the window frame*

fabric requirements remember to allow a 1-inch turnback either side of the blind.

MAKING UP. The number of festoons per blind depends on the width of the window. Two or three lines of gathering is right for narrow windows, giving you three or four swags as the case may be. Festoons should be about 1 foot wide to look effective; anything narrower looks fussy. Having cut and seamed up your blind material as necessary, stitch a narrow (1-inch) hem at the top and bottom and turn back 1 inch at both sides. Fold the material into three, or four, lengthwise, depending how many festoons you have planned for, and iron carefully along these folds. This gives you guidelines for stitching on curtain tape. You need narrow white curtain tape into which small brass split rings can be inserted. Tack and then machine the tape down (on both sides) along the ironed creases, and along both outer edges of the blind. Insert brass rings 4 inches apart all the way up these tapes. Small weights stitched at the bottom of the tapes will improve the hang and drawing up of these blinds. You now need a large quantity of thin white cord – about 1½ times as much cord as curtain tape (it's quite cheap so don't be mean) – a thin wood lath or batten the width of the window – 3 inches by ¾ of an inch in section – and some brass screw-eyes. If you look at the illustration (figure 15) you will see that the cord is threaded through the rings up each tape, then turns off at right angles to pass through the screw-eyes, all the cords finally converging into a pull cord at one side. Thus the cord farthest from the pull side will be the longest, and so on, getting shorter and shorter at each tape. Allow a good margin for error because knots won't go through the screw-eyes. To assemble the blinds first screw brass eyes into the lath at distances corresponding to the tapes on your blind. Then screw the lath to the top of the window recess. Stitch the lengths of cord securely to the bottom of each tape, then thread up through rings and finally through the brass eyes attached to the lath. When you have adjusted the cords so that pulling on the whole bunch raises and lowers the blind evenly, bind them all together with wire or thin twine and then plait the rest together to make a neat pull. Do this with the cords fully extended, and remember that you will have to unfasten them to take the blind down for washing.

A slightly more laborious, but cheaper (no tape, or rings) way of making up blinds like these is to sew narrow (1-inch) strips of the blind fabric, cut from leftovers, up the creased folds instead of tape. Use the side hems as channels up the outer edges. Sew the strips as you would a band of bias binding, turning in the raw edges each side and machining down close to the edges. The cord is then threaded up *inside* these narrow channels. Use a length of stout wire, with one end bent to make a loop and the other sanded smooth to stop it catching, as a bodkin for this operation. Tie the cord to the loop. One advantage of this method, which may or may not weigh with you, is that they look better from the outside of the house. They may not draw quite so easily as the other sort – extra weights, or a fringe sewn along the bottom, should correct this.

Alternative ways of finishing off the bottom of festoon blinds are a bobble fringe, a band of coarse lace, a gathered or pleated frill of the same material, or a silky tassel stitched to the bottom of each tape.

FLOORS

Floors are apt to be the biggest headache when furnishing a place on very little money. The sheer acreage of them, uneven, thick with old paint and varnish, bristling with nailheads and splinters, is enough to fill even a keen do-it-yourselfer with despair. The only quick, easy solution is to pay someone else to cover them all up with fitted carpeting, but the cost of this transformation puts it right out of the pauper bracket. However there are alternatives, and in this section I shall be dealing with some that are cheap, attractive and practicable, starting with ways of rehabilitating the bare boards themselves and finishing up, via advice on re-laying secondhand carpet, with patterns for rugs you can make yourself to strew upon them. It may be comforting to know, if the vision of wall-to-wall Wilton dies hard with you, that some of the ideas listed below – painted floors, for instance – are all the rage among folk who could well afford to carpet their dwellings with cast-off St Laurents if the fancy so took them. The fact is, the fitted carpet, once a potent symbol of the rich life (remember Chandler's private eye wading through pile up to his knees?) is becoming a cliché. Your super snob relegates it to the bathroom.

Stairs, halls and landings

This is the worst bit if you live in a house on more than one floor. The surfaces to be dealt with seem interminable, take a tremendous beating and are the first thing that confront you (or the health visitor or your mother-in-law) as you open the front door.

I'ts a mistake, if you decide to cover it all up, to go for a cheaper grade of new pile carpet because these look beat-up in no time. If you have this amount of money to spare, choose a good-quality haircord in a vivid but darkish colour – the lighter shades show up every stain and haircord is difficult to shampoo successfully. Sisal floor coverings are in the same sort of price bracket, and come in lovely colours, but again they stain easily and the nice tweedy texture soon looks dingy under really hard wear. Good old-fashioned coconut matting is tipped for revival (*see* cheap floorings). Immensely tough and resilient, its breakfast cereal colour would look pleasant in a brightly painted hall and stairway.

Lengths of old stair-carpet often go cheaply in sales, and are worth considering if you can find a piece in a good colour and quality. Badly worn bits can be cut out and the edges stitched up again (*see* below for how to go about this), and with a bit of juggling you can re-lay the remainder so that the scuffed parts go up the risers and the unworn bits cover the stair treads. Old brass stair-rods are easy to come by because people can't be bothered with cleaning them, and they improve the look of any stair-carpet. You could lacquer the brass to stop it tarnishing.

The cheapest solution of all is to forget about coverings altogether and strip the stairs back to the bare wood – usually a good-quality pine. Hall and landing floors can be sanded to match. I did this in one house I lived in and it looked very effective with white wainscot and banisters, bright yellow walls and the odd rug. Cleaning off old paint and varnish is a slow business but the beauty of it is that once finished, your worries are over. Carpet wears out, paintwork needs refurbishing but stripped wood goes on for ever and fluff, dust and dogs hairs show up much less than they do on carpeting. I used a blow-lamp to burn off the paint, followed by sanding to smooth the wood and bring up the grain. Scrubbing with caustic will remove obstinate traces of paint, but be careful if there are kids running about. If the wood is too yellow you can cool it down by bleaching (*see* wood finishes). The bare wood can be finished by oiling, waxing or a coat of floor seal. Waxing builds up a rich patina, but it could be slippery unless you polish away like a washerwoman. Floor seal is quick to apply but wears off rapidly on surfaces which take a lot of traffic, and seems to absorb grit and grime.

I settled for oiling with boiled linseed oil which gradually builds up a resistant surface, and an occasional scrubbing to remove ingrained dirt. For larger areas like hall and landings hire a sanding machine. Any sanding should be done before re-decorating as the fine sawdust settles on everything.

Painted floors

Brightly painted floors, sometimes decorated with a stencilled border, are coming back into fashion and are both practical and pretty for rooms which need frequent sweeping out – children's bedrooms, dining-rooms. They were a frequent feature of Early American interiors, the perfect complement to demure printed calicos, patchwork quilts, rustic furniture and hooked rugs. Updated versions tend to be more elaborate – one painted floor I heard of was hand-decorated to look like blue and white china. A properly painted and varnished floor wears astonishingly well. The American Museum has most of its rooms and corridors painted and stencilled and, despite the heavy traffic, they look immaculate.

The Early Americans favoured sensible dark colours like turkey red, dark green, sometimes enlivened by coloured stencils, but there's no need to be bound by tradition. A white or yellow floor would cheer a dark north-facing room. Bright red, with a striped rug, would be nice for a cold bedroom. And a subtle khaki or denim blue would make a pleasing background to a Persian rug. Obviously it would be foolish to paint over a fine polished wood floor but for rooms where the flooring is nothing special, and you want some colour without the expense of carpet or lino, paint seems a sensible answer.

Instructions

A painted finish, as the experts never tire of reminding one, is only as good as the surface beneath. A floor won't need to be as flawless as a painted piece of furniture of course but some preparation is necessary. Punch down any protruding nails, and go over splintery parts with sandpaper, working from coarse to medium-fine grades. Ideally, any varnished or previously painted areas should be sanded down to the wood, but this is a counsel of perfection. What is essential is to clean off any grease and dirt. A strong sugar-soap solution scrubbed well in and rinsed off with clean hot water should do the trick. Really grimy areas – near the door for instance – may need scouring with wire wool and Vim. A glossy painted finish shows up cracks and craters so its as well to deal with these now. Fill holes and fissures with plastic wood, sanded smooth when dry. Wide cracks between the floorboards are best dealt with by hammering thin wood laths, planed or sanded to a fine edge along one side, down between them. Smaller cracks can be stopped up with papier-mâché pulp, made by soaking torn bits of newspaper overnight in cold water, squeezing out and mixing with flour-and-water paste or Polycell. Push this down between the boards and leave to dry hard.

Now give the floor a coat of undercoat, or primer on new wood. Start painting at the corner farthest from the door, use a wide brush and kneel on an old mat. Use a good-quality paint for the topcoats, preferably in a semi-gloss finish. If you can't get the exact shade you want in any of the commercial ranges, get a colour close to it, but lighter, and tint to the right shade with artists' colours – oils for oil-bound paints, acrylics for the plastic based variety (see painting wood for instructions). Give the floor two coats of paint, allowing plenty of drying time in between. Any decoration should be applied before varnishing. You can make your own stencils (see stencils) from stencil board, obtainable from most artists' supply shops. Use a Stanley knife to cut the pattern out cleanly. The stencil should be painted in the same type of paint as used for the floor because it will need to be durable. A thickish brush like a sash tool (decorators' supply shops) or even an old, cut-down, shaving brush is best for stencilling. Finally, give the whole floor one – preferably, two – coats of protective varnish. A clear polyurethane varnish is adequate, but better still, if you can get hold of it, is a fast drying, extra tough varnish for floors called Universal Medium (Suppliers' Index). To keep the room as dustfree as possible while putting on the varnish and while it is drying, keep door and windows closed and stick something over the fireplace if there is one. If the weather is chilly leave a heater on to help the varnish flow freely, and speed drying.

The floor may need revarnishing occasionally. First make sure the floor is clean and free of grease. Mop it with warm water with a little detergent and soda added, and rinse. Any ingrained dirt should be gently cleaned off with a Brillo pad. But try not to rub so hard that you remove the paint. Any badly worn patches should be touched up with paint, and rubbed down to level them with surrounding paintwork before varnishing.

Some shops still stock a range of special floor paint, chiefly intended for use on cement or lino though they can be used on wood. They are very durable but come in rather drab colours. A gayer finish for cold concrete is to apply brightly coloured gloss paint thinned half and half with white spirit, using a rag swab – an old-fashioned floor mop might substitute.

Old rugs for new

One of the most attractive ways with sitting-room floors is to scatter the bare boards – waxed, sanded or painted – with old and mellow Persian, Turkish or Kelim rugs. These are not outstandingly expensive unless you insist on fine specimens in perfect condition. I have seen attractive rugs in reasonable nick and large enough to cover most of a small sitting-room floor go for between £20 and £30 in country salerooms. If you are not deterred by such flaws as frayed edges, worn patches or the odd hole (which can be patched up) you will be able to pick up pretty ones more cheaply still. Even when shabby these hand-made rugs retain their distinction. If you stick to an overall colour – deep rose is a common one – several rugs overlapping like playing cards will cover most of the floor and provide an inimitable stretch of pattern and richness underfoot. One great advantage of a rug collection, if you aren't yet settled in a permanent home, is that when you move you simply roll them up and cart them away. I have several which have moved with me three times in the past seven years and more than anything else I own they seem to humanize any surroundings they find themselves in, covering up dingy carpeting, cheering dark landings and accommodating themselves to some very random collections of furniture.

If you doubt your ability to distinguish between a genuinely old handmade, natural dyed rug and a machine-loomed imitation, look up a book on Persian rugs in the local library. Do not get too bogged down in nomenclature and knots per square inch; the most valuable rugs are not always the most attractive.

Rugs, but particularly old and fragile ones, need some sort of underlay to cushion them against wear. Rolls of old underfelt go cheaply at sales.

Alternatively, thin foam underlay is not expensive. Cut the underlay a fraction smaller than the rug – a dab of Copydex here and there on the bottom of the underfelt will help to stop it slipping about.

Cleaning and repairing

The best way to clean rugs – I have this tip from a professional – is to beat them. This shakes out dust and dirt which has worked down into the fibres. Vacuum cleaners tend to loosen and finally to swallow the knotted loops. You can use a tennis racket to beat rugs with. Suspend them over a strong clothes-line and thud away rhythmically. Then shampoo the surface with one of the proprietary brands of carpet shampoo, wetting it as little as possible. Plop on handfuls of foam and rub gently with a soft brush, following up with an old clean towel to remove as much grime as possible. Soft water – rainwater or distilled water – gives the best results.

Minor repairs are not impossibly difficult, and they prolong the life of a rug enormously. How skilfully you blend a patch or darn into the original will depend on your patience and care, but any sort of patch is better than a hole and a bit of cheating with paint can help a lot.

One of the first parts of a rug to get worn away is the oversewn wool edging along both sides. Replacing this, or patching it up will stop the actual jute from getting nibbled away. Use a matching wool – embroidery or knitting wool doubled will do – and a blunt tapestry needle for this job, and don't pull the stitches too tight. Where the jute edging has small bites out of it, I find one can tidy up the frayed patch considerably by knotting together any long ends and then darning backwards and forwards with ordinary string to make a new firm edge. Frayed ends are best left alone apart from coating the back with Copydex and sticking on a piece of cotton tape. Worn patches can be strengthened by sticking on a patch of some soft material (hessian or sacking with the dressing washed out is best) from the back with Copydex. Actual holes must be patched otherwise you will enlarge them every time you vacuum-clean the rug, let alone the times you trip over the hole. A crude but adequate patch can be contrived by sticking or stitching a piece of hessian, sacking or embroidery canvas on from the back and painting it to match the rug pattern. More elaborately the patch – embroidery canvas this time – can be worked with wools to imitate the original and then stuck or stitched into place from the back. (Always use a latex adhesive like Copydex because it has some elasticity in it.) This can be done very successfully with the woven type of rug – like a Kelim. The main difficulty, as a rule, is matching the original, natural-dyed colours. Embroidery or tapestry wools come in the best colour range. Use two or three lengths twisted together. A knotted pile rug presents greater problems. A perfectionist would learn up how the original knots were tied – I'm afraid I simply stick on a strengthening patch and stand a piece of furniture over the spot wherever possible.

Re-laying secondhand carpet

A snag with secondhand carpet is that you will probably have to cut, stitch and re-lay it yourself unless you know someone in the business who will do it in his spare time. If your piece of carpet is larger than the room it is to go in, you may only need to cut it down to fit. But if your room is irregularly shaped you may need to add bits on, and if the carpet has already seen plenty of wear you may need to cut out and replace badly worn parts.

Before starting work on the carpet, give it a good cleaning. If you have somewhere to beat it, this will loosen clouds of embedded dust and grit. Otherwise Hoover it on front and back. Next, clear as much furniture as possible out of the room and lay the piece of carpet down to decide which way round suits the room and furniture arrangement best. If one corner is badly worn or stained and you can contrive to hide it under a bed or sofa that's clearly a wise move. Decide which bits need to be lopped off or replaced, and where the replacements should come from. Try not to unpick any more of the original stitching than necessary.

In the way of tools and materials you will need a Stanley knife with spare blades, some chalk, a carpet needle (included in household packs) and a ball of twine, which can be purchased at most ironmongers. Copydex is invaluable for sticking down the edges. Adhesive carpet tape is handy for strengthening seams, but not essential. Finally, a large box of 1-inch bayonet tacks, a tack hammer, and a tape measure or wooden rule.

Turn the carpet wrong way up and mark the parts you want to re-place with chalk. Cut from the back with the Stanley knife. Fix small

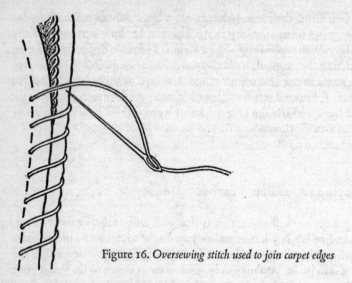

Figure 16. *Oversewing stitch used to join carpet edges*

patches in place with carpet tape and/or a square of hessian or sacking cut several inches larger than the patch and glued over the back with Copydex. Woven edges of carpet are stitched together with an oversewing stitch (figure 16). Cut edges should be treated first to stop them fraying. To do this pull off ¾ of an inch of pile along the cut edge to expose the backing. Fold this back and glue it down with Copydex. Then oversew as for a woven edge. Use fairly large stitches and check from time to time that your stitches are neither too tight nor too loose. Finally chalk a guideline for cutting right round the carpet, leaving a 1- or 1½-inch turning allowance, and cut.

When the carpet is done, bundle it out of the room while you tackle the underlay. This can be underfelt (rolls of secondhand felt can be bought at sales and some junk shops), foam underlay, an ancient carpet cut down to fit or, if you are really skint, innumerable sheets of newspaper. A layer of newspaper spread over the floor is a good idea in any case as it intercepts draughts and dust coming up through the floorboards. Cut the underlay to fit and tack it down here and there to keep it in place while you tackle the carpet. Stretch the carpet out smoothly on top. It's a good idea to leave it like that for a few days before tacking it into position because walking about will probably spread it a bit, particularly if you have restitched much of it. When tacking down begin by folding over the turnback along one side and tacking down every 6 inches or so. Pull or 'walk' the carpet smooth and taut before tacking down along the opposite wall. Repeat for the other two sides. Finally go over the carpet with one of the proprietary shampoos, wetting the backing as little as possible. Rubbing as you go along with an old towel helps to clean off clinging grease and grime.

Cheap floorings

The two cheapest floor coverings I have come across are coconut matting and printers' felt. Coconut matting can be bought in various widths up to 6 feet, and thicknesses varying from about a $\frac{1}{4}$ of an inch to 1 inch. The cheapest works out at not much more than £1 per square yard. It comes in red, blue and green, but the natural fibre colour is the most attractive. The suppliers, Jaymart Ltd (Suppliers' Index) will cut it to the lengths you require but you will have to stitch it up yourself, using the technique described above. Cut edges should be bound with thick cotton webbing. Underlay is not necessary but makes it springier to walk on. Ideal for playrooms, halls and stairs (use stair rods), and sitting-rooms.

Printing felt is a thick felt used in the printing process, but enterprising people have been spreading it over their floors. It is thick, hard-wearing and cheap – at the time of writing £12 buys a roll large enough to cover an average (10 × 12 feet) room. The snags are that you have to collect it from the paper mills yourself (Suppliers' Index) and, of course, do any cutting, stitching and laying. The standard colour is a pleasant greyish buff. Excellent for bedrooms, where it won't have too much wear. A nice background for patterned rugs, or you can use it as underlay.

Kitchens, bathrooms: chipboard panels, tacked and glued down over the existing floor and heavily sealed make a cheap, resilient, easy-to-clean surface which looks like cork. Spills and stains show up less than on plastic flooring. The floor beneath must be level, and the chipboard needs re-sealing once a year.

Make your own rugs

Hand-made rugs are part of the folk art of almost every country. The patterns were usually traditional, often symbolic, and colours used could be bright or muted but were invariably obtained from natural dyes which is one reason why they age so gracefully. They must have been prized family possessions – perhaps the one touch of luxury in an austerely furnished farmhouse. Some of these traditional rugs are intricately knotted, others more simply cross-stitched, others even more simply made of coloured rags or felt stitched to a strong jute backing. Most of the research and practical work in this section was done by Lesley Wright, a young art teacher with a special flair for improvisation and problem solving. One of the interesting snippets of information she came up with is that until quite recently, when they switched to telly to while away those long, dark, storm-lashed evenings, rug-making was a favourite hobby of lighthouse keepers. They evolved their own method, using narrow strips of thick felt stitched to a backing made of old flour sacks, each strip doubled and stitched down through the centre. If you come across any off-cuts of heavy felt, it's an idea worth copying.

The points we kept in mind when choosing rugs to make were cheapness, speed and design. Cheapest of all is the coiled rag rug, made from old odds and ends one would normally throw away. The tile rug goes quickly, as a small piece is easier to work than a large one. Locker stitch covers the ground fast, and gives a lot of texture for a small amount of wool. We worked out a broken stripe pattern for this rug, using wheat colours – green, yellow, off white, sandy brown, a little orange. You could substitute bright primary shades, or dark subtle ones for a quite different look. More ambitious, but worth the effort, is a large – 6 feet × 3 feet 2 inches – cross-stitched rug in four colours based on a traditional Greek peasant design. You may have seen similar designs on those good-looking woven wool bags holidaymakers bring back. The patterns are simple geometric ones which are best suited to the large cross-stitch used, and the general effect is bold, unfussy and handsome. The colours we chose were as close to the original as possible – peat brown, cream, burnt orange and pink. Some came from one range of rug wool, some from another. This is the best course to follow – wool firms have an annoying habit of chopping and changing the colours in their range, so there's not much point my giving names and numbers. Wool for a rug this size can't be cheap, but for the money you have an article with real style which will last and last. Incidentally, the large cross-stitch goes relatively quickly – Lesley worked this one in under six months.

Coiled rag rugs

Absolutely the simplest type of rag rug is made by coiling a plait of coloured rags snail-wise and stitching it down as you go. Northern Italian peasants make and use rugs like these on their stone floors and I'm told they are lovely things, a mosaic of colours, almost every inch differ-

Figure 17. *The start of a coiled rag rug showing the plait being stitched into place*

ent from the next. My own attempt has stuck at bath-mat size, but I intend to finish it one day. It's a marvellous way of devouring old bits of material, old tights, clothes, scraps. Stretchy stuff like the kind used for tights is ideal as it is soft to sew, and doesn't fray. You can either make your plaited strip first and then sew it, or plait as you go along. The only tricky part of making the rug is joining the lengths of rag together. I found by tucking the end of the new strip into the end of the old one, one could plait it in with the other two strands without having to sew the pieces together. Strips approximately $1\frac{1}{4}$ inches wide – tear the strips rather than cutting wherever possible to save time – plait down to a plait just over $\frac{1}{2}$ an inch wide. But of course this will vary with the thickness of the cloth used for the strips. Try to keep the plait reasonably even throughout its length.

STITCHING. I used a large, strong darner and button thread, with a thimble on my finger to push the needle in and out. The needle has to be passed in and out of the new thickness of the plait and the one before (figure 17), using a diagonal stitch, and backstitching now and then for strength. Or you could use a curved upholstery needle in a fine grade and push straight in and out of the two layers. Otherwise there's nothing to it, just plait and stitch away till you have something large enough for your purpose.

Locker rug

Using a locker needle and locker-rug canvas – see Suppliers' Index – you can make a good-sized rug quickly and cheaply. A locker needle is a

Figure 18. *Locker needle*

simple implement looking much like a crochet hook at one end and a giant needle the other. The rug design shown here, which measures 2 feet 2 inches by 4 feet 8 inches (a nice bedside size), took about three weeks to make, working mainly in the evenings. Locker stitch gives a thick, ribbed effect, not unlike elephant cord, but richer and softer. It won't cope with intricate patterns or curved lines but combines pleasantly with broken stripes and a cool, unfussy, Scandinavian look, both of which we tried to incorporate in the design. Diagonal overstitching down both sides and a short knotted fringe at each end give a professional finish. This design, by the way, has been worked out to give you lots of practice with straight runs of the stitch before you hit the more complicated pattern sections.

LOCKERSTITCH. It reminds me a little of picking up stitches in knitting, but is much less exasperating. If you are starting to work the design proper (not playing about experimentally) fold back the first eight rows

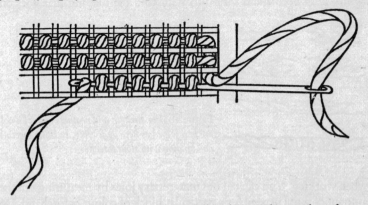

Figure 19. *Locker needle in action – the principle is akin to picking up dropped stitches in knitting*

of the canvas and work it double thickness for a strong edge. (Do the same at the other end of the rug, folding back the last bit of canvas so you work the last eight rows on double thickness.) To work, pull a good length of wool from the skein. *Do not cut* it off, but thread the end through the eye of the locker needle. With the needle in your right hand, working from right to left (reverse everything if you are left-handed) bring the needle and length of wool up through the first hole at the end of the first row, leaving your skein of wool dangling below. Now poke the hook end of the needle through the next hole to the left and pull up a loop from the skein. Keeping this loop over the needle repeat the process, working in a straight line along the row, till you have a dozen or so loops over the needle (figure 19). Then pull the needle through the loops, which locks the stitches into place. Continue along the row in the same way, picking up a needleful of loops and locking with the wool on your needle. When you get to the end of the row, pass the needle and locking thread down through the last hole and up through the one immediately below. Turn the canvas round and you are ready to begin on the next row.

JOINING THE WOOL. Joining the ends is the chief problem with locker stitch. Too many loose ends darned in might weaken the rug. The best and neatest way is, when your locking wool is almost used up, to fray the ends to be joined, interweaving as shown in figure 20, then binding tightly with needle and thread to withstand the tugging that goes on

Figure 20. *For strength and neatness ends of wool are best joined as here by fraying, twisting together and binding with stout thread*

when working. You can cut out unnecessary joins by measuring out the amount of wool needed for a particular block of colour beforehand. Do this by laying the wool along the rows to be worked, doubling to allow for loops, and adding 3 inches or so to be darned in. Mark the point on the wool and pull through as far as the mark. Darn in loose ends by weaving backwards and forwards across the wool to be looped where possible. Otherwise leave them loose till the rug is finished when they can be darned in with a rug needle.

THE DESIGN. Study the design and work out a plan of campaign before you start, filling it in block by block, colour by colour. You save time and wool by plotting the starting points and direction of working beforehand. See figure 22 for a suggested line of approach.

WHERE TWO BLOCKS OF COLOURS MEET. Overlap a join between two blocks of colour – a gap looks mangy. The joins should always overlap in the same direction to avoid breaking up the ribbed surface – upwards to the right and downwards to the left, as shown in figure 23.

Start here ↓

Figure 21.
*Rectilinear pattern
in five colours
suitable for working
in locker stitch. We
used soft,
complementary
colours for a
wheatfield-in-the-
sun effect. For a
dramatic, quite
different look you
could choose deep,
strongly contrasted
shades*

One 2-ounce skein does approximately 8 rows
The canvas has 100 holes across its width
One square represents one stitch

Colour key
□ Off white
╲ Light yellow
✕ Deep yellow
⊠ Burnt orange
■ Light khaki

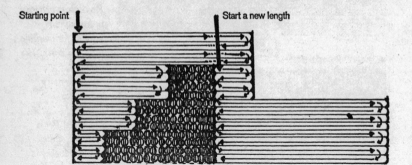

Starting point | **Start a new length**

Figure 22. *Suggested method of tackling a new colour-block*

Figure 23. *Overlap wools where two colour-blocks meet to prevent canvas grinning through*

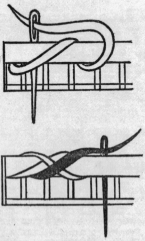

Figure 24. *Binding stitch gives a firm rolled edge to rug*

FINISHING OFF. Cover the selvedges either side of the rug with a binding stitch worked like this. Take a large-eyed rug needle threaded with a good length of wool – the predominant colour in the rug looks best. Darn the end into the selvedge at one end, then bring the needle up through hole one, over and up through hole four, then over and back up through hole two, then over and up through hole five, then over and up through hole three, then hole six, then back up through hole four and on to hole seven (figure 24). Continue this way till you have covered in the selvedge. This binding stitch gives a neat, thick, welted edge.

Fringe the ends with 7-inch lengths of wool – using all the leftover rug colours. Fold each length in half and pull through the holes from front to back with the locker hook, then slip the ends through the loop and pull tight. Repeat with all the holes.

Figure 25. *A simple knotted fringe is optional but looks rich*

Backing the rug with hessian will prolong its life if it's to be laid on a bare floor or lino. If it's going over carpet, this reinforcement isn't really necessary. Most rugs tend to twist a little as you work them. This will right itself in use, but you can speed the straightening-out process by pressing the back lightly with a steam iron, or ordinary iron over a damp cloth, and then coaxing it back into shape. The canvas may 'grin' through at first, but this rapidly disappears as the wool gets flattened with wear.

NOTE. Locker-rug canvas is particularly coarse meshed and liable to catch on stockings and knits, so it's a good idea to lay a piece of old sheet or something like that over your lap as you work.

A pile rug from knitting-wool tiles

The least cumbersome way of making a wool rug is by making lots of small separate tiles or squares, and stitching them all together when you have as many as you need – the rug can be any size, depending on the number of tiles. The tile pattern given here is a 12-inch square (figures 27 and 28), which is a handy size to work on your lap. They are made from ordinary 4-ply knitting wool, using a Danish carpet needle, hessian for the backing and a wooden frame. Crafts Unlimited (Suppliers' Index),

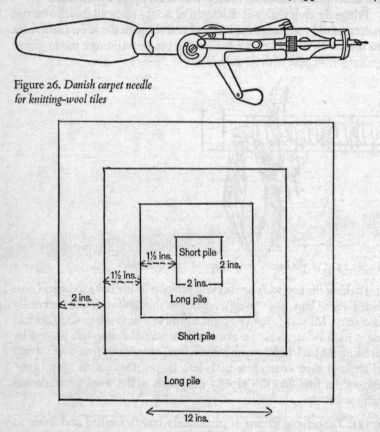

Figure 26. *Danish carpet needle for knitting-wool tiles*

Figure 27. *Diagram for working a tile, using long and short pile for contrast*

have both needle and frames, but since the needle is on the expensive side – about £2.50 at the time of writing – you might like to save a couple of pounds by making your own frame, out of four 18-inch lengths of 2- by 1-inch deal section nailed or screwed together at the corners. Alternatively use a flat wood picture frame approximately the same size. The Danish carpet needle looks complicated, but once you have mastered the threading (instructions come with it) it is simple to operate. It works a bit like a shuttle with a needle at one end which forces loops of wool through the hessian from the back. You can set it to produce loops of different lengths – short, medium or long. A combination of short and long, as in the pattern given here, gives an interesting textured effect, especially when the rug is worked entirely in one colour. The tiles go very quickly – you can work one in an evening if you keep

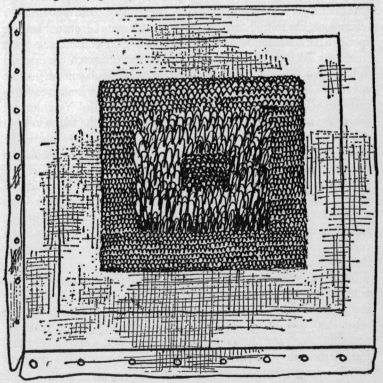

Figure 28. *Hessian tacked in place over frame and a partly made-up tile*

at it. The pile is dense and feels luxurious underfoot, and a rug made like this is excellent value for money – wool for a 3 × 6-foot rug can cost as little as £3 or £4 if you use a cheap line of knitting wool. Allow 6 ounces of wool per tile. The pile needs to be sealed from the back with carpet glue (Crafts Unlimited) or a latex adhesive like Copydex, which incidentally creates a non-slip backing.

There is a certain amount of wastage with the hessian, as the frame and each square of hessian backing need to be at least 4 inches wider than the finished tile for easy working – you can't get the carpet needle right up to the frame edge. The cheapest way to get hold of large widths of hessian is from an upholsterers' suppliers (Suppliers' Index).

METHOD. The first step is to get a square of hessian stretched taut over your frame. (When making the frame, incidentally, there is no need for refinements like mitred corners, butt joints are quite adequate.) Lay the frame on the hessian and cut a square large enough to pull and tack down round the sides of the frame – this allows you to stretch the material tighter. If you add another couple of inches on all round you can fold the edges back and tack them double, which will make the hessian easier to manage – it is stretchy stuff and liable to fray when pulled. You must get the weave of the hessian running at right angles to the frame in both directions, lengthways and across. If you don't square it up properly the hessian will stretch and your tile won't be a proper square. Fold the hessian in half, first one way and then the other, checking that the creases follow the weave to make a cross-shaped crease. Mark the middle of each side of the frame and lay the hessian on top so that the cross lies directly over the marks. Pin securely with drawing pins at these points, stretching the hessian taut as you do so. Then pin the hessian down at the corners. Carry on round the frame, stretching and pinning, till the hessian is as tight as a drum.

Using a felt-tipped pen and ruler, or T-square if you have one, mark out the pattern in the middle of your hessian square. Don't sweat to get it accurate to a hairsbreadth – with a thick pile rug like this small inaccuracies won't matter. Mark the pattern on the front of the frame but remember that your tile will emerge on the back. It will be more comfortable to set the frame on a flat board – drawing board, tray – on your lap, than prop it on your knees.

Thread your carpet needle with the wool, following the instructions given in the manufacturer's leaflet. Begin in the middle of the design, marking out the smallest square with the needle set on the shortest loop. Then fill in, working the needle backwards and forwards, and leaving just a little hessian showing between the rows of stitching. Let the wool run freely and make sure you always keep a few feet of wool loose on the surface of the hessian. If the flow of wool is checked, it will alter the tension and change the loop length. Be careful of knots too as the needle won't take them, and cut off any free ends as soon as possible (no need to darn them in as the carpet glue seals them in place) because the needle tends to trip up over them.

When you have finished the small square, cut the wool off close to the hessian. Set the needle to the longest loop and mark out the outer edge of the next largest square with two rows of stitching. Fill in the same way, as evenly as possible. Carry on in the same way, using shortest and longest loops on alternate squares till your tile is finished. Remove drawing pins. Trim the hessian to within 2 inches of the tile all round. Spread special carpet glue or Copydex over the back of the tile, turning back the extra hessian all round and pressing down firmly while the glue is tacky.

MAKING UP THE RUG. Joining the tiles from the right, or pile side, is easier as you are less likely to catch the loops in while stitching. Use a carpet needle and stout thread – carpet thread, or linen thread run over beeswax to strengthen it. Put two tiles back to back, and stitch two edges together with an oversewing stitch (*see* re-laying old carpet). Continue till you have stitched them all together. The long pile round the outer edge of the tiles will hide the seams.

Cross-stitch rug based on a traditional Greek design

A rug this size – 38 × 72 inches – is not something to take on if you must have quick results, although compared with the tiny *petitpoint* of so many needlework rugs, the large cross-stitch used here covers the ground at a gallop. It's a job for long winter evenings in front of the telly, or whiling away the last months of pregnancy. Cross-stitch (figure 29) is one of the simplest canvas-work stitches, gives a pleasant texture, and is very hard wearing. The design, once you have mastered the basic motif repeated round the border and plotted out the large cross-shaped motifs in the centre, is not a difficult one to follow. As illustration, we have

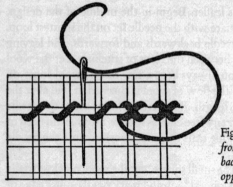

Figure 29. *Cross-stitch is worked
from left to right as shown and then
back over your tracks in the
opposite direction*

included a photograph of the finished rug, so that you can see how to
position the central motifs, and how many of the border motifs are
needed along the sides, plus charts for working a section of the border
and for the individual cross motifs; figures 30, 31 and 32. The design is
worked mainly in off-white on a peat-brown ground, with a little pink
and orange in the border (*see* colour key).

MATERIALS. You need 2⅛ yards of jute canvas from the Needlewoman
Shop (Suppliers' Index) and forty-eight 2-ounce skeins of rug wool in
these proportions – twenty-eight skeins of the background colour,
sixteen of the colour used to work crosses and the basis of the border
motifs, and 2 each of the contrasting colours worked into the border.
Also a tapestry needle, and a length of hessian to back the finished
rug.

METHOD. The easiest way to work the border pattern (*see* figure 30) is
to fill in the basic dark colour first, which leaves the motifs standing out
clearly. Work the ends of the rug first because rug canvas frays at alarming speed – turn back 2 inches of canvas at each end and work the first
few rows on a double thickness to prevent this. When you have filled in
the border background, fill in the motif in three colours as shown in the
key. Keep the two contrast colours in the same position in the motif
right round the rug.

Now count out the large cross motifs (*see* figures 31 and 32) in the
centre, marking them out with a felt pen, or alternatively following the
same procedure as with the border – i.e. working round the motifs in

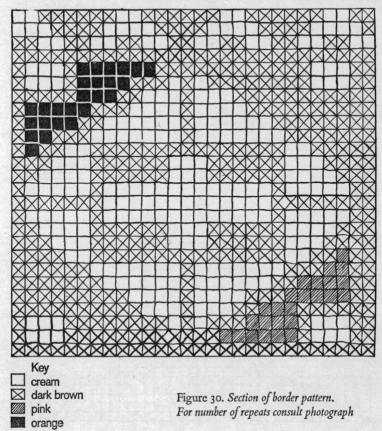

Key
☐ cream
⊠ dark brown
▨ pink
▩ orange

Figure 30. *Section of border pattern.*
For number of repeats consult photograph

the background colour, counting as you go. Don't drive yourself crazy counting all the holes one by one till you get the exact centre – simply folding the rug in half will give you the middle, give or take a hole or two. If this shocks you, I can only say that a touch of asymmetry is an accepted feature of folk designs, like the Hopi Indian woman in Lawrence's poem who leaves a loose thread at one end of her mat so the spirit can escape. Now fill in the centre motifs. The rug will be pretty heavy by this time. You will find it easier to manage if you fold up the part you aren't working on and stitch it at a table. This also helps prevent it getting pulled out of shape by its own weight.

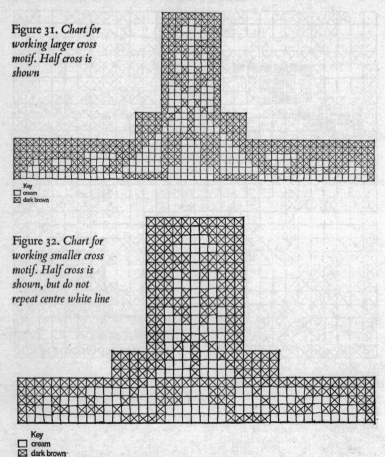

Figure 31. *Chart for working larger cross motif. Half cross is shown*

Key
☐ cream
☒ dark brown

Figure 32. *Chart for working smaller cross motif. Half cross is shown, but do not repeat centre white line*

Key
☐ cream
☒ dark brown·

The rest is plain sailing, a matter of filling in the background colour, working large blocks at a time. Cover in the selvedges on either side of the finished rug with the background colour, using the binding stitch shown with the locker rug instructions. Add a short fringe if you like, or leave the ends as they are. You should really slipstitch a hessian backing to the rug if you are going to put it on a bare floor, that is if you want it to last for a hundred years. On the other hand, with a rug as heavy as this, adding hessian might make it almost too weighty to handle easily.

FURNITURE

Close covering

Close covering – replacing the original tacked-on outer cover – is the only way to rehabilitate chairs and sofas with exposed wood frames. A loose cover draped over knobbly arms and carved wood back looks slightly sinister. It is also a good way of facelifting a stuffed armchair which has begun to sag and lose its shape. The thought of renewing the outer skin of a piece of furniture may sound drastic, if you have never attempted it, but apart from being a bit rough on the hands it is quite easy to do and takes less time than making a loose cover. If you prefer using a hammer to a needle, it is also more fun.

You do not have to be expert to get good results, just methodical. Doing the job yourself saves a lot of money – £15 upwards for a chair, and more for a sofa. You don't need many specialized tools. Upholsterers use ripping tools for removing old tacks, and special hammers, but a light tack hammer and screwdriver are quite adequate substitutes. You also need a curved needle – sold in household needle packs – thin twine, and two or three boxes of ½-inch upholstery tacks. For a chair with an exposed wood frame, gimp or ½-inch grosgrain ribbon are needed to hide the tacks. In some cases – see below – you may also need unbleached calico, hessian, curled hair and cotton felt (see Suppliers' Index).

Removing the old cover is the most tedious part of close covering. You should not just rip it off though, because the old cover pieces make useful templates for cutting new ones, saving a lot of calculating and measuring. Remove the old tacks one by one. Do this by setting the screwdriver at an angle to one side of the tack and banging lightly with the hammer. This levers them up and they can then be prised up with the screwdriver or forked end of the hammer. Obdurate tacks should be banged flat.

Remove the old cover in this order. Turn the chair upside down and take off the dust cover on the bottom. Outside arms and back come off next. Start by removing tacks fastening these to the bottom rail and then work up round the sides and top. Next come inside arms and back, and lastly the seat cover.

Lay the cover pieces out flat, with the straight of goods – lengthways weave – all going the same way, to give you an idea how much fabric you need for the new cover. Allow a couple of inches extra all round each piece because the old ones will have stretched in use. Most upholstery fabrics are 50 inches wide, or more. Odd scraps can be used for covering piping cord, if you are using it.

Fabric

Close covering looks best carried out in a close-woven, medium- to heavy-weight fabric with a little stretch to it. Thick, tweedy textured fabrics are excellent for beginners, being firm and stretchy, and the texture disguises flaws in the workmanship. Most good-quality up-

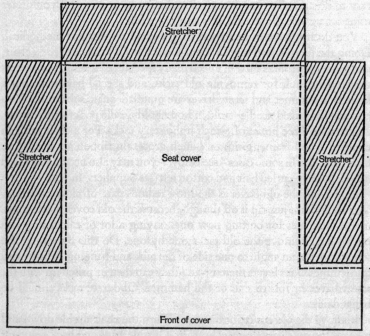

Figure 33. *Pieces of scrap material can be used to economize on chair fabric, and the pieces saved used for covering seat borders, arm panels or piping. The scrap pieces are called stretchers. Measure seat at widest point both down and across and add on 1 or 1½ inches to determine stretcher size. Use a double row of machining when attaching stretchers to seat cover as the seams take a lot of strain*

holstery fabrics are expensive. You can save material by using cover stretchers – pieces of tough scrap material machined to the cover pieces where they will not show, which means from just below the cleft running round the seat to the point where they are tacked to the bottom rails (see figure 33). If your chair has a loose seat cushion, you can save a bit more by covering the underside of the cushion and the back part of the seat-cover proper with more scrap material. Use something strong though – denim, ticking, canvas. Where every penny counts, go for a cheaper material as long as it is strong. Denim, ticking, holland, tailor's canvas, sheet canvas (available from marine suppliers) are all suitable. Canvas can be dyed either professionally, or at home (see marbled canvas, p. 82). Handle these fabrics respectfully and smarten them up with fringe, braid or contrasting grosgrain ribbon, and they can look very distinguished. Their disadvantage, as with all smooth-textured fabrics, is that they show dirt more quickly. Keep your eyes open, too, because you might stumble on something quite special which could be used to re-cover a chair – a piece of old Kelim rug (they often turn up at sales of household effects), Indian woven-cotton bedspreads of the crunchy thick kind, secondhand velvet curtains, often complete with yards of fringe and braid which can be used to embellish the chair. Avoid the edges of old curtains where possible because these are usually worn as well as faded – cut pieces from the centre, avoiding seams.

Undercover work

To look really sleek and classy an upholstered piece should have a calico undercover, usually overlaid with a layer or two of cotton wadding or felt. The outside arms and back should be covered in with pieces of hessian too to prevent that caved-in look. If your piece was properly upholstered in the beginning, it will already have these, and you can go straight ahead with recovering. If not, it was a shoddy job, and you might well consider improving its looks by adding these underpinnings yourself. The materials are cheap, and fitting a calico undercover is good practice for installing the final one. You can build up meagrely stuffed arms, seat and back at the same time, which will make the whole chair more comfortable and twice as good looking. Use curled hair to build up the stuffing. This can be salvaged from an old chair or stool, or bought from upholstery suppliers. A $\frac{1}{3}$ of a pound of hair per square foot gives approximately 1 inch extra padding when compressed by the cover. Pick hair over to break up lumps, and then pack it on generously where it is needed – usually a thin layer over inside back, a thicker one to correct hollows in the seat and a good puff over each arm. The calico undercover will keep it all in place.

Use the old cover pieces as a rough guide when cutting the undercover, adding on a few inches all round to accommodate the extra padding and allow for beginner's mistakes. Fit on and tack down as for the final cover (see below) but set the tacked edges, which should be double thickness, i.e. folded back, for strength, $\frac{1}{2}$ an inch or so within the tack holes marking the edge of the old cover. Cut pieces of hessian or strong scrap material to cover in the outside arms and back and tack these down, folding edges in, round sides and top, but not the bottom rail because the outer cover pieces will have to be pulled through here to be tacked down. Set the tacks close together – $\frac{3}{4}$–1 inch apart.

Cutting and fitting the cover

Again, use old cover pieces as a pattern. Lay the new fabric out flat and arrange the old pieces – reconstituting their original shape carefully – on top, allowing two inches all round to allow for the old material having stretched. When covering over a chair you have padded up, allow more where needed. *Important:* all the old pieces must be laid out with the straight weave of the cloth corresponding to the straight of the new fabric. Squeezing odd bits out on the bias will boobytrap your work, because bias stretches just where you need the cloth to be taut. Mark the outlines in chalk. Make sure you have not overlooked a vital piece – front arm panels – or forgotten to cut two of a particular piece. Then cut them out. Any joins should look meant – down the centre of a sofa back and seat for instance. Machine these up first, using a medium-sized stitch. The cover pieces are fitted, or installed as upholsterers say, in the reverse order from the one in which you removed them – seat first, then inside arms and back, outside arms and back and any borders (the part from the seat to the bottom rail of an armchair) and arm scrolls, finishing up with a new dust cover and any gimp or braid trimming.

Stretch the seat-cover fabric smoothly over the seat, pushing the sides and back well down till the fabric hangs over the bottom rail. If you have followed the old seat-cover you will have nicked pieces out to fit round the back posts (wooden uprights continuing up from back legs) but you may have to slash these further for a snug fit. Do this carefully at first – cut a small Y-shaped nick, prongs facing the post, and cut deeper if necessary as you fit the cover. It takes some trial and error to get the cover pieces smooth and taut, without wrinkles, pull marks, or slack, so do not hurry this part. Begin tacking with slip tacks, or tacks driven only a little way in so they can be removed easily, while you are adjusting the piece. The object of all this fiddling about is to get a really tight fit, keeping the weave of the material in both directions running straight across and up and down the chair seat. Sliptack first at centre front and back, then in the middle of each side, straining the cover smooth and tight each time. Go on straining and sliptacking round the seat, working outwards from your first tacks. When the whole piece is sliptacked into position, give it a last critical smoothing over with your hands and correct any slackness by removing the relevant tacks, tightening and re-tacking. When you are satisfied you have got a perfect tight fit, pull out the centre tacks, fold the cover edge under and re-tack, driving the tack home this time. Repeat round the seat. A double, folded edge stands up much longer to heavy wear – single thicknesses are liable to tear. Make

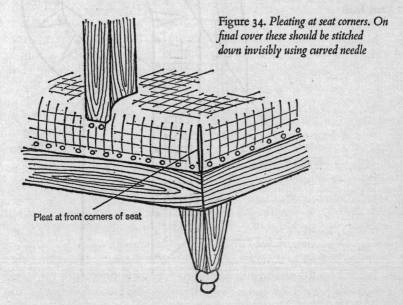

Figure 34. *Pleating at seat corners. On final cover these should be stitched down invisibly using curved needle*

Pleat at front corners of seat

any further nicks needed to fit the piece smoothly round the back posts and arm posts, folding the slashed edges in a little and tacking down firmly each side of the post. The cover may need pleating to fit smoothly at front corners (*see* figure 34). You can leave the pleat as a pleat, or blind-stitch it (*see* figure 37) with curved needle and thread.

Do the inside back next, which is generally straightforward unless it needs buttoning. On a stuffed chair the back cover should be nicked to follow the curve of the arms. Push the raw edges well down into the fold here before tacking side pieces to the back posts and the bottom edge to the bottom rail. Turn all edges under again before tacking down. The inside arms are often the trickiest part of a cover to fit well, as some

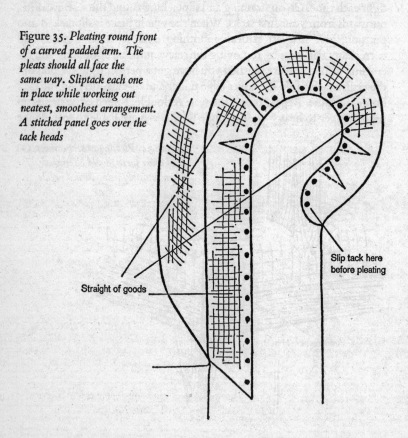

Figure 35. *Pleating round front of a curved padded arm. The pleats should all face the same way. Sliptack each one in place while working out neatest, smoothest arrangement. A stitched panel goes over the tack heads*

Straight of goods

Slip tack here before pleating

pleating may be needed to fit the piece neatly round the arm front, and any bungling will show. The fewer and smaller pleats (*see* figure 35) you can contrive, the better – this is done by working the fabric tightly round the curve, and keeping the whole piece with the grain or straight weave running vertically up the inside arm and over the curve. Begin by sliptacking the piece down at the outer corners, keeping the weave vertical. Next sliptack the centre of each side. Sliptack right round except for the part to be pleated, making sure you get a smooth curve over the arms. Now make some experimental pleats, following the diagram, holding each one down with a sliptack. When you are satisfied that you have got it just right, tack down permanently all round. Trim any extra fabric off round the pleated curve. Tear a strip of cotton wadding to pad out the narrow panel, or scroll, down the centre of the arm front. The

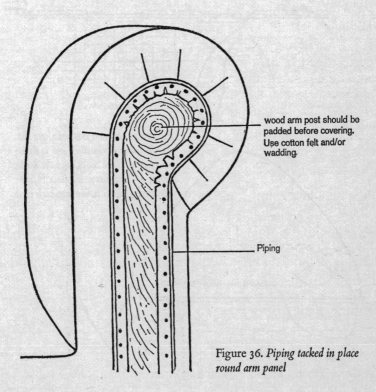

wood arm post should be padded before covering. Use cotton felt and/or wadding.

Piping

Figure 36. *Piping tacked in place round arm panel*

scroll cover piece is blindstitched down over the top. If the scrolls are to be piped, tack the piping down first as shown (*see* figure 36). Use hatpins to skewer the scroll piece into place before turning edges under and stitching. An upholsterer's trick is to blindstitch it from the top using two curved needles, one down either side simultaneously. This prevents it being pulled out of true. For blindstitching *see* figure 37. The front border (part between seat front and bottom rail) of a sofa or chair should be tacked or stitched into place invisibly. Do this by laying the border

Figure 37. *First method of blindstitching two cover-pieces together. Dotted lines show hidden path of curved needle. Note that stitches are at right angles to edges being joined*

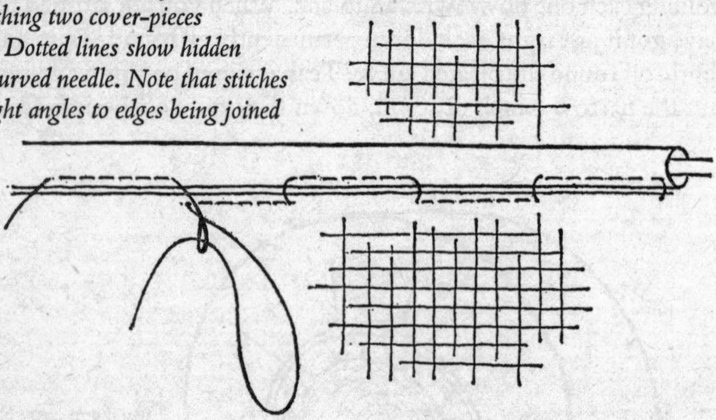

Figure 38. *Second method: here the needle takes a backstitch and is then run two or three times over the loop of twine to form a running knot before continuing. Pull twine taut each time*

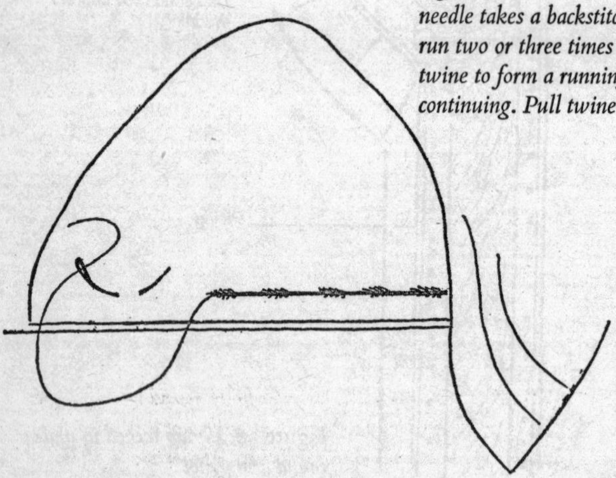

Figure 39. *Cutaway section showing a piped border blindtacked into place along seat front*

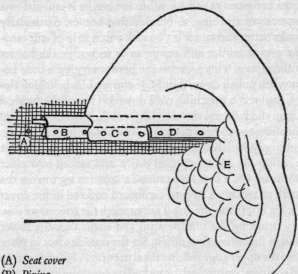

(A) *Seat cover*
(B) *Piping*
(C) *Border cover*
(D) *Cardboard strip (optional)*
(E) *Padding or hair stuffing*

   Cardboard strip tightens a blindtacked edge. Stuffing or wadding should be packed over tacked edges to give a smooth curve when border is pulled down and tacked

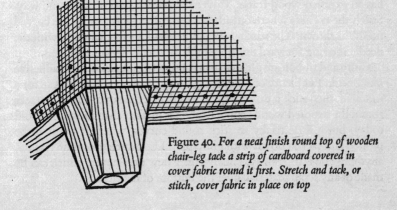

Figure 40. *For a neat finish round top of wooden chair-leg tack a strip of cardboard covered in cover fabric round it first. Stretch and tack, or stitch, cover fabric in place on top*

piece, wrong side up, over the front of the seat so that the border edge meets up with the edge of the seat cover and then blind-tacking or stitching as shown in figures 38 and 39. When the border is pulled down you cannot see tacks or stitching. A blind-tacked border, particularly when piped, looks better and tauter if you tack a thin strip of stiff cardboard down on top of border and piping so as to wedge the border tightly against the piping. This prevents the border sagging a little between the tacks when pulled down tightly. If you are blindstitching this piece down, you can sew a matching cord down on top of the finished join to neaten it up and hide any tiny sags between the stitches. Sew cord round the scroll pieces too to even things up. The border itself should be padded out generously with hair and felted cotton or wadding to give a smooth curve before the cover is pulled down and tacked into place under the bottom rail. For a neat finish round a wooden leg top use the upholsterer's trick of tacking a strip of cardboard covered in the cover fabric round the leg first (*see* figure 40). Tack or stitch the cover over this.

Before finally installing the outside arms and back, tack the lower edges of the hessian undercovering down. Set the outside arms in place first, making sure the upper edge follows the arm curve. This edge can be blind-tacked in position, or stitched, or tacked on from the outside, the tacks then being covered with glued-on gimp, or ribbon. This depends on the style of chair – gimp and trimmings look appropriate on Victorian furniture, but fussy on large stuffed chairs. A first-class upholsterer would neaten these edges with piping, but this is not necessary. The bottom edges of the outside arms and back should be brought right down under the bottom of the chair before being tacked down, unless the chair has an exposed wood frame. Cover the outside back in the same way. Stitch the corners where outside back and arms meet using the curved needle as shown. The stitches should be small horizontal ones, with the needle moving forward invisibly underneath (*see* figure 37).

Gimp and ribbon are glued in place, using a colourless instant adhesive like Bostik. Put plenty of glue on the wrong side, leave it to soak in for a moment, then stick it down a small length at a time over all visible tacks round the exposed wood frame. Ribbon is prettier than most gimp sold today, but a little tricky to stick round curves, where it needs to be pleated and tacked down with gimp pins. Use $\frac{1}{2}$-inch grosgrain ribbon, anything else is too flimsy. Finally tack a new dust-cover, which can be made of any scrap material, over the bottom of the chair.

Buttoning

Buttoning looks complicated, but again, if you use the old cover as a guide, and go about the job methodically, you can get very good results. Shallow buttoning is easier to do than deep buttoning, where the fabric has to be pleated symmetrically in a diamond shape between the buttons. In some cases you may find a Victorian chair or ottoman was upholstered for buttoning but has since been close covered flat, without buttons, to save fabric, time and money. This never works very well, unless the stuffing is completely re-laid, because the original loose stuffing retains the old hummocks and hollows, and a cover can never be stretched quite tight and smooth over the top. Run your hand over the piece – if it was once buttoned, you can distinctly feel the curves of the stuffing and locate the old button sites. Re-buttoning the piece as you cover it will improve its appearance dramatically, tightening up all the outlines. Cutting a new cover piece for the buttoned area will be a bit more difficult as the old unbuttoned cover can't be used as a pattern. Instead, use unbleached calico as an undercover, cutting it generously larger all round. Poke the material into the button sites experimentally and then draw it down round the sides to give you an idea how large to cut the final cover. Then use the calico as a pattern for the final cover before installing and tacking it. A calico undercover is a good idea in any case, as it gives you invaluable practice in pleating, stitching, etc., and greatly improves the final look of the work. The calico is not buttoned at the button sites – that comes in the final stage – instead take a long straight upholstery needle threaded with a long piece of twine – 2 feet or so – up through the webbing or hessian backing and then out through the button site then take it back down again $\frac{1}{2}$ an inch or so to one side of where it came out, then up again and back at right angles to the first stitch – like sewing on a button with four holes – and then tie the ends of the twine in a reef knot over a tiny bit of wadding or cotton wool to prevent it cutting through the webbing.

Get the buttons professionally covered. A local upholsterer might do them for you, otherwise consult the Suppliers' Index for details of a postal service. The do-it-yourself kits for home dressmakers are useless for this sort of job because the covered top tends to come adrift after a while leaving a sharp, conspicuous metal shank. Alternatively you might like to add a decorator touch with looped tufts reminiscent of the cotton

Figure 41. *Tuft of looped piping cord stitched to a circle of cover fabric*

tufts on old hair mattresses. These were secured to pinked leather circles. The decorator variety are made of loops of thinnest piping cord (you could substitute ordinary string) dyed to match the cover and caught down with stout thread to a small pinked edged circle of the cover fabric (figure 41). Glue a piece of the cover fabric, using a strong solution of decorator's glue size for the job, to a backing of tailor's canvas or similar stiffening material. When the size, which stiffens and sticks in one operation, is quite dry, mark out the circles with a 10p coin and cut round with pinking shears. To make the loops, wind cord or string several times round three fingers, slip these loops off and stitch down securely across the centre of the bunch to the centre of the fabric circle with a strong needle and waxed button thread or twine. If this tuft looks skimpy, stitch down another bundle of loops at right angles to the first. When the tuft is stitched into place the tension will keep the loops bunched together.

Cut the cover piece to be buttoned using the calico undercover as a pattern. Chalk the button sites on it carefully. To be on the safe side allow two or three inches extra all round. Begin with a central button, or tuft. Align the chalked button position on the cover with the corresponding hollow in the stuffing beneath, poking it down a little way. Thread a long length of twine into an upholsterer's needle (Suppliers' Index) and stab this through the stuffing from behind the chair back or beneath the seat as the case may be, so that the needle passes out through the chalked button site on the cover piece. Now pass the needle through the button shank, looping it once to make it easier to pull tight and stab through the button position again and out at the back close to where the

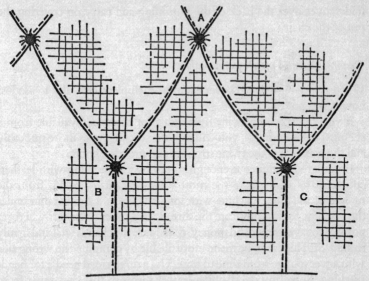

Figure 42. *Order of fixing buttons or tufts, and direction of pleats in between*

needle entered. This may take a little practice to get right, but after a while you will find you can do it without thinking. Draw the two ends of twine up tight over a scrap of wadding or cotton wool (to prevent the twine cutting through the webbing) but do not knot permanently as yet. Next, attach buttons in the same way at the two points which form a triangle with the first (figure 42). Then button at the point next to the first, and so on, across the back or seat. Pleat the fabric between the buttons with a sharp pointed tool like an icepick or knitting needle as shown in the illustration. The pleats should all face downwards, so as not to harbour dust. When all the buttons and pleats are in place study the effect to gauge whether some buttons need pulling tighter. Having adjusted these, begin knotting the twines at the back, using a reef knot (*see* figure 71, p. 130). Do not pull the twine ends too tight. A buttoned surface should be firm and resilient but not rock hard. The extra fabric round the edges should be neatly pleated from the nearest button point to the edge of frame or seat. Keep these pleats straight; vertical at top and bottom, horizontal at the sides, angled like wheel spokes round curves such as one finds on a buttoned Victorian spoon-back chair. Now tack a hessian undercover over the back of the buttoning and carry on covering the rest of the chair.

General tips and points to remember

When removing the old cover examine each piece carefully to see just how it was put on.

If you run stitching twine over a cake of beeswax (available from a chemist) before using it, you will find the stitching goes more smoothly and the wax makes the twine stronger and prevents knots.

If you are adventurous enough to re-cover something with leather, cut the parts which take the most wear (seat, arms, back), from the middle of the hide, machine with long stitches and rub paraffin under the machine foot to lubricate the thread. Use cover stretchers wherever possible to save leather and money. Make sure the chair is well and firmly stuffed. Stiff hides can be made more pliable by damping the wrong side with a wet sponge from time to time. Use a three-sided needle for hand-stitching. Skive any overlapping leather pieces so that they taper from about half an inch from the end on the wrong side to a sharp edge. Use a sharp blade, lay the leather down on a smooth board or marble slab and slice diagonally.

Clean upholstered surfaces by going over them frequently with a vacuum cleaner, banging the stuffing back into shape at the same time. Shampoo with suds only – an eggwhisk froths up a splendid amount of suds.

Some Victorian pieces look better lowered by lopping off an inch on the legs, or simply removing the castors. Deep fringe (*see* trimmings, p. 291) tacked round the bottom makes them look twice as luxurious.

Marbled canvas for upholstery

One does sometimes hit upon successful ideas by accident. I bought some canvas – ordinary sheet canvas, medium weight – to upholster a Victorian chair because I was looking for something strong and cheap, and canvas cost less than £1 for a yard 72 inches wide. I decided to dye it because I thought the natural cream colour would get dirty much too quickly and, after failing to find the sludgy green colour which I was after in the Dylon range, bought two colours – a bright green and a warm yellow – which I thought might combine to give the shade I wanted. For some reason I decided to dye the cloth in two stages – one colour first, then the other. What I had not reckoned on was that to dye canvas evenly one would require a huge dye bath because it is much too rigid to pack down into a smallish tin sink-bowl, which was what I was using. The result was that the canvas came out blotchy. Thinking that a second coat of a darker dye might correct this I dyed it again. It looked horrible when I hung the stuff up to dry, like camouflage of the dingiest sort. My husband suggested I would do better to chuck it away. But to my great surprise, when dry and ironed smooth, the blotches looked decidedly attractive – not like blotches at all but a quite subtle dappled effect, with the paler greeny yellow showing through the darker green haphazardly, like sunlight through leaves. The chair, upholstered, buttoned and edged in gimp dyed to match, looked decidedly handsome. The canvas has stood up to hard wear extremely well. It can be cleaned successfully with the usual upholstery shampoo. The only snag is that these Dylon dyes do fade. The fading looks quite attractive, since the general effect is dappled anyway, but if you want to keep the fabric more or less as it started out you should stand the piece out of strong sunlight.

To get this dappled effect the trick is to fold the piece of canvas several times, and keep moving the unwieldy bundle about in the dye, opening it up from time to time to make sure the dye gets in to all the folds, otherwise one area may remain almost blank. Do not be put off by the look of the stuff wet because canvas darkens appreciably when wet. Two colours of the same tone seem to work out best – though I did get quite an attractive crushed rose-petal effect with a greeny mushroom shade re-dyed a pink-mauve.

Making loose covers

Short of completely redecorating, nothing so radically improves the look of a room as re-covering the main pieces of furniture. The shabbiest sofa and chairs, uncut moquette and all, take on sleek and prosperous airs zipped into fitted covers in good plain colours or brilliant prints. Covering a chair is a bit like dressing a problem figure – there is a lot one can do to disguise its bad points. Soft or neutral colours play down ugly shapes and lumpy contours. A corner-pleated valance or quilted band round the bottom hides bulbous feet and gives furniture a streamlined look. Under-stuffed chairs and sofas are greatly improved, both in comfort and looks, by a plump seat cushion (two in the case of a sofa) covered in the same fabric.

Anyone who can make clothes can make loose covers. I should explain, incidentally, that 'loose' in this context just means removable; a loose cover can and usually should fit like a glove. Once you have grasped the principles of cutting and fitting, it is actually easier to make a well-fitted cover than a well-fitted dress. The chair does not move or scream when you stick pins in it, or mysteriously expand between fittings. Its contours are large and simple, and you can take as long crawling round it adjusting seams as you like. The sections of a cover are cut out in simple rectangles (measured of course), and then shaped and pinned and tacked *in situ*, and finally machined up in one operation. Piping is inserted at the pinning stage. Piping is invariably used by professionals, because it looks neat and reduces wear on the seams, but it is a bit tricky to handle if you have never piped a seam before, and it does emphasize the shape of the chair, which might not be a good thing. Also it takes more material, unless you use some suitable scraps you happen to have.

Making your own covers saves a lot of money – the cheapest sewing lady seems to charge around £10 to cover an armchair these days. That does not include the cost of the fabric. Doing it yourself costs approximately half what it would cost if you handed the job over to a professional. And if you take some care over it, you may well get better results.

Before buying the material it is worth spending some time measuring up the piece – or pieces – with some care. Any standard yardages that might be quoted to you by shop assistants, magazines, etc., invariably err on the generous side and you may be left with a piece of material too large to throw away and just too small to cover anything else with. If you have some idea of the particular fabric you want, so much the better, because furnishing fabrics come in varying widths. Standard British width is 4 feet but some imported fabrics are 5 feet wide and more. Any of these widths will accommodate the average armchair without joins in any of the main pieces – I suggest you begin with an armchair for this reason – but the really wide fabrics also allow you to cut most of the smaller pieces from the off-cuts.

To measure up

First consult the illustrations (figure 43). There are ten sections to measure up for a cover for the chair shown, and these are designated by alphabetical letters. A band or pleated valance round the bottom will require extra material, as would a seat cushion – incidentally, this type of chair

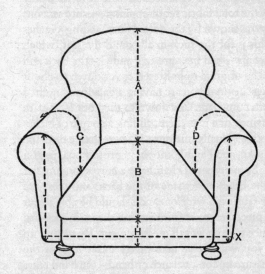

Figure 43. *Measuring up an armchair for fabric requirements*
(A) *inside back*
(B) *seat*
(C) *inside arm*
(D) *inside arm*
(E) *outside arm*
(F) *outside arm*
(G) *outside back*
(H) *border*
(I) *front arm quirk*
(J) *front arm quirk*
X *shows line where band or valance should come on a chair of this shape. If the chair has a seat-cushion this line would be set higher*

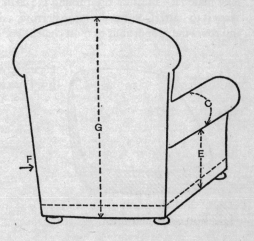

looks twice as luxurious with a cushion. The actual cushion need not cost much if you use the innards of old pillows and bolsters to stuff it with. It helps to get the plan clear in your mind if you draw a long rectangle on a piece of paper representing your length of fabric and draw out the pieces on it – not to scale, but just to make sure you have not left anything out. It is only the *length* of each section you have to worry about when working out the total fabric requirement. Measure sections A, B, C and D lengthways, as shown by the dotted lines, adding 5 inches to each measurement. This is for the tuck-in all round the seat, which anchors the cover to the chair. Then measure E, F and G – the back and sides – from the seam in the original upholstered cover down to about 1 inch above where the legs begin if you are having a valance or quilted band (instructions for both come later), or down to the floor if you are finishing the cover with fringe or a plain hem, adding a couple of inches for the hem in the last case. Finally measure H, hereafter called the 'border' for simplicity's sake, and I and J, known in professional jargon as the 'front arm quirks'. Some types of chair have a corresponding flat piece (like ears close to the head) either side of the back, and these are called side quirks. If your fabric is a wide one, you should be able to cut quirks and border out of pieces left over from cutting the main sections. Add 1-inch seam allowance to each length measurement. By totting up all your measurements you will arrive at a pretty exact idea of the yardage required. To measure up for a valance or band – the band takes least material – measure right round the chair at the height where you want it to start. (Don't make it too narrow, a deep border of some kind improves the proportions of most chairs.) For a corner-pleated valance,

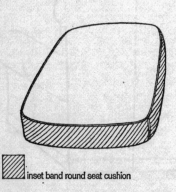

Figure 44. *Seat-cushion cover showing boxed inset band*

inset band round seat cushion

which looks smarter than box pleats, or a gathered frill, add two feet to the all-round measurement. Now measure the drop down to the ground, adding 2 inches for hems and seams. To measure up for a seat cushion, measure length from back to front of seat, add on 1 inch for seams and double the result. A seat-cushion cover has an inset band running right round it (*see* figure 44). Again you may be able to contrive this from odd pieces. If you are doubtful add 8 inches to your total.

When measuring up for a sofa cover you must allow two widths across the back, inside back, seat, border and valance or frill. Also for two seat cushions instead of one. One point to remember when making up is that a two-seater sofa is generally covered in two widths with a seam plumb down the middle, whereas a wider sofa is covered with the width of the fabric across the middle and seams at the sides. These practices may seem arbitrary, but actually they look better this way.

This may all sound like a lot of palaver just to work out your fabric requirements, but accuracy can save money at this stage. Once you have had a little practice you will be able to do most of the arithmetic in your head in a few minutes.

Cutting out

Marking out and cutting your cover sections follows much the same procedure as measuring up, except that this time you need width as well as length measurements and you chalk these onto the fabric itself. Measure every section from A to J across at the widest point, adding 1-inch seam allowance. This measurement plus the length measurement you already have gives you a rectangle corresponding to each particular section. Measure and chalk out these rectangles onto the fabric, marking each one with its alphabetical letter so that you know where you are. Before cutting make sure (a) that you have not left out any pieces, (b) that your rectangles are laid squarely over the fabric so that the edges follow the grain (a T-square could help here,) and (c) that you have not overlooked seam allowances here and there – allow $\frac{1}{2}$ an inch per seam. Cut all sections out except seat cushion and valance or border. (In making a cover do not choose a large pattern with a pronounced repeat – *Toile de Jouy* for instance – unless you are fairly experienced at dealing with them, because these create a host of special problems in measuring and cutting in order to keep the pattern properly centred on back and seat and symmetrical on inside arms and front quirks.)

Shaping and fitting

It helps to chalk lines down and across each section of material at the exact centre, and mark similar lines on the corresponding chair sections so you can pin each piece on squarely and make sure none of them get pulled askew while fitting (*see* figure 45). *All pieces are pinned and fitted to the chair inside out.* Place A section over chair back, matching and pinning centre lines. Tuck extra fabric in round seat, and into sides. Cut a short diagonal nick at both sides (figure 46) to let fabric lie flat over the curve where the arm joins the chair. Repeat for B, C and D, tucking in extra fabric, pinning at centre marks. You may need to cut nicks in C and D as for A to make the fabric lie flat over the arms. Now pin G to back, pinning G to A as these meet along the top seam line, following the

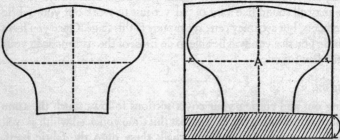

Figure 45. *Fitting. Chalk centre of fabric lengthways and widthways and pin over centre lines on corresponding chair section. With practice this can all be done by eye*

(a) *Chair-back with chalked centre lines*
(b) *Section of cover with chalked lines pinned over chair*

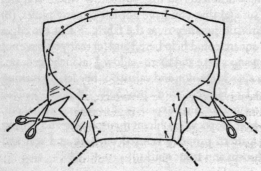

Figure 46. *Cut diagonal nicks to allow fabric to lie flat over arm curves*

curves either side. Smooth G to chair back and pin at sides. Now pin E and F to chair sides, pinning to C and D along the arms, and to G down the back. Finally pin H to chair front and then to B. I find it simplifies fitting to cut I and J (the quirks) to shape before pinning in place and attaching to the rest of the cover. To do this cut a newspaper pattern to the shape of the quirk on the upholstered cover and transfer this to your fabric pieces, allowing a ½-inch seam allowance all round when cutting. Now pin to chair quirks. You may need to shape C and D to curve smoothly over the arm fronts. This looks neatest done with two or three small darts. Pin these in place and then pin quirks to the cover sections all round – J, for instance, is pinned to H, then C, then E.

Figure 47. *Use small darts to give a smooth fit over back and arm curves*

Now, having satisfied yourself that all your fabric sections are lying smoothly and squarely over corresponding chair sections, you can begin adjusting and tightening and trimming off extra material where necessary. Section A will need darting for instance to follow the bulges either side (*see* figure 47). If the seat overhangs a bit in front you may need to take a few tucks in B at each front corner if the border is to lie flat to the chair. If your chair has sides and back which slope sharply inward, giving it a top-heavy look like a butterfly-stroke champion, all shoulders and no legs, you can disguise this by letting the vertical seams at the back and sides drop straight instead of taking them in till they lie close to the chair. When you think you have pinned your cover to perfection tack all the main seams except for those round the quirks. Pull out the tuck-in round the seat and pin and tack this all round, making a diagonal seam where A meets C and D over the bulge of the arms. Tack all seams firmly, and not too loosely, as you want the edges to hang together while machining. Unpin I and J (front quirks), machine any darts and machine up all seams except for one side seam at the back, where you will put the placket and fastenings for the cover. Put the cover back on the chair inside out, smoothing out and tucking in, and now pin and tack I and J in place. Then machine.

The bottom of the cover should be finished off before you sew in the fastenings. I favour a quilted (*machine* quilted naturally) band because it uses the least material, is heavy enough to improve the hang of the cover, does not take long to do and looks solid and nice. Best used on a fairly straight-sided chair or sofa. Shelving sides need a pleated valance. To make the band, cut the previously measured pieces and join into one continuous strip. Back it with something fluffy like a strip of old blanket or interlining, and a strip of plain scrap material so that you have a sandwich with fluffy filling. Turn 1–1½-inch hem up over the filling along the bottom edge of the band and tack down loosely. Fold lining material under and tack over this (*see* figure 48). Lay the band out flat and pin or tack all three thicknesses together here and there so they can be machined as one. Machine several rows all the way along your band in whatever grouping you like, a few rows wide apart, or one or two wide apart and several bunched together. It does not matter if your lines are

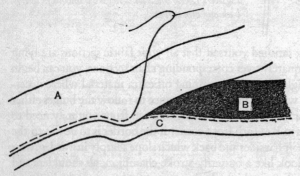

Figure 48. *Tacking hem of band before quilting*

(A) *band lining*
(B) *interlining*
(C) *fabric band*

not dead straight, and if the fabric puckers a little here and there as you quilt it. To attach band to cover, draw a chalk line right round the cover on the *right side* at the correct height. Remove cover and pin band to chalk line, keeping right sides of band and cover together. Tack in place and machine.

To make the corner-pleated valance (*see* photograph), cut your measured strip. Allow 6–8 inches at each corner for an inverted pleat. Chalk a line round the cover bottom where the valance is to start. Measure the width of each section separately along the line and mark it off on the strip, adding and marking off 6 or 8 inches for the pleats at corners. Fold pleats and tack down. Tack valance to chalk line, making sure pleat opening is exactly over chair corner and follows on the cover seam. Machine. Turn up hem round bottom and machine or hemstitch. The valance will look crisper if you line it, though this is more trouble. To line simply tack a piece of plain cotton the same size to valance before pleating, and pleat, stitch and hem as one.

If you are edging the hem with fringe, or just leaving it plain, simply turn back the hem allowance and hemstitch or machine down. Fringe is stitched into place by hand. Cotton rug fringe is cheap and looks good on matt-textured fabrics. To give a plain hem a bit more definition, you could make a rouleau edging of the same fabric, by stitching a strip of the fabric over a fairly thick cord, or even rope, if it is not too springy, as for piping (*see* figure 49). This is then machined or hand-stitched round the hem on the inside, leaving only the rouleau visible.

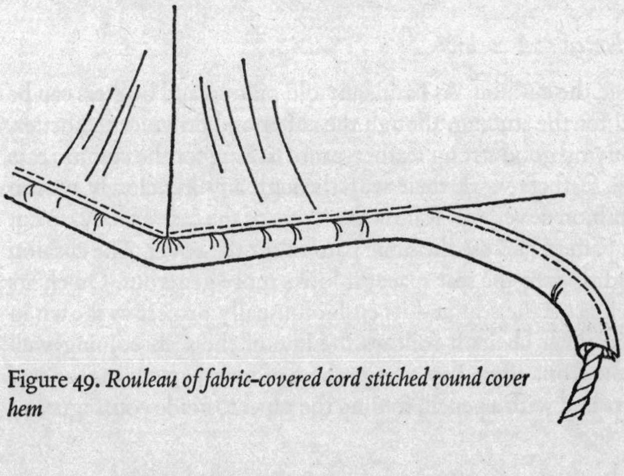

Figure 49. *Rouleau of fabric-covered cord stitched round cover hem*

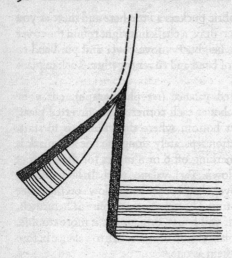

Figure 50. *Placket at side back of cover using Velcro fastening*

The easiest fastening of all, I find, is a strip of Velcro, machined each side of the back opening (figure 50). You will need to sew a strip of fabric to one side to give enough overlap for your Velcro to be hidden. Other alternatives: a zip, inserted as for a garment, with the opening at the *bottom*; press-stud tape as sold in most needlework shops, machined on as for Velcro; or, cheapest of all, and perhaps the longest lasting, good old hooks and eyes, large size, firmly sewn to a neat placket.

To make a boxed seat-cushion

First you need the cushion. As I said, any old pillows and bolsters can be cannibalized for the stuffing, though the softer and downier the better. It is worth buying good strong feather-proof ticking for the cushion case itself because feathers work their way through any less closely woven stuff. The cushion cover will follow the shape of the case exactly, so cut the case to a pattern and use the same pattern for the cover. The cushion should fit tightly into the seat space; it looks more generous. On chairs with set-back arms the seat and its cushion usually project as shown in figure 43; on other chairs it follows the line of the seat, coming well forward at the front edge. Lay a large sheet of newspaper over the seat and mark it round with a pencil, folding the paper to guide you. Figure 44 will help. Make sure your pattern is symmetrical by folding down the middle. Cut two pieces of ticking according to the pattern but 2 inches wider all round to ensure that it fits the seat tightly when sat on. Measure round the edge of your ticking pieces and cut a strip 3–5 inches wide and long enough to go right round, with one inch for a seam at the ends. This strip determines the fatness of your cushion, which will depend on the depth of the chair seat, the ultimate height from the ground (you do not want to be perched too high) and the softness of the filling. Really soft down filling is better stuffed into a very fat cushion as it squeezes down so far when sat on. 3–4 inches is right for most chairs. Tack the strip, wrong sides out, to both cushion pieces to make a bag, making sure the pieces are squarely on top of each other – pin first. Machine up, leaving ends of the strip open. Insert stuffing here in handfuls till cushion is plump. Overstitch the gap in the strip with small tight stitches. Make the cover the same way, but sew up the strip and leave a section of the cushion-cover seam open at the back so that you can get the cushion in. These openings are usually finished with a long nylon zip, inserted as for any dress opening.

Your completed cover will be much stronger if you oversew the seams. Worth the effort if you have bought a good, expensive fabric and want to get the most wear out of it.

Piping

Figure 51 shows a clever way of cutting material for piping that does not leave you with dozens of lengths to join separately. Piping cord should always be boiled, to pre-shrink it (if the cover is washable) before making up. Cut strips $1\frac{1}{2}$–2 inches wide depending on the thickness of cord and material. Fold the strip over the cord and machine, using special piping foot, as close to the cord as possible. Covers are usually piped along all the outside seams, but not round the tuck-in, or down the seams where the arms join the back. It is inserted, raw edges outwards, along all the seams after the sections have been shaped and fitted. Pin and then tack through cover edges and piping thicknesses all at once, tacking as near to the cord as possible. Don't pull the piping too taut, or the cover will pucker, but don't let it slacken either. I think it is best to machine up the main seams with piping first, leaving the quirks to be fitted and seamed separately, because it may take a little adjusting before you get

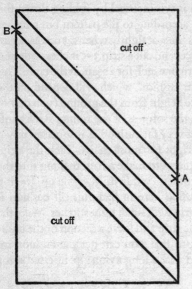

Figure 51. *A convenient way of making a continuous bias strip for piping. All the joins are done in one operation. Find the direct cross of the fabric, which can be any width. Cut off corners top and bottom as shown, then machine the two edges of your diagonal strip together matching A and B as marked to make a bias ring or tube. Starting at B, cut continuously round it, like paring an apple, to the width you require. 1½ inches is standard. You can pencil or chalk guidelines on the strip as shown before machining up the tube*

both quirks exactly symmetrical, with the piping evenly distributed round them. Machine up with piping foot, as before.

Stair-rod tables

For occasional tables, old brass stair rods, a dime a dozen now that people prefer clips, provide smart scaffolding for blockboard shelves. Four rods plus three ½-inch blockboard shelves, 14 inches square, make a handy little bedside or phone table, with shelves for directories. Two larger shelves – approximately 18 × 27 inches – plus the rods, make a nice looking sofa table for lamp, ashtrays, drinks, etc. with a shelf for magazines below. One either side of the sofa looks better still, especially if you bind the edges of the shelves with brass half-round or D strip to hide the sandwich effect of blockboard.

The structure is held together with split metal pins and Araldite. Rigidity depends on a tight fit – the holes through the shelves must fit tightly round the brass rods. The Araldite is to stop the shelves sliding up once in place. Both shelves and rods must be drilled. For the shelves, use

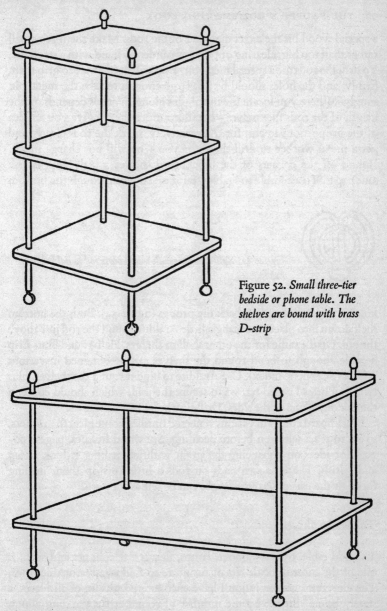

Figure 52. *Small three-tier bedside or phone table. The shelves are bound with brass D-strip*

Figure 53. *Sofa table*

a special wood bit the exact diameter of the rods. Make them too small rather than too big, clearing out the remainder by hand with a small file. To drill the rods use a special metal bit. You will need a vice to grip them firmly, and the holes should be just large enough to take the metal pin snugly. Where you locate the metal pins along the rods depends on the length of the rods themselves – the illustrations should give you an idea of the proportions to aim for. Alternatively, mark the rods clearly and get a metal worker to drill them for you – he will not charge much. Round off the corners of the blockboard shelves a little with coarse sandpaper. To assemble the tables, push metal pins through the bottom

Figure 54. *Split-pin bent back round brass rod to hold shelves in place*

holes in the rods, bending back the prongs (figure 54). Push the bottom shelf down into place, smearing a little Araldite round the rod just above the pin. Do the same for the other shelf or shelves. Half-round brass strip flexible enough to bend round the shelves can be obtained in various widths (Suppliers' Index). Use Araldite to bind it round the shelves, plus two tiny brass headed screws to secure the join, which should come in the middle of one of the sides. Drill tiny holes for the screws.

Blockboard comes in various veneered finishes, some nicer than others, so ask to see a selection before deciding. *See* wood finishes, pages 196–206, for ideas on enhancing the grain without making it look cheap and garish. Flatten acorn ends on rods a little to stop them drilling through the carpet – round knobs can be left as they are.

Tables in skirts

The odd table, to carry books, lamps, flowers, telephones and such, is one of the most difficult bits of furniture to find at a reasonable price. The cleverest cheap solution I have encountered was in, of all places, a stately home. Struck by the number of round tables standing about, demurely skirted to the floor, I lifted up the skirts of one, expecting to see some little bit of Chippendale, only to find a crude scaffolding of rough deal supporting a circular blockboard top.

Skirted tables like these have a cosy charm which looks right in almost any setting except the most rectilinear. Round tops seem to fit better into odd corners and gaps between chairs, and appear to take up less space than rectangular ones. You can change the covers to suit the seasons – cotton in summer, velvet in winter. And, by making it yourself, you can have a table just the height and diameter you need – from a little thing to hold a bedside lamp and clock, to one big enough to take four people at meals.

The table design shown here is intended to be as simple to assemble, and as rigid, as possible. You should be able to make it even if you have

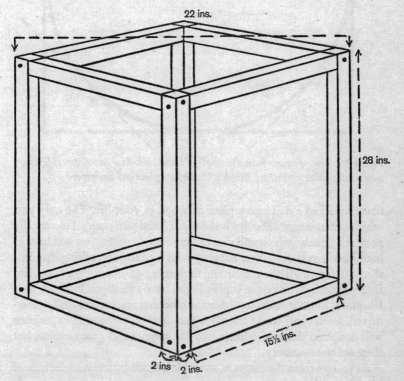

Figure 55. *Frame to support a two-foot table top*

s–c

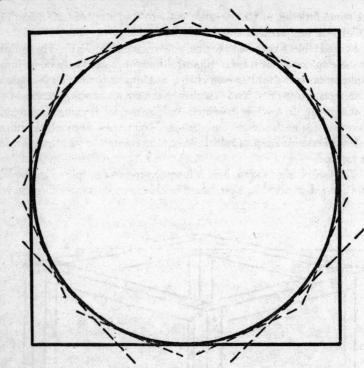

Figure 56. *Sawing a circle from a rectangle of blockboard. Saw across corners first, then tackle smaller projections. Finish with Surform plane and sandpaper*

never knocked a nail into a piece of wood in your life. The only part which presents any difficulty is the top. Unless you own an electrically powered jig saw, which will slice cleanly round curves, you will have to hack your circle out rather roughly with a panel saw, taking diagonal slices off (figure 56), then trimming the larger jags off with your saw, and finally sanding with coarse paper till you have a clean-cut circle. A little laborious, but not difficult. Other tools needed are a wood drill, screwdriver, screws and wood adhesive. People with carpenting experience will doubtless think of refinements like tongue and groove joints but these are not necessary.

As you see from the diagram, the table is made by screwing a circle of blockboard (or chipboard, cheaper still) to a box-shaped frame made from lengths of 2 × 2-inch section, screwed and glued together. The frame should extend almost the full diameter of the top for strength – a narrow pedestal will not be stable enough. If you are planning to make a larger than average table – 2-foot diameter is about average – choose a thicker deal section, $2\frac{1}{2} \times 2\frac{1}{2}$ inches, and screw metal shelf brackets, obtainable from any do-it-yourself shop, into all the inner corners of the frame to brace them before fitting on the top. The measurements given here all apply to a 2-foot diameter table. For a larger one increase the size of the underpinnings proportionately.

You need 20 feet of 2 × 2-inch section for the frame, and a 2-foot-square piece of blockboard or chipboard for the top.

To make the frame

Saw the section into four 28-inch lengths for the uprights and eight $15\frac{1}{2}$-inch lengths for the crossbars. Sand the ends of the cross bars smooth with coarse sandpaper, for a tighter join later. Now drill holes for 3-inch screws on adjoining faces at both ends of each upright. Use a wood bit the same diameter as the screws, or a fraction larger – the screw should move freely in this end of the join, or you will not be able to get a purchase on the other piece of wood. As you see in the drawing, the screw-holes must be set a little distance apart on the two faces, otherwise the screws will collide head-on. About $\frac{3}{4}$ of an inch is safe, making sure the top hole comes less than 2 inches from the end of the upright. Mark the spots with a felt pen. If you have a vice to grip the upright while drilling, this will make it easier. Otherwise lay the upright on the floor, stand on it with one foot and drill down as vertically as possible, stopping short before you fasten yourself to the floor. Drill holes in this way in both ends of all four uprights. Now screw uprights to the crossbars, assembling one end of the frame at a time. To find the continuation of your screw holes on crossbar faces, push the screw into one of the holes, align the crossbar correctly and tap the screw with a hammer to make a little dent on the crossbar. Using a bradawl, or slightly smaller wood bit, drill a little way into the crossbar to start the thing off. Then smear some wood adhesive on the crossbar face, realign, and screw home tightly. Carry on till you have finished the bottom of your frame, then turn round and repeat with the top. If you are using right-angled metal brackets to strengthen the corners, screw these in place in the inner corners now, holding them in position, marking holes with a pen, and using $\frac{1}{2}$-inch screws to secure them. Sand the top surface of your frame, paying particular attention to the tops of the uprights which should be flush with the crossbars to let your top sit flat.

To make the top

First draw a 2-foot circle clearly on your blockboard square, using a compass or at a pinch a 12-inch length of string attached to a pen one end and fastened to the centre of the board with a drawing pin at the other. Rule guide lines for sawing at angles as shown in the illustration. Don't shave the circle circumference too close, unless you are very expert, because it is safer to sand away a little excess board later. Now saw off the remaining protuberances, cutting closer and closer to your perfect circle. A tenon saw is easier to handle for this stage of the operation. Finally, when you have a near circle, sand vigorously round the edge with coarse sandpaper to remove remaining jags and give a nice smooth clean edge.

To join the top to the frame, lay your blockboard circle on the floor or a table, set the frame on top, aligning so it comes 1 inch or so from the circumference at the four corners. Then drill down through the crossbars, using a bit corresponding to a $2\frac{1}{2}$-inch screw – the screw must not be so long that the top protrudes through the table top. Two screws per crossbar is enough. Spread wood adhesive over the top of the frame, and then screw the top into place.

The cover

Please yourself how elaborate a cover you make for the table. The simplest kind to make are from felt, which has enough body to stand out without assistance and of course needs no hemming. Most craft shops sell coloured felts in extra wide widths. A cheaper, and in some ways more practical, answer is to make a good solid underskirt out of something like old army blankets, and cover it over with some washable, pretty material which goes with the rest of the room. This washable cover could be gingham, poplin, cotton lace, denim. If you look around street-market stalls you might come across one of the old chenille covers made for tables like these around the turn of the century. These often have a deep fringe, and can be very attractive.

TO MAKE. The same instructions apply to underskirt and cover. First measure across the top of the table and down to the floor at an angle on both sides. This is the diameter of your cover. All but the very widest fabrics will need seams to make up the necessary size. Arrange these so that they come to the sides of your circle rather than across the middle, where they will show. The easiest way to join them up is in three widths of the material, making up a square the same width as the circle. Lay this square flat on the floor and mark out the circle's outer edge, using a long piece of string measured to the radius of the circle, with a piece of chalk tied to one end, and the other pinned to the floor in the middle of the square. (The radius is half the diameter in case you have forgotten your geometry, but add on for a hem.) Cut round the chalked line. Turn up the hem all round by hand or machine and there is your cover. It will look prettier if you sew fringe round the bottom – cotton rug and lamp-shade fringes are the cheapest, and washable. For a grand velvet cover make your own deep handknotted fringe – (*see* trimmings, page 291). Alternatively, try bobble fringe (but not with small children around) or rows of rickrack or bias binding in various widths and colours.

If the cover is not washable, a circle of glass cut to fit the top is a sensible precaution. A table you plan to eat at is best protected by a plastic table-cloth on top, or for special occasions a lace tablecloth over a large piece of polythene. Really beautiful old hand embroidered tablecloths, with yards of hand-tatted lace trimming, are absurdly cheap in Oxfam shops and similar places. They need more upkeep than plastic of course, but nothing makes a prettier background to a meal. Soak them in cold water with a little bleach added to take out stains, and starch lightly.

Caning chair seats

Dining chairs are becoming increasingly rare, along with such things as occasional tables and chests of drawers. Attractive modern ones are expensive, while sets of so-called antique chairs – usually Edwardian – command exorbitant prices. The only cheap way round this difficulty – after all one gets sick of balancing plates on one's knees – is to hunt out old cane-seated chairs with the caning gone, and learn to replace it yourself. Chairs of this type, often with a piece of plywood tacked over the seat, turn up in junk shops and sale rooms for very modest prices by

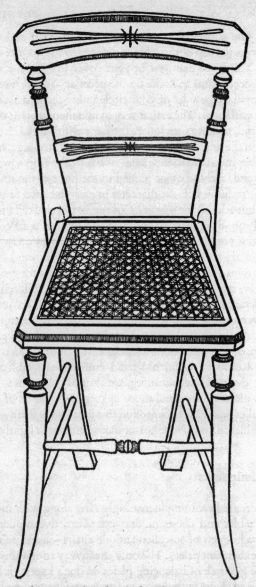

Figure 57. *A typical Victorian chair, bought for a few pence in a sale, with the caning replaced, and original decorative paintwork restored. The painted details came to light while stripping off layers of old enamel*

present-day standards. You might even be able to build up a matching set, if you do not mind waiting, because many caned-chair designs seem to have been turned out in their thousands – I found one of a pair I have on a rubbish dump, and the other turned up for 25p in an Oxfam shop.

There is less competition for these chairs, pretty though they may be, because most people cannot be bothered to find someone to re-cane them. Also, a professional re-caning job can work out expensive – a friend of mine recently paid £26 to have two small bentwood carvers re-caned. If you do it yourself the cost is minimal. Any tools needed can be improvised from what you have lying about – a length of wire to help thread the cane through, and something like an icepick to use as a bodkin in the last stages of caning.

Caning is not the mystery it looks to the uninitiated. It is a straight-forward, simple process, but slow, especially at the beginning when you keep having to check that you are doing the right thing. It is the perfect job to do sitting in the garden on a hot day.

Any mending, strengthening or titivating of the chairs should be done before caning them. Old paint and varnish may need to be stripped off. If the wood is attractive you could simply wax it. But most caned chairs were made of undistinguished wood and look better painted (see painting wood, page 241, for ideas on antiquing) or dyed a bright colour, and then varnished (see dyeing wood, page 202). Any loose joints should be re-glued with Evostick wood adhesive and left to dry under pressure – a tight bandage of tape or string will usually do the trick. The rows of holes round the seat must be cleared of old pegs or bits of cane, or old paint if you have stripped them down. Banging a sharpish tool, like a bradawl or icepick through the holes with a hammer will clear them – do not use so much force you split the wood.

Materials

Seating cane is a split cane with a hard, glossy finish on one side. It comes in various widths, Nos. 2 to 6 being the ones most commonly used for chair seats. The standard pattern for cane seating has six strands of cane woven in and out of each other and passing through the holes, so you need a narrower cane for this, Nos. 2 or 3, or 2 for the first four stages and 3 for the next two to give a bit of variety. It is tempting to use the caning patterns which use only four strands, but these are not so strong and are really only suitable for bedroom chairs or chair backs. For beading – the cane which is laid flat round the seat – choose a thicker cane, No. 6. Split cane can be bought from most handcraft shops, or ordered by post (Suppliers' Index).

Method

The cane should be soaked for a few minutes in a bucket of cold water to make it pliable before working it. I usually keep the extra cane in the bucket till I need it – take it out at the end of each stint though, or it will start some mysterious fermentation process. Keep a sponge handy to damp the cane as you work and keep it flexible.

Begin by counting the number of holes along the back and front of the chair. There will usually be more along the front as most chair seats are wider at the front. Find the centre holes. You start caning from the

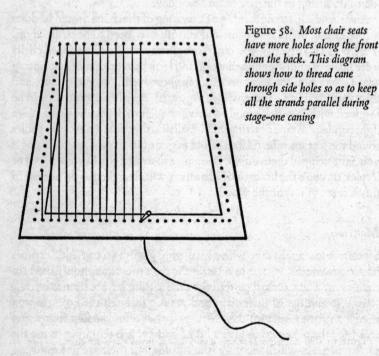

Figure 58. *Most chair seats have more holes along the front than the back. This diagram shows how to thread cane through side holes so as to keep all the strands parallel during stage-one caning*

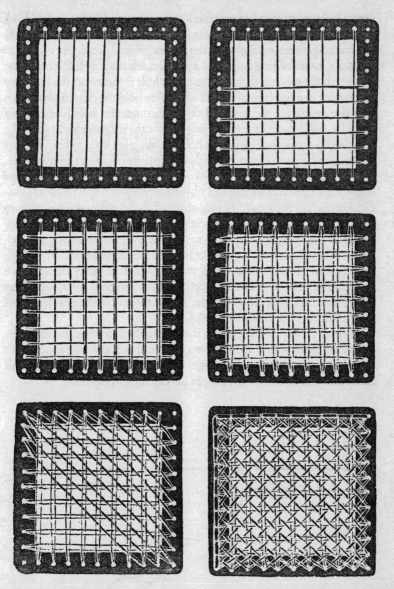

Figure 59. *The six stages in caning a chair seat to the standard six-strand pattern*

centre holes outwards because the last few strands of cane each side of the seat will have to be taken through holes along the sides (*see* figure 58) so as to keep them parallel with the others.

Take a strand of cane and make a pencil mark roughly half-way along it. Thread the cane up through the centre hole in the seat at the half-way mark, stick in a peg (a small pencil will do) to hold the cane in place, then take the cane over the seat and down through the hole immediately opposite, making sure the glossy side of the cane is uppermost. Now take the cane up through the adjacent hole, twisting it a little to keep it shiny side up, and pass it down through the opposite hole in the seat front. Figure 59a shows a frame half-worked in this way. This may *sound* complicated but it is logical and obvious once you come to do it. Continue threading the length of cane through front and back holes till you come to the corner holes at the seat front. Consult figure 58 to see how to thread the cane into side holes so as to keep the strands lying parallel. If the cane runs out before you have finished (one strand is usually enough to complete one stage of caning a seat but sometimes they break, or are shorter) run the end of the used-up cane over and over the nearest loop between two holes and pull it tight. Secure the end of the new length of cane in the same way (*see* figure 60).

Remove the peg holding down the other half of the cane and work the other half of the seat in the same way. Do not pull the cane too tight at this stage because the last two stages in working (figures 59e and f) will take up any slack, and a little give in the caning is a help then.

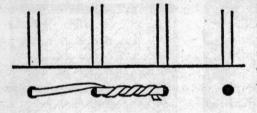

Figure 60. *To fasten off ends of cane under the seat, wrap them over and over nearest loop. Ends of new canes are anchored in the same way*

Stage two (figure 59b) is worked in exactly the same way except that the cane is now threaded across the chair seat. As before make sure that you keep the glossy side of the cane uppermost.

Stage three (figure 59c) repeats stage one exactly, taking the cane in and out through the same holes, so that it lies over the previous strands.

Stage four (figure 59d) is where the job gets slower because here the strand is woven under and over the previous ones. You are working across the seat as in stage two. The threading can be done with your fingers, but it speeds things up to improvise a threader. Use an 8-inch length of thick wire bent into a loop at one end to hold it by. Thread the wire in and out of the strands as in (d) then slip the cane in alongside and remove the wire.

Stage five is where diagonal weaving starts. First check that all your woven strands of cane are neatly separated out into pairs as in (d) as this makes the weaving easier to follow. In this stage of the caning the strand is threaded over a pair of horizontal canes, under a pair of vertical ones, and so on diagonally across the seat. Begin threading from the corner hole at the right of the seat front. Unless you make a mistake en route you should finish up at the left corner hole of the seat back. Work half the seat at a time. Note that two strands are passed through each of the corner holes to give the correct spacing.

Stage six, the final one, repeats the diagonal weaving process in the opposite direction (figure 59f). Here the cane passes under the horizontal strands, over the vertical ones. This stage goes quickly because you can see the pattern emerging, which is a great encouragement. The seat holes will be getting rather choked with canes by now, so you may have to use a pointed tool like an icepick to clear a space to slide the cane through.

Beading

A wider beading cane worked round the seat sets the caning off handsomely and gives protection against wear and tear. Use No. 6 cane for the beading and No. 2 to bind it in place. Cut one end of the beading cane into a sharp point and push it well down into one of the corner holes. Then thread the No. 2 cane up through the next door hole, pass it over the beading cane, keeping the shiny side up as usual, and down through the same hole. Continue along till you reach the next corner, where the beading cane should be cut to a point and pushed down into the corner hole. If the holes are so packed that it is difficult to get the No. 2 cane through you can cheat a bit and work it through alternate holes, though this will not be so strong. Begin the next section of beading by cutting the cane to a point and driving it well down into the same corner, as before – this will help wedge both ends of beading securely. Carry on right round the seat. If any ends of beading threaten to work loose you can secure them by driving in a peg – a couple of matches cut to $\frac{3}{4}$-inch lengths will do the trick. Check that all cane ends are neatly fastened off underneath, and trim off any excess. You can give the caning a protective coat of clear varnish or leave it as it is.

Caned sofas, etc.

Larger caned pieces – daybeds, sofas, bentwood rockers – can sometimes be picked up quite cheaply where the caning is badly damaged. Re-caning them is a long-drawn-out business, but if you have the necessary perseverance the results are well worth the labour as pieces like these are nearly always simple and graceful and pretty. You can paint them, and cushion them, or leave them just as they are. If you are undertaking a large area of caning use a four-strand pattern (figure 61) for the back and sides of your sofa, chair or whatever, because this is quicker to work and strong enough for parts which take less strain. Keep the six-strand pattern for the seat though. The four-strand pattern shown uses No. 6 for stages one and two, and No. 3 cane for the next two. In stage three the No. 3

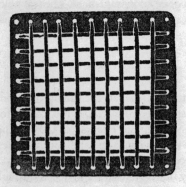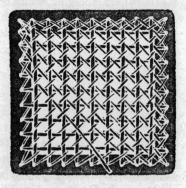

Figure 61. *Quicker four-strand pattern suitable for caning arms and backs of larger pieces*

cane is woven diagonally from left to right, over the vertical canes and under the horizontal ones. Stage four repeats this operation in the opposite direction, passing under the verticals and over the horizontals.

Duvets

A duvet, should you not have noticed those ads showing a couple sexily snuggling under their continental quilt, is an extra large and all-enveloping down-filled quilt which replaces the conventional top sheet and blankets. They are traditional bedding in countries with icy winters like Scandinavia and Germany, and are becoming increasingly popular over here and in America – chiefly, I suspect, because a duvet combined with fitted bottom sheet cuts bedmaking, that dreariest of chores, to a quick tweak and shake in passing. Mothers of lazy adolescents swear by them. They are also extraordinarily light and warm, and if made with the best materials will last a lifetime.

I must admit, though I detest bedmaking, that I had never given serious thought to duvets because of their price. So I was interested to learn that an enterprising aunt of mine made her own duvet very successfully for a fraction the cost of the shop sort. She was lucky enough to have the down filling to hand – an old down eiderdown and pillow supplied enough for a double-bed duvet – so her whole quilt cost no more than the special cambric used for the cover, plus a bit more for the washable detachable cover. If you can get hold of any old down-filled cushions, pillows or quilts – down is the stuff which squashes down to nothing in the hand, plumps up at a shake and weighs next to nothing – this would be the cheapest way of making your own. A double-bed size duvet needs 3 pounds of down, single size 2 pounds. Failing this, you will have to buy the down filling which brings the cost of the quilt up, but a home-made one is still much cheaper than the commercial variety. For children's duvets you could use a cheaper 50 per cent down, 50 per cent feather mixture, or terylene filling, which is washable. The Russell Trading Co. supply everything you need to make your own duvet at what they rightly call 'keen' prices (Suppliers' Index).

For a double-bed duvet you need 6½ yards of special quality cambric for the actual bag and 3 pounds of down to fill it with. Over this goes a washable, zip-up cover which should be cotton – not nylon – and can be any quality and print you fancy.

Instructions

To see how a duvet is constructed study the illustration (figure 62). Basically it is a large (72 × 78 inches) bag divided up by narrow cross strips into six down-filled channels or sausages going the length of the bed. A generous overhang is allowed for at the sides and foot of the bed. To make the bag, fold your 6½ yards of cambric into three, and cut along

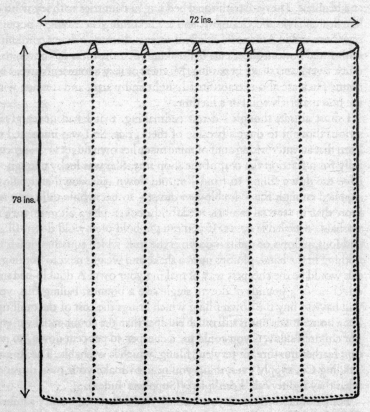

Figure 62. *Duvet-case ready for stuffing with down showing six channel pockets, top-stitched side and bottom seams. The top opening can either be topstitched the same way or handsewn with two rows of overstitching to keep the down in*

fold lines. From one of these pieces cut a strip 35 inches wide and the full 78 inches long. Join the two large pieces and this narrower one to make a piece of cambric roughly 144 inches wide (allow ¾-inch seams) and 78 inches long. Double machine, or hand oversew these seams for extra strength. Now cut five strips 2½ × 78 inches from what's left of your cambric. These are the cross pieces which make the channels in your bag. Fold the cover fabric in half, seams outward and on *one half* measure out and mark at 12-inch intervals. Tack your strips to these and machine down. Now fold your piece of cambric in half the other way, with the strips inside and chalk or pin seam lines on the other half immediately opposite the ones you have machined. Starting with the inmost strip – the one nearest the centre fold – tack and machine the strips down to these guide lines. Join the open side of the bag up – you will have to top stitch from the outside as shown in the diagram – so that you now have a bag open at each end and divided into six compartments. Stitch up the bottom of the bag, making sure you catch the bottom of the strips in securely – I would tack and then topstitch twice by machine. Now fill the channels with down, allowing ½ a pound of down per channel. It is as well to be fairly accurate about this if you fight about the bedclothes anyway, so borrow a weighing machine if you do not own one. Tack up the top of each channel as you fill it. Now machine across the top, as you did the bottom, and your duvet is done. To make the washable cover you simply make a bag large enough to go over your quilt, with an extra large zip on one side-seam to get it in and out through.

REPAIRS AND RESTORATION

The danger with becoming at all skilful at repairing and restoring damaged things is that one begins to look about like a surgeon in quest of new clients – one *prefers* things a little imperfect or, as the trade says, 'slightly faulty'. My home has been a casualty ward for years, full of chairs with one worm-eaten leg (just needs replacing), cracked plates, chipped candlesticks, leather-bound books hanging together by a thread, papier-mâché objects with great bites out of them, ornaments missing a limb or a handle. Still, as aberrations go, it is a harmless one provided you do not allow yourself to be rooked over the starting price –

damaged goods should be reckoned in pence, not pounds – and cherish no dreams that your pretty rose-decorated Coleport plate with a small chunk missing only needs a dab of Araldite and paint to be tripled in value. The way to look at it is that by buying something 'faulty' and mending it, you can own something you could not have afforded if it were in perfect nick. Then there is the very real pleasure of rescuing it from the dustbin and restoring it to circulation.

Here I shall only be dealing with a few simple restorer's tricks which I have tried out myself and found successful.

China, ceramics and pottery

Everyone knows that the epoxy resin adhesives like Araldite will mend a broken object so strongly that the mend is actually stronger than the object. But you may not know how to get a really tight, near-invisible mend; or that Araldite, mixed with various substances and a little colouring can actually be used to build up missing chips and chunks.

To do a really first-class job with Araldite you need gummed brown-paper strip and meths, and both the broken object and the Araldite should be warmed beforehand in a low oven. This makes the adhesive flow over the join thinly – the thinner the film of adhesive on both surfaces the better. Excess adhesive which oozes out can be wiped away easily. If, despite precautions, you get Araldite over everything, it can be wiped off with a little cotton wool dipped in meths. Use this for cleaning off the surface of the broken object, but do not take it right over the join or it will weaken it. Brown gummed strip, wiped over with a sponge both sides till damp and sticky but not sopping wet, makes an excellent bandage to hold the broken pieces together till the adhesive sets hard, because it shrinks as it dries and this gives extra pressure on the join as and where you need it. For simple mends – a bowl cleanly broken in two – just wrap a good tight belt of the strip round in such a way as to exert the utmost pressure on the join while holding the various parts together (figure 63). Where the object is broken into several pieces, the repair may have to be done in stages. A dry run, fitting the jig-saw together, will show you whether this is necessary. Again, bind the pieces with gummed strip. Breaks which cannot be held together with gummed strip can sometimes be stuck with the help of gravity, by burying the object in sand

Figure 63. *Gummed brown-paper strip used to bind a simple break while adhesive is setting. Stick first strip across the break, using the rim and base for extra leverage; stick the next right round the bowl*

or sawdust (or salt or flour) so that the broken-off piece can be balanced delicately in place on top.

Araldite which runs out along the mend can be trimmed off with a razor blade while it is still pliable, and before it has set hard. Inaccessible bits can still be pared away when hard, but take great care as the adhesive can lift tiny chips with it. It always lifts lustre, so with this take extra care beforehand, wiping the mend quite clean with rags or tissues. Another way to remove excess adhesive is to break it down by rubbing gently with glasspaper.

To rebuild small areas with Araldite – chips round the rim of a bowl, or base of a pot – mix the warmed adhesive very thoroughly with a little titanium dioxide (I sometimes use gesso powder) or kaolin, both obtainable from chemists. All these mixtures are sticky, so keep some meths handy to dip your tools into and dab a little of the powder over your fingers. Damp the knife blade or whatever you are using as a tool with meths, take up a little of the adhesive mixture and press it down over the missing place, shaping and smoothing till it matches up with the surrounding area. Take care no air bubbles are trapped underneath – pricking the mixture with a needle will cure these. Large flat chips can be filled more easily if you smooth a little plain adhesive over the surface before pressing on the filler. There are two approaches to replacing missing portions – you can either get there gradually, a bit at a time, or stick on a rather crudely matched lump which will be abraded and filed and carved to match when it has set hard. Method 1 is slow but worth it when you are dealing with a fragile piece of china, where anything less than perfection will show up annoyingly, while Method 2 is adequate for patching up objects of the sturdy and useful variety. Araldite filler – i.e. Araldite plus one of the above powders – goes through a pliable stage prior to hardening when it can be further shaped and worked on. Finally, when hard, it can be smoothed finely with glasspaper, carved with sharp blades, or filed if necessary.

I often use plastic wood to rebuild missing parts of ceramic objects intended for decoration rather than use – candlesticks, bowls. The rough surfaces of the earthenware provide a good key for the plastic wood, and though it takes a long time to build up a sizable chunk, layer by layer, it is very easy to handle and mould, and to shape and abrade once it has set hard. It has an annoying tendency to shrink, so always fill it 'proud', i.e. higher than the surface around it, and abrade down to the right level afterwards.

Now, overpainting. The Araldite fillers dry out to an opaque non-shiny biscuit colour. You might decide to colour the filler itself, rather than overpainting it afterwards. This is best when the object is going to be used and washed frequently. Colour with artists' oils, or powder colours, mixing very thoroughly. With a little experiment you should be able to get a near perfect match. To glaze it, paint over with a little polyurethane glaze, or better still Darwi varnish (art shops) which is a particularly shiny, tough, glaze finish. If you prefer to paint over the filler, what you use rather depends on how much money you feel you want to spend. For a simple colour – black or white – ordinary lacquer or paint you may have around will do quite well, if you apply two or three coats and rub down with glasspaper in between to get a dense covering surface. Varnish to finish off. Artists' oils mixed with Reeves' Artists' Gel as the medium will allow you to get a much wider range of colours. It is harder to get an opaque colour with these, but several layers will usually build up a solid coat. A little dryer mixed in will speed the drying. The ground colour can be overpainted to match any existing decorations on the piece, in the same way. But note whether the original painting is thick and opaque looking or transparent and glowing. The transparent effects are got by washing one thin glaze of colour over another till you have the tint you want. Thus a leaf may begin with a fairly thick coat of green, but over this, when dry, go a brown glaze for shadows and a touch of yellow glaze for highlights. Acrylic paints provide a good opaque finish, and their own glaze medium will give a high shine.

For a really perfectionist job where the object is handsome enough to be worth restoring perfectly, you could buy some of the Darwi paints specially evolved for use on china. They stock a range of transparent and opaque colours and a glaze and varnish to give the effect of fired glazes without firing.

Papier mâché

Papier mâché is the restorer's dream. A piece of china skilfully repaired may fool the eye but the only way to reproduce the exact texture and ring of the original is to model and fire a new bit of china to replace the missing one. However, with papier mâché you can build up quite large missing chunks which look, feel and *sound* – when tapped of course – like the real thing.

Rebuild fairly small pieces – chipped corners and feet on papier-mâché boxes, small bites out of the sides of trays and little plates, small chunks out of chair frames – with plastic wood, building it up layer by layer as described for the ceramic repairs above. For black papier mâché mix in Indian ink, or black lacquer, or artists' oils with the plastic wood. For coloured papier mâché, overpaint the finished mend. Build your plastic filling up proud, and then whittle it with a knife or razor blade and sand-paper till perfectly smooth. Finish with glasspaper for a really fine surface, damping the paper slightly to lubricate it. Take care not to scratch the sound papier mâché all around – this may mean folding your abrasive papers into little points or wrapping them round the end of a pencil. When counterfeiting black papier mâché the important thing is the finish, built up with layers of transparent varnish, lightly rubbed down in between. If your plastic wood filling is not quite black enough, give it a coat of black paint, then varnish several times over the patch, thinning the coat out as it comes to the edge of your repair – otherwise you will get a ridge of varnish all round your mend. Finish off by giving the whole object a coat of varnish, rubbed down gently when dry with a ball of finest grade wire wool, or better still – if you can be bothered to hunt it up – fine powdered pumice applied with a damp felt pad. Ordinary Vim can be used instead, with care.

You might be lucky enough to have an old piece of coloured papier mâché to restore. This usually comes in subtle, rich colours like garnet red, salmon pink, or a light but moody green. When matching up these colours remember that the colour you are imitating is made up of paint plus glaze or varnish. The glaze or varnish will almost certainly have yellowed a little with time, and this vitally affects the colour beneath, as you will know if you have seen a painting before and after cleaning. For the best match, work out just what tone of colour plus a slightly yellow tinted glaze equals the original shade. For a salmon colour, for instance, a light peach pink plus one or two coats of yellow tinted varnish (a little yellow ochre) gives the intense colour of the original, together with a certain depth obtainable in no other way.

Gilding and painted decoration should be applied before the varnish. See gilding, page 175, for a simple way of laying on gold leaf. Colour the size with yellow ochre so that you can see what you are doing with it, and use a sable pencil to paint fine lines or delicate filigree patterns. Tone the gilding down to match the rest by tinting the glaze or varnish with a little raw umber. If there is any flower decoration that needs restoring – most Victorian papier mâché was decorated with posies of poppies, convolvulus, lilies of the valley, roses, etc. – either get hold of a book on papier mâché with colour plates you can pinch ideas from, or make up your own bouquet with blooms copied from Dutch flower paintings. Finish with several coats of varnish, carefully rubbed down for a soft sheen rather than lacquered brightness.

When replacing large pieces of papier mâché you will have to make some sort of armature to strengthen your repair work. Use a medium-weight wire, flexible enough to bend fairly easily. With a drill and very fine bit, or sharp tool like an ice pick, bore $\frac{1}{2}$ an inch or so into the papier mâché either side of the missing piece. Run the wire into these, fixing it in place with a little plastic padding or Araldite (figure 64). Check that the wire framework follows the line of the tray or chair, or whatever it is you are repairing. Over this armature paste little strips of newspaper soaked in wallpaper paste. Continue till you have built up a strong core. Leave to dry hard, moulding from time to time with your fingers to

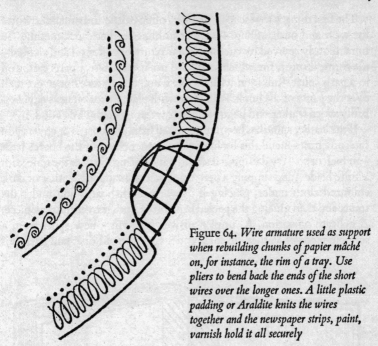

Figure 64. *Wire armature used as support when rebuilding chunks of papier mâché on, for instance, the rim of a tray. Use pliers to bend back the ends of the short wires over the longer ones. A little plastic padding or Araldite knits the wires together and the newspaper strips, paint, varnish hold it all securely*

make sure it is drying to the right shape. Over this continue building up with plastic wood as above till your replacement matches the original perfectly. Finish by sanding smooth, and painting, gilding and varnishing as above.

Old books

It is rare for an attractive old leather-bound book to reach one in good condition, at least at pauperish prices. Usually the binding has split down the back, and the front cover is half off. A complete re-binding job is the ideal solution, but it is expensive, and only worth considering in the case of a really superb edition of a favourite book. It is possible to repair damaged bindings neatly, if not invisibly, and stoutly enough to give the book many more years of active life.

The first thing is to rescue the leather, often brittle and much the worse for wear and mishandling. Really crumbling leather can sometimes be miraculously revived by rubbing in a mixture of castor oil and alcohol – use surgical spirit, for which you need no licence. Use 3 parts castor oil to 2 parts spirit. Rub it on with cotton wool, taking care not to get it all over the pages of the book. Follow up with plain castor oil next day. Less badly worn leather will be improved by treating with Hide Food.

If the leather spine has become detached from the boards or covers you can sometimes mend this by lifting the leather cover of the boards back $\frac{1}{2}$ an inch or so – try damping it slightly and paring away at the glue with a knife blade – and slipping a very fine piece of matching leather or dark coloured cloth under, glueing it down to both boards and under the spine, and then glueing the peeled back bit of leather over the new piece. A delicate operation. A simpler answer is to cut a new spine from a suitable piece of leather, an inch wider than the old one, and stick this

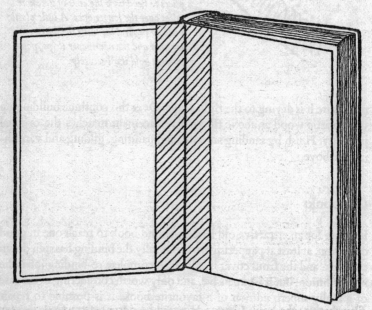

Figure 65. *The simplest way of sticking back an end board using a strip of Sellotape X. Glueing new endpapers on top will disguise the repair*

down over the top and over the boards, allowing enough play for the book to be opened out flat when read. If the old spine has gone completely, replace it in the same way, but stick a piece of canvas or cloth inside the leather to stiffen and strengthen the replacement. A strip of Sellotape X is the easiest way to stick a half detached board back into place (figure 65). You can disguise this by sticking new endpapers down on top. Removing the old endpaper on the cover will make a neater job of this.

Stuck together pages often respond to steaming. Hold the book in the steam from a kettle for a minute or so and gently try to separate the pages, one at a time. Dabbing with petrol or benzine will remove greasy fingermarks from endpapers and pages. To save a valuable book which has been dropped in the bath put sheets of blotting paper or tissue paper between the pages through half the book or so (if you cram paper between all the pages the book is liable to burst at the seams) and dry out in a warm place under a weight. When dry do the same for the remaining pages, which may need steaming to get them apart.

Handles and hinges

Handles and hinges are the weak point of many bits of furniture. What usually happens is that the screws have worked loose and gradually enlarged the hole they were meant to fill. With the old china-knob handle on drawers, the type that screws into place, the strongest type of repair is to plug the hole with a new piece of wood and screw the handle back into that. However, this takes a bit of finesse to do neatly. I find plugging the hole with Araldite filler (see above) and screwing the handle in while it is pliable, and then leaving to set hard, works quite well. The same thing can be done with hinges, especially tiny hinges on little wood and papier-mâché boxes. If the old screws have gone they can be difficult to replace, as ironmongers tend not to keep such tiny screws in stock. Try Beardmore and Co. (Suppliers' Index).

Bamboo furniture

Elsewhere in the book I have advocated buying up attractive pieces of bamboo furniture, which can still be found cheaply, though my guess is that it is just poised to make a comeback. In simple modern settings its whimsicality looks just right, and adds a nice touch of the fantastic. It is unusual to find a piece in perfect condition because though the basic structure – usually deal – is solid, bits and pieces of bamboo are often missing, particularly the narrow beading used to frame the panels of woven matting, imitation lacquer, etc. Bamboo can be found quite easily – most garden supply shops stock the narrower sort, for staking up plants. I spent a long time pondering how to reproduce the brown mottled finish, and discovered the solution by accident. The brown tortoiseshell marks are made by scorching the bamboo over a small flame – a lighter flame would probably work, though I used the old style gas-stove lighter. Copy the markings on the remaining pieces. Then give the bamboo a coat of shellac – golden, not white – to give it the proper tawny colour and faint sheen. Shellac is not that easily obtainable unless you have a trade shop handy – 'there's no demand for it', I keep being told. If you can get hold of it, it is useful stuff, dries almost immediately, and can be used as a light finish and seal for wood, as well as to give painted wood a wonderfully satiny finish (*see* painting wood, p. 215). You could use blonde button polish, which is a simplified French polish, instead.

Do not nail bamboo as you would wood because it is brittle and may split. I have a hunch the people who made the original furniture made holes by running a red hot needle or wire through the bamboo. I have not plucked up courage to try that myself yet. I use a fine wood drill to make the holes, and very fine nails like panel pins. A bit of wood adhesive at the joins helps to make a solid job of it.

Basketwork

One can often pick up attractive baskets – relics from our colonial past – which are in quite good condition except that the vegetable dyes used have faded to near colourlessness. I bought a handsome Ali Baba type of basket large enough to take a seven-year-old child, whose original indigo and dark brown patterning had become faded and worn to milky blue and buff outside, while still bright and fresh as new inside. I wiped the basket down with warm water and a little salt then, using the interior as a guide, mixed Artists' Inks (drawing inks) to matching colours and painted them on with a brush. The colours were not a perfect match – vegetable dyes have a pure intensity of colour which no synthetic can quite reproduce – but the basket looked quite like its old self by the time I had finished. Then I coated the whole thing with a mixture of white beeswax dissolved in benzine as a preservative and to give it a faint gloss.

LAMPS AND LIGHTING

Almost anything that can be persuaded to support or contain a light fitment can be made into a lamp, and some of the unlikeliest things are the most successful. An actor I know, who lives in a Parisian garret straight out of *La Bohème*, all pitched roofs and beams and crooked little windows looking out over slate roofs and eccentric chimney pots, made his lamps from, of all things, the wooden hubs of old cartwheels. With the spokes removed, they look like lanterns a medieval woodworker might have designed, with stout iron bands above and below, and they exactly suit his quirky but comfortable environment.

Old wooden cartwheels are not as easy to come by as they once were – people buy them to convert into gates, or prop outside country pubs – but ransacking a local junk yard might produce something equally convertible. Turned wooden balusters from an old staircase, or the wrought iron variety, are one possibility. You would need professional help to convert a metal post or bracket into a lamp. Genuine old oil lamps fetch high prices, converted or not, but you can sometimes pick up the glass or metal bases for them, minus paraffin container and wick holder, in out-of-the-way junk shops quite cheaply – the glass ones are often mistaken for vases with the top broken off – and they can sometimes be adapted for use as table lamps simply by plugging in one of the Woolworth's fitments based on a large cork. I think everyone knows about the possibilities of bottles and wine jars and decorative chemists' jars and those handsome japanned tea containers – there is a booming trade in repro. tea caddies. Similarly, figures in spelter and Britannia Metal, once relegated to the back of junk shops, are now eagerly sought after for conversion into lamps. You might find a damaged piece cheaply. Damaged parts can be restored with plastic padding and breaks mended with soft solder, and the figure can be made into an attractive lamp by setting it on a plain polished wood base and running an inconspicuous metal rod up the back to hold the light fitting. Britannia metal takes a good polish, something like pewter. Chipped vases, too badly damaged to stand proudly on the mantelpiece, can be restored carefully (*see* Repairs and Restoration, pages 111–21) and made into lamps with the light-fitting set rather low in the neck of the vase (use a piece of shaped cork or wood glued into place) so that the shade conceals the worst of the damage which is usually round the top. Some stoneware hot-water bottles or water filters make surprisingly chic lamps, because of their plain shape and neutral colour, and a whittled cork or wood plug can usually be used for these too. Turned wood lamp bases, which can be bought quite cheaply from most craft shops or good lampshade shops like the one in Berwick Market, Soho, seem to have been somewhat unfairly despised in the search for original lamps. They are not intrinsically unusual, of course, but they could be marbled, or painted decoratively (get ideas from old china and pottery candlesticks) or given a polychrome finish (*see* Wood Finishes). Or, if your taste runs to the plain material unadorned, a driftwood finish can be got very easily by the rub-on rub-off painting method (*see* Wood Finishes again) to get rid of that pallid raw wood look. Interestingly shaped baskets can be made into lamps with two bulbs, one pointing down inside the basketwork base and one up under a raffia shade. They give a pretty, warm, broken light, but you must be prepared for the fact that the heat of the light bulbs will eventually dry out the wicker or cane and crack it. String or cord soaked in size and then wound round and round a glass jar or bottle looks more original than plain glass, and means you can weight the thing invisibly by filling it with sand or small pebbles before fixing in the light holder. Or try the Victorian idea – decalcomania – where small coloured cut-outs soaked till pliable in wallpaper paste are rolled very carefully round a pencil or something similar, lowered into the bottle and then pressed up against the glass, coloured side out, and smoothed out with the end of your implement. The Victorians used coloured scraps, specially printed and sold for such hobbies, but cut-outs from the usual Sunday supplement and magazine sources could be used instead, with a few old family snaps to make the collage more personal. The inside of the bottle or jar should be fairly densely covered with cut-outs, and then filled with sand or salt to make a background which will show them up well, as well as weighting the container itself.

Wall light fittings are always a problem, if you cannot afford the austerely elegant modern kind, or the few pretty old ones which turn up from time to time. One suggestion might be to buy the smallest, cheapest wall fixture available and then cover it up. Instead of a conventional shade, you might experiment with punched tin (*see* Ideas to Try) which gives a very pretty pin-prick pattern of light. Tin is amazingly pliable and easy to work, and small pieces can be soldered with a small soldering

Figure 66. *Wall-light holder made of tin and wire. The lamp attachment is shown sideways on to give an idea of the relative scale compared with flower stalk and leaves. Make flower stalks from heavy wire, leaf stems from thinner wire twisted round at the base as shown. Leaves and flowers are cut from tin (empty cans) and veined by pressing from the back with a sharp point. Crimp petals like pastry flowers. Fix inner discs to flowers with brass split rivets. Solder wires to back of leaves and flowers, or use plastic padding or Araldite. A spray of flowers like these can be attached to a small, cheap, wall-light fitting*

iron. A half cylinder of punched tin, painted or left plain, could be attached to the wall, completely covering the light fixture. Or you could make a large daisy shape in tin, fixing the petals together with rivets and Araldite, and wire this to the back of the light fixture for decoration alone. The French make charming wall fixtures based on sprays of stylized flowers and leaves, shaped from light metal, and gilded or painted (figure 66). This idea could be copied in tin and strong wire with a soldering iron. An idea stemming from this, which I have seen used very effectively, is to make up a wreath of artificial flowers or a posy to twine prettily round the lamp fixture, which is then given a very small, discreet silk shade. This sort of decoration looks best on the candle type of fixture, which is small and usually unobtrusively painted in cream or off-white.

Fabric lampshades

Well-balanced lighting makes all the difference to the look and atmosphere of a room. Two or three lamps giving a well-diffused amount of light in different spots round a room create a much softer and more peaceful atmosphere than one very powerful light source, especially if that one comes from a ceiling fixture. Women, I think, grasp this truth instinctively while men are usually quite happy with the multi-watt overhead bulb and the interrogation-cell bleakness it creates.

For the best diffusion of light, a light which is warm, even and soft, the classic fabric-covered shade still leads I think. Because they must be hand-sewn, they are very expensive to buy ready-made. You can make your own, on the other hand, remarkably cheaply. Large department stores and craft shops supply a wide range of frames from the pumpkin and Tiffany shapes most popular today, to the most elaborately fluted and scalloped throw-backs to the 1930s. You need very little fabric to cover an average sized shade – 1 yard of 36-inch width is usually enough. I think natural fibres give a pleasanter light than synthetics, but this is a small quibble. Anyway, there is a wide range of materials you can use – lawns, jap silk, muslin, odd remnants of wild silk, plain cotton, linen, cotton lace, to name only a few. I often use odd scraps. That peach-coloured silky stuff – crêpe de chine, or a rayon or art-silk imitation – used for ladies' underwear in the good old days is excellent for lining lamp shades as it gives a flattering pinky glow. It can be covered with something less boudoir-like. You can find old slips and nightgowns – if the idea does not repell you – in Oxfam shops up and down the land. On the whole a limp, close textured fabric with plenty of stretch is the easiest to work with. And as far as colour goes, its best to curb your adventurous spirit – the traditional pale shades from off-white through to pale pink and tawny yellow give much the nicest light. You will also need a fairly large roll of white or cream bias binding to bind the frame with, a large box of sharp pins and something to cover the edges of the finished shade with – this can be a braid or gimp edging, or a bias strip of the lampshade fabric.

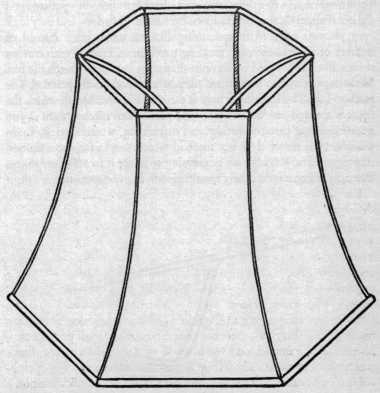

Figure 67. *A frame like this is a good shape for beginners to cover*

It is only fair to say at this point that making fabric-covered lamp-shades is – or can be – a rather painful business. The thing seems to bristle with pins and it is hard to avoid pricking yourself while stitching away. The preliminary stage of binding the frame is tedious, and the whole operation in fact is liable to be punctuated with curses and groans. *But*, as I said before, you literally save pounds by making your own, and results do repay the toil involved.

Instructions

Choose a simple shape to start off with. One with a slight concave curve to it like the frame illustrated is the easiest to cover for a beginner. Traditional shapes like these are coming back into fashion – perhaps you did not realize that there are fashions even in lampshades – and they look very pleasant covered in something like off-white linen instead of swathes of ruby chiffon or crackling parchment. Frames with convex curves, like the beloved mushroom shape, are harder to stretch the bias fabric over evenly so leave those till you have had a little practice. The method I shall be describing here is the simplest possible, in which the shade is covered one half at a time and pinned and stitched to fit as you go, eliminating patterns, fittings and machining, which is tricky to do with bias-cut material. It is a method which works for most frames, though as I said it takes a bit of cunning to adapt it to a Tiffany shape. The only frame it is definitely unsuitable for, in my experience, is a plain

Figure 68. *Binding metal frame with bias binding or tape*

drum shape because the bias-cut cloth sags between the struts giving it an unpleasantly bony, starveling look.

The first thing to do is cover the frame, yes, all of it, with bias binding wound round and round in a spiral. Perfectionists paint or varnish the actual metal frame before binding and covering to stop it rusting with time and washing. (Fabric-covered shades can be washed very easily by dipping them into warm soapy water, brushing with a soft brush, rinsing and standing in a warm place to dry.) Cover the uprights first, one by one, bringing the bias over the top and bottom at either end and pinning or stitching it securely. Wind the bias good and taut, each twist just overlapping the edge of the one before. It has to take a considerable

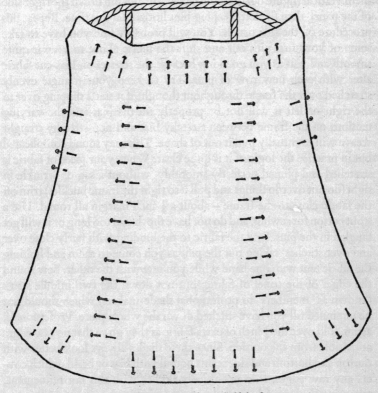

Figure 69. *Cover being stretched and pinned over half the frame*

strain when you start pinning the cover to it and any slack binding will give. Then bind the top and bottom of the frame, pulling the binding extra tight over the joins where your previous bias strips were fastened off, so that you have no lumps.

Now cut your square of fabric into two triangles. (Incidentally, if you plan to line the shade, the procedure is exactly the same for lining as for cover.) Cut the corner off the apex of your triangle, not a huge piece, just enough to give you the true bias of the piece by keeping this cut edge parallel with the top of the frame when you start pinning. Centre the middle of your triangle over the middle of your centre panel (you are covering three panels at a time), and pin the fabric along the top and bottom of the panel, sticking the pins through the binding and keeping them vertical (figure 69). Pull the fabric taut and pin down the right side of the panel, then the left, keeping pins horizontal this time. Repeat this procedure on the side panels. You will probably find you have to take some of your first pins out and shift the fabric about to keep it quite smooth and taut as you go along because the stresses on bias-cut fabric alter with each new row of pins. Try to keep your triangle evenly stretched over the frame throughout though; if it starts slipping over to the right or left it will not be properly on the bias and the varying tensions on the frame between stretchy bias and non-stretchy straight weave will eventually pull it out of shape. This may sound complicated but in practice the logic of it is quite clear. When your piece of fabric is stretched and pinned perfectly smoothly, without a sag or wrinkle in sight (do not overdo things and pull it so tight the frame buckles) trim off the fabric close to the frame – about a $\frac{1}{4}$-inch margin all round. Use a stout cotton for sewing, and do not have the thread too long or it will get tangled in the pins. Sew the fabric to the binding with fairly close over and over stitches, taking out the pins as you come to them and holding the fabric taut with one hand while you sew with the other. Sew round the edges of the panel of fabric, but not down the two middle struts (known as 'members' to professional shade-makers) which should not be unpinned till you have stitched down the whole piece. Professionals, again, fold over the $\frac{1}{4}$ inch of extra fabric as they go so that no raw edges are visible from the outside. Since these shades always look better with the top and bottom and side seams bound with bias or braid, which covers any raw edges, I do not usually bother with this last refinement, trimming the extra fabric off close to the stitching instead.

Repeat this procedure with the other half of the frame, keeping the fabric on the bias, stretching and pinning evenly, etc. The side seams will be stitched over the previous side seams. If you are making a shade with lining and cover, the two are stitched one above the other in exactly the same way. The only exception to this rule is if the two layers of fabric are so thick they would create a ridge down the sides, in which case it might be better to have the side seams of the cover down different 'members' from the lining. Unless your seams are incredibly neat, you will probably have to glue or sew braid down all the members then, because the lining seams will show through the cover slightly. Otherwise you can finish off this particular shade with braid or bias, sewn or glued down the side seams and round the top and bottom. Braid or gimp is quick – choose a plain one in a matching colour and use a clear impact adhesive – but bias looks sleeker. Cut your bias strips the width of standard bias binding, fold edges in and iron flat. Cut the strip to roughly the right lengths before glueing otherwise you may find yourself trapped in a perfect cocoon of sticky tape. The bias should be glued so that about half is outside, half inside the frame – you may have to make nicks in the inner edge to fit it smoothly over the members.

String lampshades

Ordinary string, the sort you buy to tie up parcels, makes excellent lampshades wrapped round the standard wire frames. The look is cool, like solid geometry, and so is the light – ideal for ceiling lighting in halls, on landings, and anywhere else you need an unobtrusive overhead light.

They are made in the same way as raffia lampshades. They take a bit longer to make, since string is much narrower than raffia, but they can be washed easily and last for years, unlike raffia shades which tend to scorch and crack as the raffia dries out.

Lantern shapes, either round or melon shaped, make the best string shades as the bulb is well hidden. If plain string colour seems dull you can buy brilliantly coloured balls of string in most stationers – red, emerald and bright yellow. Or you can dye the finished shade in Dylon cold-water dyes though the result will not be as bright as the shade on the dye card.

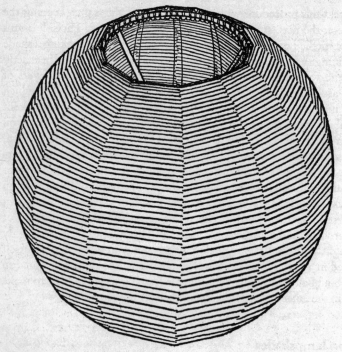

Figure 70. *Completed string shade*

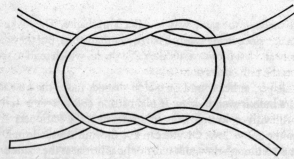

Figure 71. *Reef knot*

To make

Begin by buttonholing round the top and bottom of the frame. This is not essential but gives a neat finish. Knot the string round the frame to start, buttonholing the loose end in as you go round. When the string has to be joined, tie a reef knot, which will not slip (figure 71) and arrange it so that it comes inside the frame. To start the shade proper unroll enough string to make a little ball you can hold in your palm. Tie one end securely to the top of one of the 'staves', or upright wires, and take it over the next stave, under the next, pulling it taut. Keep pushing the strands of string up close to each other as you work round the frame, otherwise you will have glimpses of bare bulb through the chinks. When joining two bits of string arrange it so that the knot comes just beyond the next 'stave', and is drawn behind it when you take the string under and over again. Use reef knots everywhere because they will not work undone. The last inch or two of the shade is a little trickier to do because the holes you are pushing the string through are getting smaller all the time. It helps to work with short lengths of string at this point, and to use a large blunt needle, like a tapestry needle, to weave the string in and out for the last $\frac{1}{2}$ inch or so.

GROWING THINGS

There is no need for a green plot to have the pleasure of watching things grow; basement areas, balconies, windowsills can all burgeon with life in the blackest city environment. I have seen basements and railings in central London festooned with wistarias, clematis, even vines; sometimes as many shades of greenery as a salad bowl; window-boxes frothing with flowers and trailing foliage all spring and summer long. If you cannot provide even a sunny windowsill you can still nurture a handsome clump of indoor plants: shiny green climbers, prettily striped Tradescantia and spider plants, overflowing a trough or tub in one corner of the sitting-room. Everyone should treat themselves to at least one green, living link with the natural world; there is balm for the soul in caring for plants and seeing them respond, grow greener and glossier, shoot up, bud, flower. The cost of this is small, out of all proportion to the improvement a splash of green makes to your environment. What is needed is a certain amount of hard work (to get the thing started, hauling back sacks of peat, mixed soil and tubs), commonsense backed up by a little research (choosing the right plants for the right situation), perseverance, and patience. The term 'green fingers' suggests a sort of imaginative identification with the plant world, and it is extraordinary how plants flourish in the care of a person who wishes them well. I had a small experience of this with an azalea which some friends bequeathed to me one spring, when all its flowers were over, with the advice that I kept it well watered. For some reason – perhaps it was all my previous failures in the pot plant line prodding my conscience – I really committed myself to that azalea. A friend agreed to let me have rainwater from his barrel and two or three times a week I would trudge up the road and back with my bucket of water. The azalea thrived, and every new batch of delicate green leaves was a personal triumph. Then, drama! Left in the care of friends during our summer holiday, 'Azalea' (by now a positively unique character in my mind) was unwatered for a fortnight and I returned to find her withered and shedding leaves like confetti. I *willed* that plant to survive, and sure enough, after much patient nursing she pulled through, determinedly replacing each withered leaf with a new green one, and even putting out six charming pink and white striped flowers as a Christmas bonus. Six flowers is not much by azalea standards but each of *my* six was like a word of thanks which went straight to the heart.

In this section I shall suggest how the would-be gardener can set about creating a green spot in adverse conditions. It would take too much space to give detailed instructions on how to care for each of the plants mentioned, not to mention an encyclopedic knowledge which I cannot claim to possess. Most indoor plants bought from florist shops come with their own little leaflet of instructions on how to care for them. Where this is not the case, consult the supplier, or get out a book from the local library. Growing things from pips and stones is perhaps the headiest form of gardening magic, which everyone should try at least once, and I shall touch on this subject. More practically, there will be advice on growing herbs in water on your kitchen windowsill. Then, for the lucky readers with a cold greenhouse (or use of one), I shall describe some out-of-the-way, spectacularly pretty things which can be done with quite ordinary plants and climbers, mostly for display indoors. And finally, to add interest cheaply to a small backyard or garden, there is some advice on making a sink-garden and laying a cobbled terrace, patio or tiny area just big enough for a chair and yourself. As you see, this section does not pretend to do more than touch on the vast subject of growing things, but I hope it may inspire some of you to start, if you have not already, and provide more experienced gardeners with one or two new ideas.

Indoor gardening

No sensible plant would choose to spend its life indoors, but given reasonable care, some will do very well where indoor conditions are close to those of their natural environment. On the whole, green plants – leafy and climbing types – do best under usual indoor conditions, i.e. not much light and a rather dry atmosphere frequently laden with cigarette smoke. You could make up an attractive clump of greenery with a climber or two like the large and showy Monstera, one of the green ivies, or *Cissus antarctica*, the Kangaroo Vine, which has bright green leaves like beech leaves, all standing together in a trough with one of the delicately striped trailing plants like Tradescantia, or Spider Plant for contrast. It is not only what plants you put together, but how you present them, that makes the difference between a half-hearted bunch of plants and a really eye-catching showpiece. Climbers need something to climb up, naturally, and make the best show when they are trained to twine round and twist themselves into a luxuriant bank of foliage. Do this by fixing three bamboo stakes tepee-wise into the pot and giving the climbing tendrils a bit of encouragement now and then. The stakes can be quite long – 4 or 5 feet at least. Monstera will reach greater heights if properly supported. All these plants benefit from constant humidity, so standing them in a trough on a layer of pebbles surrounded by water or damp peat is a good idea. The water should come just to the top of the pebbles, but the pots should not be standing in it. The trough can be made of any material. You could make your own wooden one, incorporating metal liners in the bottom (baking tins at a pinch) to prevent the wood getting sodden and rotting away. You should water and feed (with Baby Bio) plants often during the summer growing-season, cutting down on both during the winter. Syringing the plant leaves once a week or so perks them up and makes them look more attractive – dusty indoor plants are depressing. Tradescantia looks best planted in profusion – four little plants to a pot. The Spider Plant grows plantlets at the end of long drooping stems. Pick these off in April or May and stand in a glass of water till roots form, when they can be planted in pots in the usual way.

Plants with variegated, mottled leaves like the ivy Canariensis or Scindapsus (Devil's Ivy) make a handsome show, but they are more difficult to grow than the green-leaved type as they need lots of light and a warm, even, draught-free atmosphere. For advice on training variegated ivy into a cone see below.

You cannot beat Geraniums (proper name, Pelargoniums) for a bright show of flowers and leaves on a sunny windowsill. There are dozens of different colours to choose from, and you can mix ordinary Geraniums or Regal Pelargoniums (the ones with blotched ruffled flowers) effectively with the trailing ivy-leaved variety. Geraniums need regular watering and feeding during the summer, and should be kept cool and almost dry during the winter. Pick off dead flowers. Another windowsill favourite is Busy Lizzie, which likes lots of sunshine all year round, flowers almost uninterruptedly and needs water and feeding in summer but almost no water in winter. Pick out new shoots now and then to make the plant bush out nicely. Pink is the usual colour, but red and white kinds are also obtainable.

Watering

More plants die from over-watering than any other reason the experts say. Gauging just when a plant needs water is not so easy for the inexperienced, though after a while it becomes almost instinctive. Here are some pointers.

Water when the surface soil is dry, and the pot gives a sharp ping, when tapped, rather than a watery thud. The drying of the soil gives the roots a chance to breathe, which they cannot do if permanently waterlogged. But do not let it dry out to the point where the plant is starving, leaves drooping, flowers dropping. All plants need frequent watering during their growing season, especially those with large leaves – one to three times a week is the rule in summer.

In winter, when most plants are dormant, watering should be cut down to between one to three times a month. Humidity round the base (the pebble tray idea) is helpful at all times, and helps relieve your anxiety about their dying of thirst in the winter. Spraying the leaves of indoor plants from time to time also helps counteract the dry indoor atmosphere. To water, either use a can with a narrow spout (an old teapot does the job admirably) and fill the space between the rim of the pot and the top of the soil, letting surplus water drain away, or stand the pots in water up to the level of the soil till the soil looks wet and then drain. The first method is right for most indoor plants, but I usually try the second in emergencies – when a plant looks dried out. If the water runs straight through the pot, the soil has shrunk away from the sides and the pot should be watered by the second method. If the water is not absorbed, the surface soil has caked to the point where it is water resistant. Prick the surface with a fork, and then water by the second method.

Herbs in water

Fresh herbs do a lot for simple meals, especially in summer – chives sprinkled into salads, thyme with almost anything grilled or roasted, mint for new potatoes and so on – and if you have a friend or relation with a herb garden, who will let you have some well-rooted, established plants, you can keep these alive and well in a pot full of water and pebbles on a sunny windowsill. The secret is to add a few nuggets of charcoal to the water to keep it sweet. Choose a deep pot (watertight of course, not a flowerpot) fill it with pebbles and water adding the charcoal here and there. Wash the plant roots and then bed them down among the pebbles, respecting the root formation, and weighting gently with pebbles. Feed regularly with Baby Bio, and keep the water topped up. Herbs to try include chives, mint, parsley, thyme, fennel, but make sure they have roots and are lively looking to start with.

Growing from pips and stones

Everyone knows that plants and trees grow from pips and stones, but it still seems quite extraordinary and magical when it happens in a little pot right under your nose. It gives one quite a different feeling about eating tangerines, grapefruit, and avocados etc., not excluding pineapples, which produce an attractive little palmate bush. Almost all the infant trees (which is what they are) and plants in this section can be started indoors then put outside in a sheltered, sunny spot when the frosts are over and their growth well established. If you can provide the right environment – humid in most cases – in winter, they will continue to grow, blossom and even set tiny fruit. Otherwise you may have to begin over again – but pips and stones are giveaways with your morning grapefruit or Christmas tangerines, so it is hardly an expensive hobby. And nice things can happen – a friend of mine has been growing a baby oak tree on her windowsill for years now. When last seen it was about four feet high, and flourishing.

AVOCADO STONES. Wedge the stone into the neck of a jar of water so that the bottom just touches the water. When it shoots and a few leaves appear, plant it in a pot of John Innes Potting Compost, with two thirds of the stone under the soil, one third above. Keep it in a damp environment – either sink the pot in a larger one with damp peat packed round the space between, or stand it on a dish of pebbles with water just up to the level of the pebbles. Stand in a sunny window, and keep the soil moist.

CITRUS PIPS. According to connoisseurs, lime and tangerine pips produce the most attractive baby trees, with sweet-scented blossom and, if you are lucky, miniature fruit. Pips cost nothing (except limes, which are rare and expensive to buy) so do not be niggardly – plant lots of them to increase your chances of raising a sturdy crop.

Plant the pips – six in a tiny pot – by shoving them into potting compost with your thumb. Put them in a warm place to germinate – next to the window of a heated bathroom is a good choice. The soil should be loose, and keep it well watered – every time it feels dry on top. It takes a good month for the pips to germinate. Let the plantlets grow to a good size – 4 or 5 inches – and then re-pot. For their first winter they need a light place with a temperature of between 40–50 degrees. After their first year you can put them out in the summer, watering often and spraying the leaves regularly in a hot, dry summer. (Use rainwater if possible.) If the weather is right they should blossom. After their first winter they can be kept in a cool, but frost-free place during winter.

Re-pot as necessary after December, which is the dormant season, in soil compost with a good layer of charcoal at the bottom.

TROPICAL FRUIT. Dates, lychees, mangoes, etc. These must have heat in the early stages of germination, and extra humidity. Stick them in a pot of compost, watering the compost well first, and tie a plastic bag over the top with string or a rubber band, propping the bag up on a little stick. Put the lot in a warm place like an airing cupboard and watch it carefully. If drops form inside the bag, it is too wet – take it off, turn inside out and replace. When green shoots appear leave them to form a pair of leaves on a little stalk, then take out of the dark and set by a window in a damp, warm room – the bathroom for choice. Re-pot when the plants begin to look pot-bound – to judge this, turn upside down and tap the pot sharply to extract the root-ball – if this is all writhing root and no soil, pot on.

PINEAPPLE TUFTS. Cut the centre tuft away with a ½ inch or so of flesh. Leave for two days to dry out. Then stand on a bed of clean, firm, damp sand in a well-drained pot. Throw a little sand over the skin to hold it firm. Keep the sand moist but not sodden. When roots form, pot in soil compost, with a good layer of crocks at the bottom to ensure drainage. Water by filling the little vase in the centre of the tuft so that it is always full of clean water.

NOTE. With all these pip and stone ventures the secret of success is to provide the young sprig with an environment as close as possible to its natural habitat – warm and humid for the tropical exotics, sunny and sheltered for the citrus fruits.

Basement areas

Basement areas are not the ideal conditions for plant life, but a bit of green is so necessary for the morale when one lives half underground that it is worth the extra feeding and care of your plants in order to be able to look out on a swag of leaves rather than the same dismal, damnable wall. Pots and tubs, provided with good drainage in the way of a layer of crocks at the bottom and filled with sacks of John Innes compost, are the basis of your garden. You can make them yourself by sawing old barrels in half and drilling plenty of drainage holes in the bottom, or scrounge likely containers wherever they turn up – I found a mysterious but useful wooden tub, metal lined, on a rubbish dump once. I suspect it was once used for loading coal onto freight cars. Anyway, it only needed a few stout slats of wood nailed across the bottom to make a homely but attractive version of the Versailles tub – that white wooden box with four round balls at the corners which costs a fancy figure at shops where they supply such things.

Given good conditions – a light, sunny area – almost anything can be successfully grown in pots and tubs: Camellias (provided the roots are shaded), variegated ivies, tubs full of bulbs in season, hanging pots loaded with Tradescantia, anything in fact which will do all right in moderate sunlight. If your basement is dank, dark and gloomy, do not despair – plant Clematis montana (*Clematis montana rubens* Elizabeth is a particularly pretty pink variety) in a good-sized tub, feed it well and water it often from spring onwards and it will shoot up towards the sunlight. Other plants which will grow successfully in a dark basement are Bay Trees, Fatsias, ferns and Hostas, all in tubs. Fuchsias too – although the hardy Fuchsias are a little dull on the whole. Ask for *Fuchsia gracilis* Tricolor or *Fuchsia magellanica* Gracicolor. You may not get a wealth of flowers, but the plants have graceful shapes which combine well with the broad-leaved Fatsias and Hostas. Whatever your type of basement, but particularly if it is badly lit, remember to feed your plants very generously – use general fertilizer from April to July and fade off afterwards – and water often, especially during a hot summer. Things *will* grow well in tubs and pots, but only if you lavishly supplement the deficiencies of their limited environment. Climbers – jasmine will grow in a sunny basement too, and smells delicious – need something to scramble up. A grid of stout wire fastened to nails is adequate and cheap, but wooden trellis looks nice during the bleak mid-winter. A nicely clipped Bay Tree in a tub looks elegant. Fatsias are evergreen, which relieves the winter bareness. London Pride is a sturdy little plant which can be planted round the base of other things in tubs to cover the soil. One of the quickest coverers of all, *Polygonum baldschuanicum*, otherwise known as Russian Vine or Mile-a-Minute, will whisk over everything in sight in summer, though not perhaps the purist gardener's choice. And do not forget the useful bulbs, pressed down into your tubs, and flowering first every spring – Aconites, Snowdrops, Anemone nemorosa – most poetic and Virgilian of flower names.

NOTE. The advice for basements applies also to poorly lit, not very sunny backyards, cemented over or paved, or where the soil is too rancid and dubious to plant. Using tubs and pots again, make a feature of climbers to relieve that wedged-in feeling, or to score a decorative point – a Clematis montana racing up that sooty tree-stump covers it with glory for a few weeks each year and veils it with green for many months more. Encourage a Wistaria (if there is enough sun) to festoon the back door. If you have a greenhouse grow mop-head Pelargoniums (*see* below) to stand in tubs in sunny corners. If the sun never struggles through go in for interesting greens – Hostas, Fatsias, ferns, as above. And, as with basement areas, make sure the drainage in the pots is good, and water and feed generously.

Elegant variations

Imaginative presentation, I have been told, is one of the things which distinguishes the really *recherché* horticulturist from you or me sticking things into pots and tubs. Having seen some of the results, I can vouch for the force of this remark. It is not what you do, but the way you do it – grow a Regal pelargonium the ordinary way and you have a bright, pretty plant. Prune it till it shapes up into a little mop-headed bush, studded with flowers on a thick trunk of a stalk, and you have something quite special, with the gaiety of the Pelargonium flowers but without their usual sprawling shape. Take a Morning Glory seed, grow it in a pot and train it up a pyramid of bamboo stakes and in due course you have a ravishing cascade of flowers and greenery which would poeticize a corner of any room. It is obvious, when you think about it, but the trick is to think of it first. Most of these pretty notions, alas, require a cool greenhouse.

MOP-HEAD OR STANDARD REGAL PELARGONIUM. Buy well-established plants from a geranium nursery (they must be the variety given above) or take a cutting in September in the usual way, keeping it in a light, cool place during winter and watering once weekly. Pinch out side shoots as they appear till the stem is 2–3 feet high, supporting it with a thin stake. Then let it rip till it bushes out to a nice mop shape. Water more often from February onwards and pot on into a 6-inch pot. Feed with Bio 5, and dead head (pick off dead flowers) constantly. It will flower all summer. Prune hard in September, and water once weekly except during December and January when it should be left quite dry.

The same treatment can be given to the Heliotrope, and gardeners are lyrical about the results.

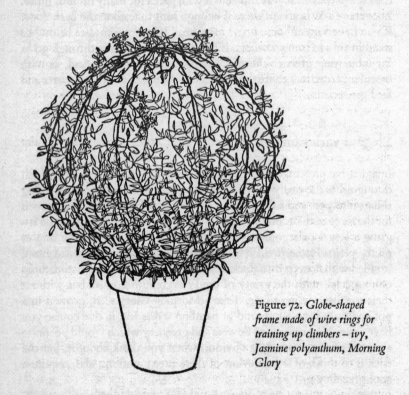

Figure 72. *Globe-shaped frame made of wire rings for training up climbers – ivy, Jasmine polyanthum, Morning Glory*

JASMINE WREATHS. Use Jasmine polyanthum, a cool greenhouse plant which can survive indoors during the flowering period. Take a cutting the usual way – a tuft of leaves on a 2-inch stalk – and put in potting compost. When well established, pot on and make a ring of stout wire about 1½–2 feet in diameter and secure this to a stake driven into the pot. Train the growing climber round this till it loops round and round itself. It needs plenty of Bio 5 during the growing period and must not be left in below freezing temperatures. Kept in a cool greenhouse it will flower in February or March. Kept at a temperature of between 55 and 60 degrees it will produce a sweet-scented blossoming wreath in time for Christmas. An even more elegant variation is to set wire rings one inside the other (*see* figure 72) so that you have a flowering globe.

MORNING GLORY PYRAMID. Soak the Morning Glory seeds in water for twenty-four hours to help start them. Sow in seed compost under a polythene bag (*see* tropical pips and stones) in March or April. When the plants have four leaves, transplant singly into 3-inch pots, in potting compost. Keep in a cool greenhouse till well established – they must not be frost-nipped. When established, pot on two or three at a time into 8- or 10-inch pots, and train up sticks or canes in a tepee, or pyramid shape. Flowers from July to September.

Given care, and a sunny windowsill, it is possible to raise this particular showpiece entirely indoors.

VARIEGATED IVIES. These are slow starters, but they can be trained up sticks as above to produce a handsome hank of variegated foliage 4–5 feet high which will stand up to three months display indoors. Two stationed either side of a sunny landing or hall table, or wherever you fancy a rather grand note, look very effective. They will be happier if your house isn't too hot or dark, and like all indoor plants will benefit from a spell outside in summer.

Fuchsias as indoor plants

Fuchsias were grown indoors with great success by the Victorians and Edwardians. Then fashions changed and the secret of getting these gorgeously pretty plants to flourish indoors was lost. They are coming back into favour, and for those who would like to grow them, here are the tricks of the trade.

Choose from the varieties the Victorians and Edwardians went for – Fascination, Ballet Girl, Mrs Marshall, Scarcity and Achievement. If you are using a clay pot, paint the inside with polyurethane varnish so the moisture won't evaporate. Plant your fuchsia in John Innes Compost No. 2. Buy a strong young plant in spring, and ruthlessly pick off any premature buds, flowers or seed pods. Give the plant the lightest, airiest inside windowsill you have. If you are a net curtain fancier loop the curtains behind the plant on grey days, but put them back when the weather turns sunny. Pot your plant on into a 5-inch pot as soon as roots are visible round the soil ball. Water very thoroughly, then leave till almost dry before watering again. Spray leaves daily.

For a well-shaped plant, nip out the tallest growing shoot when the plant is between 4 and 5 inches high, and support it with a thin cane. This will give you five or six flowering branches. At the first sign of drooping leaves rush for the watering can.

Feeding: follow the manufacturer's instructions. As with all indoor plants, *don't overfeed*.

From mid-September gradually water less, till only enough is given to keep compost slightly moist. Leaves and flowers will drop. Keep the plant in frost-free garage, shed or cellar, and look at it every fortnight to make sure it hasn't totally dried out (should this happen, the emergency drill is to soak it in a bucket of water), or is breaking into premature growth, in which case move it somewhere colder.

Fuchsias outdoors

Ask for the hardy varieties like Madame Cornellison and Tennessee Waltz. They need lots of water in summer, good feeding and protection against frost in winter – heap sand or leaves over the stems. Unlike most flowering plants they don't mind shade. Plant with violas which share their tastes.

Gardens in sinks

Those old stone sinks which got chucked out when the change-over to shining, easy-to-clean porcelain took place, are now so much in demand from gardeners that they cost more than a brand new stainless steel sink unit. (Moral – never throw anything away, today's rubbish is tomorrow's treasure.) Miniature gardens in sinks are very attractive; you can either treat them as a separate entity, a little Japanese scene on their own, or plant them as an extra flower bed. I have never much fancied cement imitations of stone, but after seeing an ordinary porcelain sink given a rough stone look with a liberal icing of cement, I had to admit that it looked quite good, certainly next best to a real stone sink. Brushing a little milk over the cement encourages green mould to grow, which antiques the thing effectively.

You will need an old glazed sink, a bonding agent – Polybond – and some cement, sand and peat mixed in the proportions of two peat, one sand and one cement. The peat admixture not only gives the mock-stone a better colour, it lessens any toxic effects the concrete might have on plants – though as the concrete won't be covering the inside of the sink, you shouldn't have to worry about that. Prepare the sink by cleaning it scrupulously inside and out. When dry, cover the outsides, rim and a few inches down the inner sides with Polybond. No glazed bits should show when the sink is planted. When the Polybond is tacky, cover with the cement mixture, making it as smooth or textured as you please. Use a trowel or something like a palette knife. Give the sink a good coating. Leave to dry. When dry, raise the sink on stone or brick piers to the height you want. Choose a reasonably sheltered spot; against a wall or below a window looks right. From the gardening point of view there are two things to keep in mind when filling and planting – drainage and conservation of moisture. Tackle the first by laying something over the plug-hole, such as an old crock or a piece of perforated zinc (an old tea-strainer perhaps) and over this a layer of crocks, or gravel, well-washed cinders. Fill with a 2-inch layer of peat or, better still, well-rotted turf, turf side down. Over this, pour enough John Innes compost (No. 1 for little plants, No. 2 for small shrubs) to give a firm bed for planting. Add a few rocks, well rammed in, to give root-cover for the plants as well as a touch of variety to the sink garden. Plant with alpines, dwarf shrubs, crocuses and miniature daffodils or – if scent means more than colour – a variety of herbs, plus one or two trailing plants to spill over the sides of your sink and clothe them attractively.

Cobbles

I have long dreamed of finding a cottage somewhere near a stretch of pebbly beach so that I could cart back sacks of pebbles and lay a cobbled terrace and paths for free. It came as a sad surprise to find that finders isn't keepers in this instance, and people aren't allowed to cart home pebbles, no matter how many there seem to be stretching in all directions. However, they can be bought quite reasonably, and I don't suppose anyone would object if you filled a small sack with some specially selected coloured ones from the beach to add interest to your pattern.

A cobbled surface may not be the easiest to walk over but it is marvellously decorative, either on its own or mixed with paving-stones or bricks, and a little area paved this way adds immediate distinction and character to any garden.

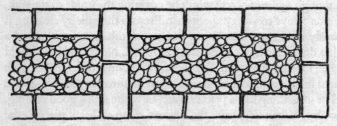

Figure 73. *Garden path combining bricks and pebbles*

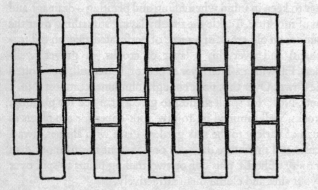

Figure 74. *Bricks alone for a cottagey path with stepped edges*

The common mistake most people make when laying their own cobbled terrace or paths is to set them in a light concrete foundation. Unless the surface is quite level the concrete tends to crack. Furthermore, frost and damp loosen the pebbles and they eventually come out, which leaves a sad blank not easily refilled. The correct way to lay them is to set them in a bed of sand resting on a levelled-out layer of hardcore made of broken bricks and stones well rammed down. If the pebbles are the right shape – a flattened egg shape – and set tight together with their long curves uppermost, feet passing to and fro on top only force them more firmly into their sandy bed. There is no drainage problem, as rain-water seeps away into the subsoil through the cracks, and little plants and patches of moss can take root here and there with attractive results.

The surface to be cobbled needs first to be cleared and levelled, making allowance for the fact that the layers of hardcore, sand and cobbles will raise the level from between 6–8 inches. A layer of hardcore 3–4 inches thick is spread over the subsoil and rammed well down. Over this goes a rather thicker layer of sand mixed with fine soil into which the cobbles are hammered.

A popular way to lay cobbles is in a chequerboard design with squares of cobbles alternating with concrete or stone paving slabs, or squares of bricks. Simple patterns like stars can be laid out using cobbles only. Peg out the pattern first with string and pegs and outline the shape with cobbles running in a continuous line, end to end. Using cobbles of a different colour emphasizes the design still more. Fill in with cobbles running in the opposite direction, towards the centre of the motif. For ideas of what can be done with these simple materials by a really imaginative worker, look up a book on early Greek and Roman mosaic floors and pavements. One of the most beautiful ones I have ever seen, a Greek floor at, I think, Herculaneum, showed two warriors sizing each other up and was made entirely of carefully selected pebbles from a near-by river-bed.

Section 2

Putting on the Style

If men on the whole are uneasy till they have assembled the basic creature comforts – bed, kitchen, easy chair – about them, no woman feels happy till she has begun adding a little colour and gaiety to her surroundings in the way of painting and papering, covering chairs, lampshades and cushions, and breaking up blank walls with pictures and prints. For this reason, I think of this section as feminine. Help from your man will be valuable for some of the decorating techniques described here – the difficulty will be to convince him that two *different* coloured coats of wall paint (dragged walls, colour washing) are better than one plain one. The corniest ruse of all, which is to begin doing the job yourself (preferably in a dark corner which won't show) rather clumsily, so that he can give a superior snort and offer to take over, is the best way of conscripting active assistance.

One subject I have so far kept off in this book is taste. Not because I haven't thought about it, but because it's hard to give any useful information about it, one way or the other. One person's taste is another's anathema. What our mothers despised we adore, and frequently vice versa. Some formulae are useful as a general guide – natural materials are generally more sympathetic than synthetic ones, for instance – but any formula too carefully followed makes a place impersonal. The soundest taste anyone can have, and it is generally acquired rather than innate – most children are cheery vulgarians – is their very own, put together over the years. It is developed in many ways – by making mistakes and living with them, by experiment, by studying grand and unpretentious interiors (barge skipper's saloon as well as Robert Adam reception room), and most of all by listening to a small, discriminating voice within which says 'no, not this, but *that*'. Taste is a living response, and the interior voice is like a pilot light which flickers up warmly when you are onto something right for you, and goes out when you toy with some uncharacteristic fancy. Forming your own taste, when you come down to it, is part of the process of finding yourself. As with cooking, it is in some ways harder to produce excellent results when all costs must be pared to the bone. Instead of going out and buying the carved Spanish chest, or lacquered clock which really speaks to you, you probably have to make do with painting a tin trunk or patiently restoring a settler's clock. A great deal of make-shift and compromise is involved in pauper homemaking, but there's no better training for the eye and imagination than trying to work a far-from-ideal jumble of possessions into a coherent, personal environment, When you bring it off, you have every right to feel pleased with yourself.

This is not to say one can't learn from the pundits, past and present. In this section I have collected together a cache of decorative ideas which may be new to you, aren't difficult or expensive to carry out, and which may relieve that feeling of frustration at always having to settle for secondhand and second best. Go for the best in a cheap commodity, like paint, rather than second best in a more expensive one like wallpaper. Colourwashed or dragged walls look more interesting than a weak imitation of a beautiful hand-printed paper. A well-framed and mounted print is worth two reproduction oil paintings. Curtains made of ticking or denim, interlined and trimmed, look more lively than fake wild silk. A solid old deal chest-of-drawers, stripped and waxed or painted up gaily, has more style than reproduction Chippendale.

Before settling on a colour for walls or soft furnishings, try out a sample on the spot and live with it before deciding – paint a piece of paper to pin on the wall, or drape a swatch of similar coloured cloth over the chair or window. It is actually a help to have to go about decorating and furnishing bit by bit, because every new colour you introduce into a room – as with painting – subtly affects those already present, and this in turn may well change your ideas about what to do next.

Colours are moody. What looked great in a friend's south-facing room, with a high, prettily corniced ceiling and a mass of bric-a-brac and pictures, may swamp a basement room furnished only with a table, chairs and a mat. Dark walls are chic and practical but unless you have a large collection of pictures, patterns and what-not to break up the expanse they can be oppressive. Alternatively, drag them, which enlivens the wall surface immediately. A little texture on the walls – brown paper perhaps – makes a room cosier and emphasizes contrasting textures like polished wood, velveteen, rush matting. Brilliant cockatoo colours look exciting by artificial light, better still by candlelight, so they are good in a dining-room. But they can be scarifying if you are feeling ill, or hypersensitive, so use them for occasional rooms. Dragging also makes bright colours softer and richer. White is perfect for an odd, or interestingly shaped room because it puts all the emphasis on the shape. In cities too, one yearns for white – but it must be thick, pure white, which means at least three coats. Pale colours are pretty and safe. Colour-washing makes them more interesting, while a glaze is useful for warming chilly pastels like primrose yellow and sky blue. Consider the view from the window when choosing wall colours – if it is natural greenery do not kill it by painting your room emerald, royal blue or mauve. Unless you know just what you are about, avoid tricks with colour like dark ceilings; they can induce panic and claustrophobia. Safer to extend a pale wall-colour over the ceiling, leaving the cornice white, if you want to bring it down a little.

White or off-white woodwork is safe with any wall-finish or colour. Gloss for rooms where the paintwork will need frequent washing, egg-shell or flat for sitting-room, bedrooms. A small, finely proportioned room gains from painting woodwork to match the walls (they can both be dragged very successfully) as this – like all-white – empha-sizes the structure, not the details. Beautifully panelled doors or shutters, on the other hand, can be discreetly brought out by painting the panel-ling in shades of off-white, palest on the frame, a shade darker on the panels and a shade darker still on mouldings. Remaining woodwork should be off-white to match.

Paint is the best disguise for the kind of rubbish furniture one buys in moments of desperation (ugly chests-of-drawers, tatty little tables and cupboards) and can't afford to do without. Paint the worst piece with care (*see* painting wood), mixing up your own colour (always more subtle than standard ones) and the improvement is astonishing. Slap a couple of coats of whatever is handy over the old varnish, however, and you will soon have a piebald eyesore. If you haven't time for perfection-ism sand the surface down hard and give it three coats of tinted or plain white undercoat. The matt finish disguises poor surfaces and imper-fections. It will wear off quicker, because undercoat is soft, but it wears away gracefully. Never paint oak, though, because the grain shows through any number of coats. Strip, bleach or dye it instead (*see* wood finishes). Some furniture, all right as it is, can be painted to change its character. I painted the dark mahogany frame of a shapely Victorian chair off-white and re-covered it in cream corduroy, and the difference is analogous to St Paul's, before and after cleaning. If you preferred St Paul's as a sober city gent, rather than a blond bombshell, leave your mahogany alone.

Picture frames are great fun to tart up, being small and quickly covered, and you can get splendid results. Ignore the glossy-mag suggestions, like giving them a quick coat of green or white gloss – it looks flashy, and does nothing for a picture. If you want a 'colour accent', as they say, get it in the picture, not the frame. A simple form of gilding (see picture frames) gives a remarkably good imitation of old gold leaf. The TreasureWax gilt finishes you rub on are easy, and handy for touching up odd spots, but I don't like them applied over a whole frame.

DECORATING

Undercover work

Walls don't need to be in such perfect shape as woodwork to get good results when you are redecorating. But an hour or two spent tidying up before you get painting or papering does make for a better finish, and saves time trying to patch things up later.

You will need Polyfilla (I use the exterior grade for filling holes in plasterwork as it dries rather harder than the standard kind), also wallpaper paste, a flexible knife, a sharp knife or razor blade, a small brush and sandpaper.

First, fill any cracks and craters in the wall surfaces and round the top of the wainscoting or door frames with a stiffish but pliable mix of Polyfilla and water, smoothing the filling down almost flush with the wall and sanding it quite flat when dry and hard. Where dents in lining or wallpaper suggest the plaster has disintegrated behind, cut the dent across with the knife, peel the paper back, brush out the loose plaster and fill with Polyfilla. When dry, sand smooth and stick the paper back in place on top or patch with a new piece, torn rather than cut so as to have less defined edges. Flatten bubbles or blisters in the old paper or lining paper (a lot of walls are lined before being painted) by slitting across with the knife and sliding a little paste inside, then resticking flat. All loose corners should be stuck down the same way. Those ugly wrinkles which happen in corners where the paper has been incorrectly hung – paper should be cut to overlap fractionally at corners, not taken straight across – can sometimes be patched up by slitting down the middle and repasting. If this looks messy, stick a narrow strip of lining paper down over the top. Or, if you are aiming for a really good finish, remove that section of paper with a commercial wallpaper stripper and re-line. Washable wall surfaces should be washed down with a weak soda or sugar-soap solution in warm water to remove grease before repainting. Gloss surfaces should be sanded as well to provide the new paint with something to grip on. Non-washable surfaces should be dusted down with a soft brush. If you don't want wall-paint to go over the woodwork stick masking tape over the top of the wainscoting and round the door and window frames. Use commercial masking tape or brown gummed strip, which can be removed easily by wetting from the back.

None of the decorative finishes I shall be describing later demand perfect walls. In fact dragged painting is quite an effective camouflage for uneven ones. The one exception is hanging expensive hand-printed wallpaper. This needs a smooth, even surface to go on easily and look as good as it should. If the walls are rough and the plasterwork isn't too good, the best course is to line them first with lining paper which is hung in exactly the same way as wallpaper. It is quite cheap and can be bought in rolls from do-it-yourself shops and most ironmongers. Butt the edges when hanging; don't overlap them or you will get ridges that show up through the final wallpaper. Paper round corners in two sections, just meeting or marginally overlapping, or you will get the diagonal creases already referred to. If the walls are papered already, and in good condition, stick the new paper straight on top. If papered, but in poor condition, I am afraid the only remedy is to strip the whole lot off, using a commercial wallpaper stripper and a stripping knife. Then patch up the plaster-work as described, re-line and then paper. Use two brushes for paperhanging, a special paste brush for sticking on the paste and a wide paperhangers' brush for brushing the paper into place on the wall. A neat little tool for rolling down the butt joins can be made quite easily by screwing an old chair castor to a small wooden handle. It flattens the edges down more sleekly and with less mess than the brush, but remember to wipe it often to remove any paste which oozes out. This is vital when hanging hand-printed papers or you may get coloured smears.

Dragged walls

For years I'd seen and admired dragged-paint effects in affluent friends' houses, assuming it was a visual treat you had to be rich to enjoy. Not so. It is not only one of the handsomest finishes, but inexpensive, quick and easy to do. I dragged the hall and staircase walls of a three-storey London terrace house recently, using two colours superimposed, for a total cost of under £4. Each coat, from top to bottom of the house, took roughly five hours to apply; trestles and boards weren't necessary, and the two colours – tawny yellow over sharp yellow – successfully masked the existing tan emulsion so that it now shows up as a shadow-stripe among the yellows. The effect is pretty, like a striped Madras cotton, faded by washing.

It may be difficult to visualize a dragged effect if you haven't seen one. Dragging is done by drawing fine stripes of one colour over another, using an almost dry brush and eggshell paint thinned to near watery consistency with a dryer added to prevent dripping. As a rule the dragged coat is close to the base colour, a couple of tones darker or lighter. My staircase painting was essentially a camouflage job, so I had to use two dragged coats to bridge the colour gap between the existing darkish tan, and the cool yellow I wanted. Normally the ground colour (emulsion applied in the usual way) sets the overall shade, while the superimposed dragged coat breaks up the surface flatness, making the ground colour look richer and softer. Dragging a room immediately makes it look larger, less boxed in – pure illusion, but effective. It is an excellent choice for long narrow halls, passages and staircase walls, where a flat, opaque colour overall can give feelings of claustrophobia. A dragged surface is *lively*, and makes a splendid background to pictures, polished wood, and any other colours around. The use of oil-bound paint makes it washable and sturdy, and any time the walls begin to look a bit scuffed or you fancy a change, you simply drag another coat on top. Add to this that it is a cheap method of transforming an existing emulsion colour you have tired of, and you can see why I feel paupers should get into drag immediately. Hitherto decorators have tended to rather sit on the process, and give the impression that dragging is a mysterious business needing the combined skills of a wizard with colour and a highly trained house-painter to execute successfully. It is true that a skilled painter will achieve a more regular, uniformly pin-striped effect, and an experienced decorator will have a surer sense of what colours will enliven a particular room, but any patient amateur with a little feeling for colours can get satisfactory results first time off. A little irregularity in the painting won't spoil the overall effect.

Any colour can be dragged with advantage. If you are unsure of your colour sense, you can't go wrong by sticking to the formula of a couple of tones darker or paler – pale brick red over darker brick red, mid leaf green over new leaf green, raw umber over buff, steel grey over dove grey, and so on. More adventurously, try out mild colour contrasts on top of each other – grey over pink, sludge green over burnt orange (some of the walls of the Victoria and Albert are dragged in this combination), grey-green over cerulean blue. It's sensible to try out your ideas on a piece of board first, painting it first in the ground shade, and then dragging when dry. You can sometimes experiment on a hidden patch of wall, behind a bookcase, or inside a cupboard, if this seems too laborious. Remember that a dragged colour always dries out paler than when wet, so leave it to dry completely before deciding. There is an element of happy accident about some effects, so keep an open mind. I tried two dragged coats, raw umber plus white, followed by burnt umber plus white (white eggshell paint is the usual medium for dragged paint colours) over the existing buff emulsion in one room, which dried out much more attractively than I'd expected, in a part-silvery, part-shadowy look like pigeon feathers. You can rescue a colour combination which misfires by dragging a further coat on top which supplies whatever is lacking – lightness, warmth or contrast. A slightly darker tone of a neutral colour like raw umber will blend most colour combinations together successfully.

What you need

Before you apply your dragged coat the walls should either be painted with emulsion in your chosen base colour in the normal way or, if the existing surface is in good condition, washed down to get rid of grease and dirt. For an average-sized room – 14 × 10 feet, say – you need approximately one pint of white eggshell paint, one pint of pure turpentine (from chemists, Woolworth's, some ironmongers), enough artists' oil colours to tint your white base to the shade you want for your dragged coat (half to one large 37 c.c. tube is usually enough for a paler shade, but dark or bright colours will use more oils unless you start with a coloured eggshell close to the final shade rather than white). The price of artists' colours varies considerably – all the cadmiums, yellows and reds, are particularly expensive. You can get almost the same effect using a cheaper shade in the same family, so study the chart carefully. You also need a bottle of Terebine paint dryer (paint shops, decorators' merchants), and a wide brush. A wide, soft, painter's dust brush, with spaced bristles (decorators' merchants) helps to give striped paint-strokes automatically, but I have used a cheap plastic-handled brush for pasting wallpaper instead, with good results. The type of brush to avoid is a good-quality, standard paint brush because these are generously bristled to *prevent* brushmarks. Another way to describe dragging might be to call it controlled brushmarks. You also need a plastic bucket, or paint kettle (an old emulsion tin, carefully cleaned out, is ideal for this) to keep the thinned paint in, preferably with a lid of some sort, and a large piece of clean rag to wipe your brush on between strokes.

How to do it

Use a white mixing bowl to mix the colour in, as white is the best background to judge colour shades against. Squeeze in a good dollop of oil colour and a couple of tablespoons or so of turps to dissolve it in. Stir thoroughly with an old paint brush, or wooden spoon, till the colour is dissolved. This is your tint. Now pour the eggshell into your bucket or large tin (don't use a bowl to carry the paint about in, because it's liable to get spilt) and gradually stir in the tint, mixing very thoroughly indeed. Try the shade out on a piece of card, or your painted test board, or the inside of a cupboard, as you go along, remembering that the colour will look lighter – a couple of shades – when dry. To darken a particular shade you can safely add a little raw umber; to warm it, a spot of red – go sparingly with red because a tiny bit makes a big difference, depending of course on the basic shade. Don't warm blue or green with red, for instance, but with a little yellow or raw umber. This part of the dragging process takes longer, relatively, than the actual painting. There is no need to get over anxious about it though – the dragged coat will be very thin, remember, so it's not as if you were mixing up a colour for use at full strength. Any oil colour added after the initial mixing to darken or brighten should be dissolved first in turps and added cautiously, mixing well each time.

When you have got your colour right, the paint should be thinned. It is difficult to give exact proportions of thinner (turps) and dryer to paint, because some walls seem to need a thicker consistency than others. I find $\frac{3}{4}$ to 1 pint of turps to 1 pint of tinted eggshell is about right. The best way to arrive at the right result is to mix in $\frac{3}{4}$ of a pint to start with, adding one teaspoon of dryer per pint of liquid, and try it out on a bit of wall or the board. If the brush strokes refuse to separate out into stripes the paint is too thick. Add more turps and dryer. If it makes stripes nicely, but trickles off at the bottom, add more dryer. If it makes a watery band of stripes which then run together, it's too thin, which means adding more tinted eggshell and dryer.

To drag, use a nearly dry brush, wiping it off frequently on your rag. Take up some thinned paint on the tips of the bristles, stroke off excess on the side of the tin or bucket, wipe lightly on your rag, and then touch the brush lightly to the wall at the top of each stroke, drawing it steadily down in a vertical line increasing the pressure as the paint runs out. Remember to dab your brush with the rag each time you take up more paint. Use lining paper seams, if the wall was lined, as a guide for making straight strokes. After a couple of trial runs – begin dragging in a dark corner – you will find you can brush a band of fine stripes of colour without too much trouble. Don't expect perfect regularity, because some stripes tend to come out a little thicker or denser, and it is well nigh impossible to avoid a slight build-up of the dragged paint at the top of each stroke, round the ceiling, and round the odd obstacle like light-switches, door frames, where you have to pause for a second. Don't worry about this. It may look conspicuous when you have painted only a small section and the paint is still wet; finish the room, leave it all to dry, and you will find the varying intensities of tone make the walls much livelier to look at. The paint dries to a very faint sheen, which gives a slight textural contrast with the matt emulsion. (If you want a particularly strong, washable finish, in a bathroom for instance, use white gloss paint as a base instead of white eggshell. This dries to a soft lustre.)

The usual way to brush on dragged coats is from the top down. If the wall surface is so high you can't cover the space easily in one stroke, but have to keep clambering down steps as you brush away (difficult without breaking the rhythm of the stroke, and possibly dangerous) you can cover the surface with two strokes instead, working from the bottom up, then from the top down, using a featherlight pressure to blend them in at their meeting point. It's a good idea to vary the height of this meeting point now and then to avoid a faint band of denser colour running round the wall. If the brush skates over some patches of wall, leaving them bare, fill in with a very light stroke. On a bumpy wall surface, your dragging will tend to be really uneven, with paint collecting on the top of each bump or ridge, missing the underside completely. Go over the bare bits again; it is better to overcolour them a little than leave a piebald effect, which looks accidental and distracting. One nice feature about dragging is that you can cover really high walls – the sort you normally need trestles to cope with – quite successfully by simply tying your brush handle securely to the end of a long stick or pole and brushing away as before. It wouldn't work with ordinary paint perhaps, but it suits very well the light touch needed for dragging. Uneven dragging shows up most on the window wall and the one opposite, so take extra care with these. If you can't manage a steady, straight stroke, and there are no lining seams to guide you, chalk a guideline now and then using an improvised plumb-line – weight tied to the bottom of a long piece of string – to help you. If you don't mind a bit of irregularity, don't bother.

You will find, with a little practice, that dragging goes very quickly and is even quite fun to do compared with the effort of getting perfect coverage the ordinary way. The trickiest part of the process, I find, is not the dragging, which soon becomes automatic, but what painters call 'cutting out' along the ceiling or cornice, round doors, window frames, mantelpieces or, worst of all, down a slanting ceiling such as the one I had to deal with on the staircase. Odd dabs of paint on the ceiling or cornice can be painted out with white emulsion later, which only takes a few minutes. Small bare spots, like the triangles at the top of a slanted ceiling, and odd gaps above the skirting, are best filled in with a small brush, keeping to the same dragged stroke. Don't worry about these details as you go round the walls – the chief thing is to keep up a smooth, even, vertical brush-stroke.

There's very little mess if you are careful when stroking excess paint off the brush on the side of the tin, so you can get away without covering everything with paper or Polythene. Keep a rag moistened with turps to wipe trickles off the wainscot or the odd spot off the floor. If you have to break off half-way through the job, cover the paint up with as airtight a cover as possible because turps evaporates quite fast. You may have to add a little more turps and dryer to bring it up to the right consistency, even so, before using it again. Stand the brush in cold water, which will prevent it drying out and stiffening, and brush out well on sheets of newspaper before using. Decant any leftover dragged paint into a screwtop jar, for touching up scuffs and scars later on.

NOTE. If you like the idea of extending the dragged finish over the woodwork in a matching colour, you can do this using gloss paint as a medium over a ground of flat or eggshell paint in the basic wall-colour. Use precisely the same technique, but a smaller brush. This one-colour look gives an elegant, 'finished' appearance to a small room, and makes it seem much bigger. It's also a good way of blending ugly doors or cupboards into their surroundings.

Glazed walls

A pretty and characteristic colour used in Early American decoration is a warm, delicate, greeny blue like a thrush's egg or the sky after sunset. The American Museum at Claverton Manor has a charming eighteenth-century panelled room done out entirely in this colour, and it makes a wonderful background for polished wood furniture and old gilt-framed pictures. The paintwork there is contemporary with the room, and if you look closely you can see how the sky-blue oil paint has been overlaid with a tinted varnish or glaze to give this particular soft colour. Glazing gives a blank painted surface depth, subtle variations in tone, and a touch of mystery – an analogy might be those richly smoked ceilings and walls in old pubs which suddenly look so impersonal when newly done out in a smooth, uniform, cream paint. It struck me, as I admired the panelling, that one could adapt the technique for ordinary emulsion or water paint to mellow the colour, much as one does when antiquing furniture. I tried it out in my kitchen, using white Walpamur tinted with gouache for the base coats and emulsion glaze, stocked by good paint shops, coloured with a little raw-umber gouache for the glaze. The glaze proved a little tricky to apply as it dries very fast, and colour build-up where brush strokes overlap makes for slight streakiness. I like the streakiness myself, and it is not at all pronounced in the final effect, but if it worries you you can almost eliminate it by using extra care when applying the glaze. I found the glaze gave exactly the effect I wanted, humanizing the rather cold, sky-blue wall colour and consorting happily with pine kitchen-fitments as well as a Morris paper in the adjoining room. (Incidentally a two-tone wall-colour like this is a good choice where you have a plain painted room leading out of a wallpapered one, because it is impossible to find a single colour which picks up the overall tones of a printed paper.)

Method

Use a standard off-white emulsion paint or other water-based paint for the base coats, tinting them with gouache colours, or buy a ready mixed colour. A small tube of cerulean gouache is enough to tint a half-gallon tin of emulsion paint. Use emulsion glaze for glazing, tinted with raw-umber gouache. Give the walls as many base coats of cerulean as necessary to give a uniform colour. Tint the glaze by dissolving a little (about a third of the tube) gouache in water and adding it gradually to the glaze. Thin the glaze to the thinnest consistency recommended by the makers, to give a faint sheen rather than a gloss finish. Test the colour out on a small bit of wall which won't show.

It takes a little practice to get the hang of applying the glaze evenly so begin on a wall which doesn't get direct light. Use a broad brush and paint the surface in big vertical strokes, working from left to right, and trying to prevent brushstrokes overlapping. Charge the brush with enough glaze to brush out thinly over a strip of wall but not so heavily that you leave a wet splodge when you first apply it. Drips should be brushed out immediately. Don't labour at covering in little gaps near the ceiling or round a light-switch – go over these later with a small brush.

If you like the idea of extending the glazed effect throughout the room (over woodwork as well as walls) as in the American panelled room, you can easily mix up a matching paint and glaze for woodwork, using artists' oils mixed with flat or eggshell paint (white) for the base coats and matt or flat varnish for the glazing.

Glazing can be used over almost any colour, except very dark ones where the glaze would scarcely show. Raw umber is an immensely adaptable colour for glazing as it does nice things to most other colours (Early Americans used it constantly), but there's no reason why you shouldn't invent your own combinations. Try out your ideas on a piece of painted cardboard first.

Colourwashing

Colourwashing is another wall treatment favoured by swank decorators which has a lot to recommend it from the D.I.Y. point of view. It is simple and quick to do, costs next to nothing (you can use leftover odds and ends of emulsion) and looks sophisticatedly pretty and special. To achieve it, two coats of tinted water-based paint, thinned to transparency, are brushed over a matt white ground so that the white glows through a soft dapple of surface colour. The effect is subtly luminous, as of a watercolour wash extending right over the walls. Used as I first saw it, in pale apricot over the walls of a small, north-facing cottage dining room, set off by rush matting and white paintwork, the impression was of spring sunshine even on a bleak, February morning.

Colourwashing is for clear, pale colours. To brighten a dark, chilly-looking room (a basement perhaps) you might choose between colourwashing in yellow, apricot, peach, pink. Conversely, in a very bright, sunny room, a wash of light pure blue or green gives a refreshing sunlight-through-water effect.

The first essentials for colourwashing are the proper brush – top quality, wide, with soft lush bristles – and a thick, even, uniform white ground. Use two or three coats of off-white, or warm-white emulsion, *not* brilliant white. For the colourwash itself you can choose various possibilities. An inch or so of the emulsion left in the tin can be tinted the shade you want with artists' gouache, or more cheaply still, with poster colour, and thinned out with water to cover an average-sized room. Alternatively, if you have a little emulsion paint in a suitable colour left over from another decorating job, this too can be thinned down with water and used straight, or, if the colour lacks something, mixed with a very little gouache in the appropriate colour. Gouache colours are particularly pure and brilliant, which is why decorators use them. A blob of vermilion will tint a yellow wash apricot and a squeeze of yellow ochre will colour a pink wash peachy. When mixing concentrated colour with paint it is vital to dissolve it very thoroughly in a little water before stirring it into the bulk of the paint, a streak of un-dissolved colour in the middle of one wall is a nuisance.

Method

First objective is to get the colourwash to the proper consistency and hue. Make sure your gouache or poster colour is entirely dissolved, then add it gradually to the emulsion, checking the colour-intensity on a large sheet of white paper from time to time. Remember that you will be thinning the emulsion base with water in proportions (roughly) of nine water to one emulsion, which will dilute your colour con-siderably. On the other hand, colourwashing requires two coats for a soft dappled effect, which will mean some build-up of colour, so keep that in mind as well. On the whole, keep it pale to be on the safe side. Gradually add water, lots of it, until your colourwash is no thicker than milk.

Brushing on colourwash is different from applying paint in the usual way. Instead of aiming at complete coverage the idea is to spread the colour rapidly, but with controlled *un*evenness, using big, free brushstrokes in all directions. Smooth out any hard-edged brushmarks, or drips, using the brush with a scrubbing motion, but aim to leave small blurry islands of white 'grinning through', as the decorators put it. The second coat will cover these with a film of colour, so they finally register as a lighter shade of pale. I find it helps, when rediscovering the proper rhythm of colourwashing, to start in a dark corner of the room (inside a cupboard is better still) and keep telling myself that I am *floating* on the colour, not brushing it on. After doing a couple of square yards, the knack is established and one can proceed with a confident swing. If you have to knock off at any point, try to paint up to a corner rather than stop half way across a wall. Leave the first coat of colourwash to dry out completely, which may take only a few hours on a warm day, since the paint is so thin. Be prepared for the first coat to look patchy. Apply the second coat in exactly the same way as the first, but this time brush over any white patches. By the time you have started on your second wall, you will be able to look back at the first in triumph, all its wisps and rag-tags of tint now resolved into a delicately luminous ebb and flow of colour.

Wallpapering

Anyone who has coped successfully with putting up cheap wallpapers might be encouraged to know that sticking up expensive hand-printed papers isn't all that much more difficult, though it is a job usually left to professionals. I papered a room recently with a beautiful Morris paper. 'Putting up this sort of paper isn't a do-it-yourself job,' the super-cilious sales girl told me. I didn't let this put me off unduly, but I must admit I approached the job with unusual care, double-checking every measurement and handling the paper as if it might come apart in my hands. Perhaps the extra care paid off, at any rate the finished room would strike anyone – except perhaps a trained paperhanger – as a smooth, professional bit of work.

There are a few special problems connected with hanging hand-printed paper. First, it invariably comes to you untrimmed, with a selvedge of plain paper $\frac{1}{2}$ an inch wide or so along both sides. This has to be cleanly sliced off, impossible with scissors because these papers are so heavy you can't avoid slight jags as you cut. Some wallpaper shops will trim the paper for you at a small extra cost. Otherwise you will need to invest in a trimmer, a neat little gadget with adjustable roller blades. Like many tools sold mainly to the trade, these can be difficult to track down. *See* Suppliers' Index for London stockists. If all this sounds like too much of a performance you might get away, if you have steady hands, with cutting it with a sharp knife (a Stanley knife with a new blade) and a steel ruler, but pencil a guideline first and make sure you have a level surface to do the cutting on. Either way, you will find it much easier to trim each wall-length separately. Practise with the trimmer on a spare bit of paper till you have got the knack of running it along smoothly, guided by the paper edge. If the trimmer stalls, don't try to force it on but free it care-fully and begin again at the other end, trimming to the point where you stopped.

Problem two is that the colours on these handprinted papers are liable to smear and smudge if you splash paste all over them and try to rub it off. Wipe down the pasting table between pasting each sheet. Paste the paper evenly and thoroughly but not thickly, otherwise paste oozes out along the seams. Put a thin layer on the wall surface to help get a good grip. If paste does appear along the seams as you smooth the paper onto the wall wipe it off quickly – dabbing rather than rubbing – with a dry cloth or tissues which will need changing frequently. Smooth the paper out with a dry brush or your hands and/or dry cloth, washing your hands as soon as they start picking up colour. A lot of trouble, but you might as well protect your investment.

A final problem you may run across is that many hand-printed papers have a large repetitive design which needs to be carefully matched as you go along. Examine the selvedge before you trim the paper for little coloured dots indicating the beginning of a design repeat. There is usually one at the very beginning of the roll so if you take your first measured length from there, you need only hunt out the corresponding dot further along to know where to make your next cut. But make sure it's the *right* one, as there may be more than one. Old houses often have uneven walls and ceilings, so be prepared for divergences where the ceiling dips or climbs an inch or two. If in doubt add a couple of extra inches at both ends when cutting, match the paper half-way up the wall and start smoothing it flat upwards from there. Then you can trim off any surplus after you've got it correctly aligned.

Lastly, there is very little give in expensive wallpapers, unlike cheaper ones, so don't hang it with a pronounced gap between one sheet and the next and expect to smooth and stretch it to meet up. And don't leave the paper soaking up paste for too long – stick it up as soon as it's pliable.

I hope I haven't frightened you off with this barrage of warnings and instructions, but when hanging something which costs several pounds a piece it pays to be meticulous.

NOTE. A piece is usually 11 yards or 33 feet long.

Poets and brown paper

How do you imagine a poet's room? Here's a description of poet Lionel Johnson's study by his friend, W. B. Yeats: 'that room was always a pleasure to me, with curtain of grey corduroy over door and window and bookcase and its walls covered with brown paper'. A peaceful, studious retreat it must have been, one imagines, with calf-bound books ranged in the bookcases, and a bust or two. So congenial to modern tastes that it comes as a surprise to find that Yeats was writing of almost a century ago. The idea of sticking wrapping-paper on one's walls is credited to another member of their set. It's still one of the cheapest ways to paper a room and a soberly effective one, particularly if you paste the paper shiny side down to make the most of it's texture and faint pin-stripe. Wrapping-paper also comes in a beautiful deep blue, though you may have trouble getting hold of it in a decent width – 20 inches seems to be standard in blue papers.

Contact paper and board merchants (see the yellow pages in your local directory) for the paper, which comes in huge rolls – 500 yards is about average, enough to paper two good-sized rooms or the stairway of a small house – and various widths from 20 inches up to 36 inches. There are browns and browns so see your colour before ordering. The paper is sold in various weights, from flimsy to stiff. Buy one of the heavier weights for papering, as thin wrapping paper is too fragile when wet to handle easily. Use ordinary Polycell paste to stick it up with, and if the edges need trimming invest in a patent trimmer. A simple stencilled border in charcoal or dark brown would look effective with brown paper, using emulsion tinted with gouache or acrylic paints for the stencil colour (see stencils). Brown paper is neutral enough to combine well with most furniture and fabrics, except perhaps flowered chintzes. For myself, I rather fancy Lionel Johnson's grey corduroy . . .

Finishing touches

Small details can make a lot of difference to the look of a room, emphasizing an attractive feature like an irregular cottage ceiling, relieving the boxiness of a modern room, or simply giving a finished look to the decoration. All the ideas suggested here are easy to do and cheap.

Stencils

At the turn of the century, stencilled dados were all the rage and there are signs that they are coming in again. A simple pattern looks attractive stencilled in a contrasting colour round doors, window frames, skirting, in a plainly painted room. Carry the pattern on round the walls just below the ceiling. I have included some ideas for stencil patterns, or you can invent your own, remembering that the cut-out area must not be too intricate or extensive, or the stencil will disintegrate. You can buy special stencil board from which to cut the pattern, using a sharp Stanley knife, or make your own stencil out of ordinary thick cartridge paper heavily coated with shellac or varnish to make it waterproof. A stencilling brush should be a thick one shaped like a shaving brush – you could use an old shaving brush, in fact. Mix up your own colour with white emulsion or distemper (Walpamur) and artists' gouache or acrylic paints which are soluble in water (*don't* make the colour too liquid). Cut the stencil fairly close to one edge of your paper or board, and exactly parallel with the edge, so that you can use the top edge as a guide. Hold it firmly in place with the left hand while you dab the colour on with the right, and lift the stencil off quickly to avoid smudging the paint. Practise in an easily accessible spot, like round a door frame, first. A coloured stencil on white walls is an obvious choice, but colour on colour looks great too. In a small room, a stencilled pattern running in vertical stripes up the walls looks charming. Another more sophisticated idea is to stencil a large, single motif like a fleur-de-lys, or a daisy or star shape, at regular intervals all over the painted walls of a room. For this you would have to chalk guide lines on the walls using a carpenter's rule. The motif should be scaled to the size of the room, but don't make it too small – about 4 inches high would be right in an average room – or the effect will be lost.

Dull red over denim blue would look good, or sage green on pink. A fair bit of work, I must admit, but you would have the pleasure of knowing your room was quite unique. You can of course add detail in a second colour by hand afterwards. Just to give you an idea of what lengths these ideas can be taken to: I saw a beautiful stencilled sample recently, which had been commissioned by a French millionaire to cover the walls of his Paris flat. The foundation for the stencil was a homely checked cotton made for covering the backs of Louis Quinze chairs, in grey, buff and brown. Over this went a stencil in vermilion and white, of daisies linked by a delicate trellis pattern. Two or three men would be employed to carry out the stencilling, and the whole job was expected to take six months. The stencil design itself looked as artlessly pretty as one of the old calico prints.

Borders

Ordinary gummed brown-paper strip, the kind you buy in rolls from stationers, makes a cheap, instant border for painted or papered walls. If the colour scheme is appropriate you can use it just as it comes, following the line of ceiling and skirting board and outlining door and window frames. Use matt strip rather than the shiny kind. Or, for a more emphatic edging, decorate the strip with a small, continuous, stencilled pattern in a contrasting colour. This sounds laborious but, in fact, once you have cut the stencil the rest goes very quickly. One can stencil a strip about 15 feet long in about twenty minutes. Use acrylic paints, mixed with as little water as possible, because they dry extra fast and are waterproof, which means you can wet the strip for sticking up without smudging your stencil. Cut the stencil the same width as the gummed strip, for rapid alignment, but not too long, about 6 inches is a good size to handle. Stencil the strip a section at a time, laying it gummed side down on a few sheets of newspaper and take care not to get the gummed side wet. The less water you use with the acrylic paint the sharper your

Figure 76. *Suggested stencil for gummed-strip border*

stencil will be and the faster it will dry – almost instantly, in fact. But don't fret if the pattern gets smudged here or there, a bit of irregularity looks appealing. And if you really botch it, all you need do is cut that bit out and stick the strip together again. Unless you are very calm and organized you may find it easiest to stick the border up a short section at a time, damping the back *in situ* with a wet but not dripping sponge and smoothing it down rapidly. Wetting a long strip at a time is apt to lead to Chaplinesque contortions ending in a dance of fury as the gum – much stickier than wallpaper paste – fastens onto itself, you, the floor and everywhere else.

As an alternative to stencils, try a narrow, plain-coloured border to finish off a papered room or make a painted one look more interesting. Most wallpaper firms stock printed paper borders, but the pretty ones are absurdly expensive and the cheap ones are ugly. You could make your own border quite easily by cutting long strips of plain-coloured paper and glueing them all round the edges of the paper or paintwork with wallpaper paste. Alternatively use 1-inch wide cotton tape dyed to whatever colour you like and stuck on in the same way. Plain jute webbing looks handsome, finishing off a rather sober masculine sort of room (*see* Suppliers' Index, or you may be able to buy it from upholstery suppliers and some hardware shops locally). When papering any room with a striped paper, use stripes from the paper to make a narrow border. This looks particularly pretty in a room with an irregular ceiling.

Fabric on the walls

Walls covered in hessian and book-cloth are becoming a good-taste cliché – though still a handsome look, if you can afford it. There are cheaper and more imaginative ways of using fabrics to vary wall-textures and dress up a room. A film designer I know stuck panels of dotted swiss, edged with pale blue braid, over pastel walls of a small bedroom, and hung matching dotted-swiss draperies over the bed, with sophisticated–innocent effect. Ordinary hessian and jute fabrics are marvellously cheap – I mean the fabric by the yard, not the expensive, specially backed, wall hessian – but difficult to glue up successfully as the selvedges are lumpy and uneven and if you cut them off the fabric frays. Cheap dressmaking cottons, like gingham, are easier to cope with and could look pretty in a bedroom alcove. Use heavy duty Polycell for flimsy fabrics. Ordinary glue size is good for sticking coarse woven fabrics in sludgy colours as it sticks, stiffens and glazes in one operation. It does yellow the fabric a little. But most pastes and glues will yellow the material in time.

Built-in cupboards

Built-in cupboards are marvellously useful, but a large stretch of flat painted cupboard can be overpowering in a small room. One way of breaking the surface up is to back the centre panels of the doors with closely gathered fabric panels held down top and bottom with tacks or those stretchy wires sold for hanging net curtains (figure 77). The wire passes through a channel seam at the top and bottom of the piece of fabric, which should be stretched very taut, and then hooks at each end to screw-eyes in the door. Choose a fabric matching something else in

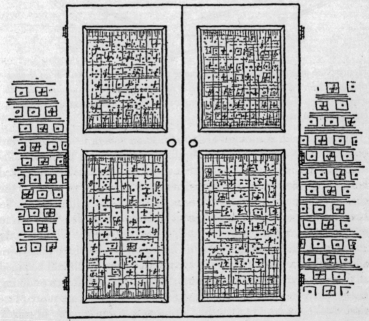

Figure 77. *To relieve the blank look of large built-in cupboards the door panels can be filled in with gathered fabric to match wallpaper or furnishings. The fabric panels are held in place by stretchy wire secured by screw eyes top and bottom*

the room or, if you want to tie it in with the walls, choose one of those fabrics printed to match the wallpaper. The size of the fabric panel depends on the design of the doors; you could have one long panel per door, or one smaller one above and one below.

Squab cushions

Silk squab cushions on painted Regency chairs are a real classy decorator's touch. My favourite, purely decorative, ones were covered in scarlet felt, on two papier-mâché Victorian chairs.

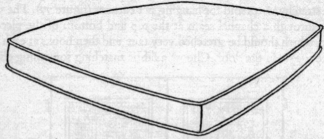

Figure 78. *Squab cushion with double row of piping and boxed sides. For an elegant chair the cushion can be buttoned. To do this stitch through cushion cover and all with a long needle and stout thread, catching in the covered buttons at the same time. The buttons have to be removed for cleaning*

The cushion itself shouldn't be too thick, an inch or less is plenty, and you can make it out of almost anything: layers of old blankets quilt-stitched together, blankets with a sandwich of horsehair or rubberized horsehair in between, underfelt, foam rubber. Trace off the shape of the chair seat in newspaper as a pattern, and cut the cushion filling to fit. To keep it in shape, this should have an undercover, made of any cheap scrap cotton you have around, machined to fit over the filling exactly and then stitched through cover and filling here and there to hold them all together. To look really good the removable cover should be piped all round, top and bottom (figure 78), but on ordinary kitchen or dining chairs where you do a lot of sitting, flat tie-on cushions are more practical. Make covers for these like ordinary cushion covers, in sturdy washable material like denim, and add piping round the side seam if you feel like it. Insert a zip, Velcro or poppers into the back seam and sew on tapes at the corners to tie the cushion to the chair back.

PICTURE FRAMES

Surprisingly, collecting decorative art-work to brighten up one's walls is usually easier, and cheaper, than finding frames to put it in. Victorian watercolours by unknown but skilful amateurs and prints of every sort can be found, unframed, at prices ranging from a few pence to a few pounds in junk shops, antiquarian booksellers and sale rooms. There are reproductions too, excellent value if you stick to drawings and water-colours which lose much less than oils in reproduction. These come cheaper by the book. A book of Turner watercolours costs over £3, but works out at 25p or so per print. Then there is child art. Children often dash off charming and spirited pictures which deserve better than a couple of drawing pins. Lastly there is a whole range of decorative items which can look interesting and attractive well mounted and framed – butterflies, old playing cards, sepia photographs, Victorian postcards, old sheet-music covers, maps.

Frames are the problem. It seems ridiculous to pay more for the frame than the thing in it. The standard mouldings art shops will make up for you into frames are not cheap, and they look brash, new and shiny.

Making your own frames

One possibility is to make your own frames from scratch. An amateur will get best results using a plain wood moulding which is then finished with paint or gilt in one of the ways described below. The reason for this is that it is very difficult to get perfectly mitred corners using ordinary tools – professional framers use an elaborate guillotine machine which slices through mouldings like cheese – and a painted finish will allow you to disguise any patching up that might be necessary. An essential tool is a metal mitre board with attached clamps which holds your pieces in position for sawing, glueing and nailing. You also need a tenon saw, a good ruler or steel measure, PVA woodworking adhesive and a light hammer and small-headed nails. Plastic wood is useful for patching up mitred corners which don't quite meet, and sandpaper for smoothing the filler flush with the frame. When measuring up your picture to decide on the measurements for the frame, it is as well to allow $\frac{1}{8}$ of an inch extra on all the measurements so that the picture doesn't sit too tightly in the frame or rebate. If you aim for a perfect fit the chances are that some of your measurements may go a fraction out in the sawing, glueing and nailing and the picture won't go in at all. If the picture itself isn't exactly symmetrical all round, as often happens with old paintings, cut your moulding to the length of the longest sides.

When you have worked out the measurements for the four pieces of moulding to be cut, mark them off on the wood, cut the moulding straight across into four pieces and set each one into the mitre and cut across at a 45-degree angle at both ends. If two mitred corners don't exactly meet when you set them in the clamp, draw the saw between them, which will remove any odd projecting whiskers of wood that may be preventing a flush fit. Assemble the frame by joining two lengths of moulding first. Glue the ends to be joined, leave them in the clamp to set and then drive two nails in across the corner, one from each side, making sure they won't collide. Join these (L-shaped) pieces together in the same way, one corner at a time. When the frame is completed, fill any gaps at the corners with plastic wood, and when this has set, smooth the join with sandpaper. Have your glass cut $\frac{1}{8}$ of an inch short in each direction, measuring inside the rabbet or rebate (*see* figure 80).

This is only the briefest run-down on the subject of frame-making. There are several excellent books on the subject which show the process step-by-step, with clear photographs, as well as giving instructions for different types of frame.

Restoring old frames

But an easier solution is to buy up any cheap old frames one comes across and refurbish them. Look for them in junk shops, dark corners, sheds 'out the back', street markets, Oxfam shops and jumble sales. If you learn to cut your own mounts and glass, which is not difficult with a little practice, a do-it-yourself framing operation works out considerably cheaper than the cheapest art-shop effort, and with a little thought and imagination you can get astonishingly good results. I framed two reproduction watercolours recently, using a pair of old frames hideously daubed in maroon enamel which I found in a junk shop for 20p each. I stripped and repainted the frames, and cut and covered mounts to fit the prints, and I swear the result wouldn't look out of place in Bond Street. Total cost per frame – around 35p. Don't think I'm suggesting that it would be an easy matter to put the experts out of business – if I had a really valuable painting I would still send it to a good professional framer. But I do think that one is likely to give more care and thought to framing one's attractive trifles than a busy professional would, and this extra effort of imagination shows in the results. An encouraging thing about framing is that everything involved is quite small, so painting, glazing and rubbing down are rapid operations.

When collecting frames, look for good proportions and not too much sugar-icing ornamentation. Learn to see beneath the skin – ox-blood enamel, Woolworth's gold paint, black treacle varnish – to the basic

Figure 79. *A small oil painting given the full treatment to make it look more important, and bridge the gap between a small picture and larger frame. Here a gilded bevel (use gold adhesive gift-wrap tape) and inked lines, filled in with a coloured wash on a card mount covered with Ingres paper. The frame can be gilt or finished in one of the ways described to give a muted but distinctive surround*

shape and possibilities of the frame. Minor damage can be restored – chipped corners, flaking gilt, small missing chunks of moulding. Avoid frames whose composition mouldings have begun to crumble through damp and exposure, unless you fancy stripping off all the super-structure to reveal the basic plain wood frame. An ebonized finish, hard, black and shiny, which one often come across, is hard to remove, needing hours of soaking in caustic and scraping and sanding, so avoid these too unless the size and shape are just right for something you want to frame. On the whole, size is not vitally important when buying frames, because most minor art-work looks better given the full treatment of coloured mount

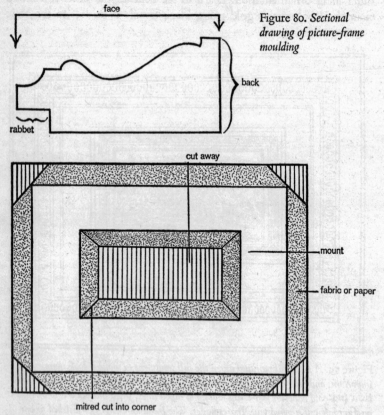

Figure 80. *Sectional drawing of picture-frame moulding*

Figure 81. *Covering a mount with fabric or paper*

and inked lines, and these will bridge the gap between a medium-sized frame and small print or picture, provided the proportions of both are similar. A really tiny picture – a reproduction of an Old Master sketch for instance – often looks well in a comparatively large but not over-elaborate frame (see figure 79).

Imaginative framing is something of an art, though scarcely – as one writer on the subject claims – on the level of painting the picture itself. Before starting on your own frames it is a good idea to study some examples of really high-class framing. Exhibitions, galleries, museums, stately homes, all offer examples of widely varying styles. Different pictures need different sorts of frame, but in every case the object should be to flatter and emphasize the picture itself. The best frames are in-variably subdued in colouring and texture, nothing too bright or shiny to distract from the subject. Gilding tends to be worn, with red underlay showing through here and there; white and pale finishes are deliberately discoloured with tinted glazes and careful rubbing down; plain wood will often have a tinted filler rubbed into the pores to give a greyish drift-woody look. When you see a framing treatment you like and think would suit something you own, it is sensible to make brief notes – i.e., 'small beach scene in oils, ½-inch off-white inset, thundery blue mount approx. 3 ins. wide with sepia-inked lines and sepia-wash bands, carved wood frame finished in pale greyish brown paint.' Good frames, as I said, are so subtly put together that if you don't make notes you will probably find your memory only retains a pleasant but vague overall impression.

The various components which can go into a frame all have their names (see figures 80 and 81 for a guide to the ones commonly used).

Cleaning and restoring old gilt and re-gilding

Old gilt frames, particularly water-gilt over gesso (you can usually tell these by the red clay ground showing through), should be sparingly cleaned. Hard rubbing can rub off the gilt, while too much water may penetrate through to the gesso and cause it to crumble. Gesso is a white powdery mixture of plaster and glue to which water is added to make a thin priming coat. Several coats are applied to get a perfectly smooth surface. It was traditionally used to prime artists' canvases, as well as painted furniture and frames of all kinds – especially water-gilt ones where the slightest surface flaws are magnified when the gold leaf is laid on. Wipe over the frame first with a pad of cotton wool dipped in a weak warm water and ammonia solution and then wrung out till damp. Gilt was sometimes varnished for protection, and the varnish may have darkened with age and dirt. Wiping gently with cotton wool moistened in turps – real turpentine not white spirits – may clean off the worst of the varnish. In some cases removing yellow varnish reveals that the leaf used was not gold at all but a cheaper metal leaf of a silvery colour, given a yellow glaze to make it look like gold. This can be pretty in its own right but, to restore, mix a little yellow ochre into picture varnish and revarnish. Small chips and missing chunks of gesso can be restored by building up the missing bits with Windsor & Newton's Wallart mixed to a thick cream with water. Lay it on with a knife, smooth off with the blade dipped in water, and leave to dry hard. Sand very lightly with fine sandpaper till smooth, trying not to scrape the surrounding gilding. If the mend is small and the frame an old, worn-looking one, the most invisible way to camouflage the Wallart filling is with paint, using artists' oils thinned with a little turps in a suitably dirtied-down shade – raw umber plus a dot of yellow ochre and black, or a touch of burnt sienna if the gilding is warm-toned. Experiment – a touch of this and that is usually what is needed. Where the gilding is water-gilding over red clay – known as Armenian bole – simulate the clay with a little Venetian red and a dot of raw umber. If this looks too bright, glaze with a thin wash of grey or brown. Over a larger area this method will probably look too garish – a large red patch in the middle of a gold frame does leap to the eye somewhat. The likeliest answer here, in my experience, is to re-gild the restored part, using the simplest gilding technique – transfer gilt over Writers' Gold Size – and deliberately aiming for an imperfect, worn finish with some red showing through. I wouldn't go to all this trouble for an old picture frame picked up for a few pence, unless it is unusually pretty, but I patched up a large water-gilt oval mirror frame like this quite successfully; in this case I didn't grudge the cost of the gold leaf and the time it took because the restoration made all the difference between a piece of junk and a really handsome mirror.

In real water-gilding more time is spent getting a perfectly smooth and flawless foundation for the gold leaf – six to eight coats of gesso followed by almost as many of red clay, the whole burnished to glassy smoothness – than actually laying the leaf. It stands to reason that the smoother your foundation is, the better your imitation will look. Wall-art dries with a slightly harsh, crystalline finish. Some sort of filler is needed to close the pores. A couple of coats of ordinary undercoat, applied thinly and sanded down with fine sandpaper, will do the trick but this will raise the level of your restored area slightly, so it is advisable to fill in to just below the gilded surround in the first place. Or use thin coats of gesso (artists' suppliers) mixed with water to a paste and left to dry in between. Smooth down with fine sandpaper. For further smoothness mix a little varnish with the Venetian red you are using to counterfeit the Armenian bole. When quite dry, paint over evenly with Writers' Gold Size, using a soft, clean, paint brush, Leave for between one and two hours, till it feels just tacky to the touch. The leaf for this job can be Transfer Gold leaf or Dutch Metal (Suppliers' Index); the latter is cheaper but shinier.

In the transfer booklets each leaf is attached to a thin sheet of tissue, which makes it infinitely easier to handle. To lay the leaf, take a sheet and lay it gold-side down over the sized area, press down, rub the back with your fingertips or a little bit of cloth, remove the tissue and the gold should be left sticking to the patch. You are unlikely to get perfect results the first time, but we aren't aiming for perfection. Continue pressing down the gold leaf in the same way till you have more or less covered the restored patch. Odd scraps of gold can be coaxed to cover gaps in the gilding if you rub with a fingernail from the back. Leave all this to dry off and settle overnight. Then, with a scrap of silk, smooth over the gilding. Never mind if a few little flakes of gold come off. The gold you have put on will almost certainly be a different colour from the original gilding, and much shinier. To camouflage these discrepancies, mix up a glaze made of a little turps and a speck of raw umber, burnt sienna or black – depending on the colour of the original gilding, raw umber gives a greeny effect, burnt sienna a warm reddish one, black just dirties it down – and paint this over your repair-work, wiping it off a little here and there to let the new gilding show through, a little dulled.

I have even used this method of faking over a whole picture frame. The same rules apply. Strip the frame down to composition or wood. Build up as smooth a surface as possible, using undercoat rubbed down, or coats of gesso. If you doubt your ability to gild a whole frame anything like evenly, a final undercoat coloured with yellow ochre will help pull the patchy gilding together. Size as above and lay the gold leaf all over, overlapping the leaves very slightly. Leave to dry overnight. Smooth over with a soft piece of silk or velvet. Glaze over. I used a neutral glaze of raw umber, burnt sienna and a little white, thinned with turps, wiping it off the raised parts of the moulding to expose highlights. When dry, the frame had something of the soft sheen of old water-gilding.

Stripping and mending

Frames which have been thickly painted and/or varnished can be stripped with one of the patent strippers: Perfecta, Nitromors, Poly-strippa, Blackfriars paint stripper all do a good job. Apply the stripper thickly with an old brush, and remove with a knife-blade or wire wool depending whether the frame is flat or elaborately moulded. Go easy at first because you just might discover a fine gilt frame beneath all the paint. Some people, it seems, couldn't stand the sight of a gilt frame with the smallest flaws in it and promptly slapped a coat of paint on top. If you proceed with great care and caution, using wire wool, rags and tissues in preference to the knife-blade, you can sometimes clean off the paint without damaging the gilt underneath. If it is real gold leaf, that is – gold paint will just dissolve with the rest. Stripper won't dissolve gold leaf, but rubbing too hard will scrape it off.

Finishes that won't respond to paint stripper, like the ebonized finish mentioned earlier, will usually surrender to caustic (see stripping wood). Scrub down with an old scrubbing brush, wearing rubber gloves, to help the process along. Let the frame dry out away from heat, otherwise it might warp. When dry, sand it with fine sandpaper to smooth the surface. Most of these ebonized frames are pine beneath, which looks nice oiled or waxed.

Wooden frames with parts missing can be restored with plastic wood, built up layer by layer and finally sanded smooth. It can be stained (use drawing inks for a small patch) or painted to match the wood.

If the frame is warped there isn't much that can be done to straighten it. You could try holding it over a steaming kettle for a bit and then leaving it to dry out slowly with a heavy weight over it. Loose corners are stuck together by running a little woodworking adhesive into the join at the back and leaving it to set in a clamp.

Special finishes

There are innumerable ways of finishing picture frames from the simplest waxed wood to the most elaborate combinations of stain, gilding, paint, glazes, spattering. Here, I shall deal only with a few simple finishes which don't require too much special equipment.

WOOD. If the graining and colour are pleasant, a wood frame looks good left just as it is. You can give it a coat of white shellac or varnish, well rubbed down with fine sandpaper or wire wool, to fill the grain, and then wax it for a subdued shine. Ordinary pine needs oiling to bring out the graining – use olive oil, which doesn't darken the wood. If the wood is too dark, and looks heavy, try bleaching it with ordinary household bleach. Use a stronger bleach if that doesn't work (*see* bleaching wood), and/or wipe it over with a paler glaze – a little white artists' oil colour with a dot of black, thinned in turps. Rub this down with fine wire wool when dry, which will force the glaze down into the pores, lightening the general effect. Give it another coat of the same glaze to lighten it still further, wiping it off the most prominent parts of the frame to give contrast. A very pallid, uninteresting wood – many frames are made of light woods like poplar – needs the reverse treatment. Try staining it with diluted drawing ink – sepia for instance. Rub it over with tan shoe-polish (quite often used to improve the colour of some wood furniture). Paint it with a grey-brown paint, using white undercoat tinted with artists' oils, and then wire wool to expose the grain slightly. Or, buy some proper wood stain. Professionals use a dark stain, like walnut, and give it a watery grey glaze rubbed down with wire wool for a driftwood effect.

PAINT. The quickest way to completely alter the character of a frame is to paint it. One of the simplest finishes, which suits most frames and pictures, is what is called an Antique White Finish. This means white deliberately dirtied down with a tinted glaze to make it look old and interesting – bright white is too glaring. For the best result this should be applied over a frame which has been stripped of its old finish. But if you are in a hurry, just clean the frame thoroughly with a rag dipped in turps and then wire-wool it to key (roughen) the surface for painting. Give the frame two or three coats of ordinary white undercoat, or eggshell, not gloss. Don't apply it too smoothly, the brushmarks should show. Leave to dry hard. Make a glaze of burnt umber and black thinned in turps and mop this generously over the whole frame. Immediately wipe off the excess with a clean rag. Enough glaze will remain to tint the frame grey-brown. When dry, rub over the highest parts of the mouldings with coarse wire wool, to expose the white paint beneath and give a pleasant grained effect.

As a variation on this finish, try tinting the top coat of paint grey or pale brown – brown-paper colour. When rubbed down to expose some white, this will give a richer, more shadowed effect. Some pictures look good in frames painted subdued colours. If you are using a coloured mat or mount (see below) a gentle contrast in the frame can look very rich. Keep the colours low-key and muted – grey-green, grey-blue, grey-brown, wiping on paler or darker glazes for a more or less shadowed effect. For the Turner watercolours I framed, I used creamy Ingres paper with inked lines and grey-blue bands of watercolour for the mounts, and painted the frames café-au-lait with the mouldings picked out in a darker slatey blue. I finished the frames off with a white glaze to soften the contrast and give an overall faint pearly sheen. The general effect is of a soft shadowy frame of colour which throws the delicate brilliance of the watercolours into relief. If you think in terms of make-up – how you would shade blue eyes or brown to intensify their colour without looking too obvious – you will be on the right lines. A conté pencil sketch (conté pencil is that soft red pencil) would look good with a brown-paper mat, with slightly darker brown bands, and a pale greyish-brown frame. Small pen and ink sketches can take a dramatic contrast, blue Ingres paper (sugar-bag blue) for the mat with a grey-buff frame.

When painting frames mix up your own colours, using artists' oils thinned with turps and mixed into a little white undercoat. Don't mix too much at a time; a small saucerful is ample. Don't worry about getting an exact match for the next coat – some of the most subtle framing effects, as I hope I have indicated by now, are achieved by superimposing layers of varying tints or out-and-out contrasts of colour, and rubbing down so that some of the underlying shade shows through. Framers often rub in colours on the painted frame, using neat oil colour – green, red, burnt siennia – the whole thing glazed over and then wire-wooled so that the frame looks mysteriously nuanced rather than spotted with colour.

POLYCHROME FINISH. For a really sumptuous effect, suitable for a fairly ornately moulded frame, try combining gold leaf and colour, rubbing down so that the mouldings are highlighted with gold against a contrasting colour, which can be soft and muted, or deep and glowing, depending on the sort of picture you are going to frame.

In Renaissance Italy the gold leaf was covered with dull red and then drab green, rubbed till the whole surface glowed mysteriously with a colour which was not one thing nor the other, but a mixture of all three. This finish is called polychrome and is still used today. The modern version often uses bronze paint, which is cheaper and easier to apply.

Professional framers frequently give the frame a coat of shellac between the different coats of gold and colour to prevent the rubbing down having such an abrasive effect and to keep the colour contrasts sharper. If you don't use shellac the final effect is more worn and aged, and I prefer it myself.

To polychrome your own frames, first prepare them with two coats of plain white undercoat, slightly thinned with turps. Over this, when dry, put a coat of dull red – Venetian red plus a little Indian red – to simulate the red clay base for old gilding. When quite dry, apply size and transfer gold leaf as described in gilding above, concentrating on the raised areas of the moulding and the inner edge of the frame. The gilding doesn't have to be perfectly applied, a patchy effect will still show up well in the final result. Or, give the frame a coat of bronze paint. Over this go the coats of coloured paint. For a delicate effect, paint the frame in the grey, buff, and antique-white range of colours. When rubbed down, with gold highlights and a hint of red showing here and there, it will look very pretty. Give it a light glaze of raw umber, or burnt umber wiped off quickly so that the glaze shadows the depressions in the mouldings. On the right sort of painting – an oil painting in rich vivid colours – the traditional red and green polychrome colours could look splendid. The red should be brick red, the green, dull olive. You will probably want to experiment with other colours – red-brown and purple, green and blue, blue and brown. Remember to allow for the gold and red showing through in the final result. For rubbing, use the finest wire wool, and keep buffing away over the ridges and high relief parts of the mouldings till gold begins to appear. An alternative, quicker, method is to brush the paint on and wipe off while still wet. When the gilding has been exposed – leave the colour in the depressions all round for contrast –

rub away very gently at it till some of the red undercoat shows through on the highest points. As well as greatly enriching the gold, this cunningly reproduces the effect of actual wear and tear on an antique frame. For further highlights, you can try the effect of rubbing in colour here and there, using a smear of artists' oils on a rag or your fingertip. Keep it very thin, just a shadow of colour. Use tinted glazes to unify the final effect.

When you are quite satisfied with your frame – one of the charms of this sort of finish is that you can go on experimenting and playing about for ever – give it a very light coat of wax, to protect and preserve it. Don't rub it to a shine, this sort of finish should look rather weather-beaten. Alternatively, finish with a coat of flat or matt varnish.

Cutting and covering mounts or mats

There seems to be some disagreement over the proper name for these cardboard inner frames which bridge the gap between picture and frame and give the picture a visual breathing space all round. I have seen them called variously slips, mounts and mats. In England, the card sold for making them is generally called mounting card, so for convenience I shall call them mounts.

You need three things to cut a mount with a neat, bevelled, inner edge – a Stanley knife with a *new* blade, a metal straight-edge, and a steady hand. Practise on a spare bit of card first. Don't despair if your first attempt isn't immaculately crisp and straight. A lot can be done to even out wavering edges with fine sandpaper and a razor blade, and the mount can be covered with paper or fabric afterwards, which will help disguise imperfections.

The inner edge of the mount, the window frame round the picture, is the opening. The opening should just cover the edges of the picture, except in the case of original etchings, woodcuts and lithographs when the edge is taken back far enough to reveal the plate marks, artist's signature and edition number. If the picture is 8×6 inches, the opening size will be $7\frac{3}{4} \times 5\frac{3}{4}$ inches. The outer edge of the mount should be cut a fraction smaller than the rabbet to allow it to drop easily into the frame (figure 80).

First measure the frame's internal dimensions, subtract $\frac{1}{8}$ of an inch all round, and transfer these measurements to the card, using a ruler and pencil – a T-square helps to get proper right-angled corners. Cut round with a Stanley knife, using another piece of card or sheets of newspaper to protect the table-surface beneath. Now place the rectangle of card in the frame and lay the picture on top. Traditionally, a mount will be slightly wider at the bottom to make up for the eye's tendency to shorten this area as it looks down at it. But framers today prefer to keep the mount the same width all round when the picture and frame are horizontal rather than vertical. I don't think these niceties matter all that much. If you shift the picture about on the card, you will get an idea of the arrangement you like best. Make four tiny pin pricks at all four corners of the picture onto the card beneath. This shows you where to rule your opening. Take the card out of the frame, checking to see that the opening window is set squarely in the mount – a $\frac{1}{4}$ of an inch to one side will look very odd. Do this by measuring to see whether the sides are the same width, and all inner edges are exactly parallel with the outside edges. Then, guided by your pinpricks, but moving each line inwards $\frac{1}{8}$ inch, rule the dimensions of the opening. To cut a bevelled inner edge, which is an edge sloping inwards at a 45-degree angle – even a tiny sloping surface like this helps draw the eye firmly inwards to the picture – lay the metal straight-edge $\frac{1}{8}$ of an inch outside your ruled opening. A strip of fine sandpaper glued to the bottom of the straight-edge will stop it slipping about. Now insert the blade at a 45-degree angle and draw it smoothly and steadily along till you come to the next corner, also an eighth of an inch in from the ruled line. This is to allow for the extra width of the bevel. Go on round till you meet up with your first cut again. If your blade was sharp and your pressure firm and even (which it won't be the first time) the rectangle will drop out leaving a lovely neat bevelled window for your picture. It if doesn't, turn the card over and score gently over the perceptible lines at the back where the blade has almost cut through the card. Push out the centre piece. Ragged edges can be sandpapered smooth. A wavering curve can be planed flush with the rest using a razor blade and paring carefully away at an angle as before. Practice rapidly makes perfect in mount-cutting. I have cut respectable bevelled edges free-hand, without benefit of straight edge. This requires magnificent breath-control.

Now you are ready for the more amusing part of mount making. You may decide to leave the mount as it is, white, cream or coloured. For a sober sort of picture like a woodcut or etching, a plain cream or white mount is quite suitable. You could add a few fine pencil lines, ruled round the opening, to emphasize it a little. Most pictures, however, are flattered by a little texture or colour on the mount. In the case of water-colours, dispense with texture but add restrained colour and emphasis to a white or pale-coloured mount by inking lines in sepia, or blue ink (use a mapping pen and drawing ink) round the opening, with one or two bands washed in with a little diluted watercolour, as in figure 79, for example. The colour-washed bands can pick up the general tone of the watercolour, or mildly contrast with it. On old coloured prints you can use gayer colour – pale clear pinks, blues and greens look pretty round an old fashion plate, or flower print.

If you plump for texture, the mount will have to be covered. Ordinary brown paper, or blue wrapping paper, used dull-side uppermost, costs next to nothing and looks distinguished. Ingres paper is not cheap, but comes in beautiful subdued shades like celadon green, deep blue, rich cream and a fine sober brown. It's not merely the colour but the finely speckled surface which makes this paper so good for covering mounts – it's astonishing how a minute variation in surface texture and colour enriches the overall effect. You can buy a book of 30 sheets of Ingres paper in assorted colours, 18 × 12 inches in size, and some art shops sell it by the sheet. Then there are fabrics. These are usually used to comple-ment a picture with its own texture, such as oil painting, but they can look very effective as a background for prints, pastels – it's up to you. For preference, use a fabric with a dull finish and interesting texture – linen, fine canvas, lawn, even plain unbleached calico. High-class framers use wild silk for exotic looking prints. On the whole, avoid cheap silk or synthetics, which are too shiny. Coloured velvet or velvet-een could look charming as a mount for a really sentimental Victorian print or painting. On anything else it looks too plushy and overpowering. If the painting or picture has any artistic pretensions, don't overdo the mount – keep the fabric neutral in colour and subdued in texture. Off-white and natural colours are better than plain white. But pretty nonsense like old fashion-plates can be camped up quite appropriately.

To cover the mount lay the fabric or paper down on the table, stick the mount on top and cut round with a margin of 1 inch or so to fold back and glue down. Cut round outer edges only. Cover the mount with glue (use wallpaper paste or flour-and-water paste), brushing it out evenly, with a stiff brush, so that no puddles or lumps are left. Make sure the fabric or paper has the right side facing down, next the table, and is stretched out smoothly. Turn the glued mount onto it, and press down firmly from the back with both hands. Look at right side to make sure it has stuck evenly. Then turn face-down again, clip off the corners (*see* figure 81) and turn back the extra fabric one side at a time and glue down. Now cut out the centre rectangle, allowing 1 inch to turn back, and cutting diagonally into the corners. Turn back and glue down. Place the covered mount between two smooth surfaces – two sheets of polythene will do admirably – lay a heavy flat book on top and leave to dry.

A paper-covered mount can be further enriched by inked lines or colour-washed bands. Some framers add a tiny strip of gold paper between the inked lines. You could improvise this from gold gift-wrapping sticky tape, or foil. It must be very narrow; no more than $\frac{1}{8}$ of an inch wide. The bevel can be gilded by sticking a narrow strip of the same stuff over it.

Fitting the picture into the frame

Take a little care over setting a picture into its frame; tacking it in properly and covering over with brown paper to keep out dust. It's surprising how quickly a picture deteriorates if you skimp this part of the job. If the picture or print is backed with strong cardboard, you will only need a piece of board – hardboard is excellent, plywood unsatisfactory because woodworms love it – cut to fit inside the frame with a fractional leeway all round. If the picture or print is not backed, cut a piece of card and hardboard to fit behind it in the frame. Clean the glass very thoroughly inside to remove greasemarks before assembling the parts – meths and a rag will do this. When dry, drop in picture and backing. You should use brads (special headless tacks for tacking the backing down all round), but $\frac{1}{2}$-inch steel pins, which any ironmonger stocks, can substitute. To tack, lay the picture face-down on a table covered with a piece of soft cloth to protect the surface. Press something heavy and solid – I use an old plane, or a kitchen weight – close up against the side of the frame you are tacking. It's amazing how much easier this simple professional tip makes it. Holding the frame steady against the weight, tack pins or brads in about 1 inch apart at a slight angle so they pin the backing down securely. But make it slight or you might skewer your mount. Carry on all round. Professional framers are generous with tacks for a nice flush up-to-the-glass look. Cut a piece of brown paper large enough to come just over the inner edge of the frame all round and stick it down neatly in place using brown gummed strip. Make tiny holes in the back of the frame with a bradawl to take screw-eyes, and thread with strong twine or picture wire if it's heavy. A picture you want to fit flush to the wall should have two small brass mirror-plates, screwed to the top corners. These are then screwed into place on the wall, using rawlplugs if necessary. A good ironmonger will stock these too.

WOOD: TREATMENTS AND FINISHES

Wood is lovely stuff to look at, touch, use and work with. Inanimate seems the wrong word to describe it, it is so much alive. As anyone knows who has planed and sanded a lump of rough deal to shining smoothness, or oiled and polished warmth and colour back into a neglected piece of mahogany, it's not fanciful to talk of wood responding – it does seem to welcome the human touch.

Think of those commonplace wooden things which human contact has casually made beautiful over the years – stile posts mellowed to the texture of old bronze, benches ribbed like a sand bar at low tide, bar counters 'glowing with the love of a million elbows'.

A handsome piece of wood needs very little attention to look good; frequent polishing with a little oil or wax will slowly bring it to a fine burnish. But most cheap furniture, old and new, is made of lesser stuff – beech, deal, the whitewoods and softwoods – which need more finishing if they are to look well and stand up to ordinary wear. There is a whole battery of special finishes which can be used to give colour or texture or shine. Most of us know about paint, stains and varnishes, but did you know that wood can also be bleached, blonded, limed, dyed, fumed, pickled, antiqued, glazed, polychromed, grained, scumbled and marbled? As for paint, which for most of us means two coats of undercoat and one of gloss, slapped on with a Woolworth's brush, in the hands of a craftsman this becomes an extraordinarily flexible finish. Used in conjunction with special varnishes or shellac, and sanded or rubbed, it can end up with a texture as hard and flawless as oriental lacquer or as worn and shadowy as a piece of ancient silk. Subtly varied shades of paint used one on top of the other, rubbed down, and finished with a tinted glaze, give colours obtainable in no other way. Wiping paint on and off, plus stains or glazes, will give a driftwood look to the most undistinguished bit of blockboard or ply, much more attractive than the brassy finish obtained with a couple of coats of sealer.

In this section I shall deal with some of the ways of treating and finishing wood which the average unskilled but adventurously inclined reader might like to try. I shall start with ways of stripping old paint and varnishes off because this is where most people first get to grips with the subject. Next, finishes, simple and not so simple, for wood you want to leave as wood. This will include ideas for restoring holes and cracks, altering the colour and improving the texture, as well as suggestions on how to re-finish modern furniture which has begun to look dingy. Then there are the complete disguises for wood you feel would look better covered up – dyes, but particularly paint. There will be instructions for painting furniture up to interior-decorator standards, for antiquing pieces which look wrong with a spick-and-span new finish, and for decorating furniture in various ways, bright and folksy, or restrained and classical.

Trying out these special effects is great fun, almost all the materials are cheap but the finished look is expensive. You don't need to be artistic, but you do need patience. Of course, these finishes need not be restricted to furniture – floors can be bleached, the front door would look distinguished with an antique rubbed-paint finish, and decorative paint-work can be applied to anything from rocking chairs to old tin canisters. For materials, hunt out a shop supplying the trade if you can, chat them up nicely and you will often find they will be immensely helpful as well as supplying you with stuff at trade prices. If you have a spare room or a shed to work in, it makes things easier, but I've done all my research into the subject in a small crowded flat with at least one child romping about, so it can be done with a bit of care. Lock all dangerous substances, like caustic, oxalic acid, even turps, away after use, try them out when small children are safely out of the way, stick newly painted or varnished objects on top of a cupboard or chest to dry, and train yourself to put paints, brushes, bottles, rags, etc. away *every time*. It is boring but necessary.

Stripping

The cheapest way to acquire any furniture, but particularly simple, solid, useful pieces like chests of drawers, toy-cupboards, dressers, odd chairs, is to buy things (sales, junk shops), thickly covered with old paint and varnish and clean it all off yourself. Of course, the dealers are on to this too – 'stripped pine' must have launched more antique shops than ever Chippendale or Sheraton did – but they haven't all got the time or facilities to deal with a really tough assignment, needing hours of work to get the old finish off and then hours more to smooth and pretty up the piece. If that sounds daunting, perhaps I should say that doing these things for oneself, with one's own dresser or chair, never seems like unmitigated slog because there's always the urge to do just that bit more to see how it will look and, finally, when you collapse into a chair, aching all over, there's the masterpiece before you, stripped and sanded to honeyed smoothness and looking as if it cost at least £75. Actually it cost £11 at the local saleroom, plus hours and hours of your labour, but somehow those you don't count.

The more paint and varnish on the thing, then, the cheaper you are likely to get it. Scrape away at the cream enamel or whatever, to see how much of it there is, what the wood's like beneath, and if the wood used for the drawers matches that used for the top, shelves, legs, and support. See what you would be letting yourself in for. There is one particularly tenacious finish, a chocolate-coloured substance half-way between varnish and stain, which only caustic and perseverance will remove. You must have a place out of doors to use caustic, preferably a cemented-over spot with a drain outlet handy, so if you are stuck in a tower block don't even think of it. Pity, though, because dealers hate the stuff too and it's likely to be a real bargain.

There are various ways of removing paint and varnish, some quicker, some less messy, and some cheaper. Here follows a breakdown of the various methods I have tried, which should help you decide what is needed for a particular job.

Burning off

Burning old paint off with a blow-lamp – paraffin blow-lamps are cheaper to buy and run, butane gas easier to light – is the only sensible solution where you are tackling large areas like stairs, doors and panelling. It is relatively quick – you can burn the paint off a door in about an hour – much less messy than caustic or solvents, rather exciting to do (the old childish thrill of playing with fire) and cheap, if you set the cost of the blowlamp and fuel off against the acreage of paint to be burnt off. The disadvantage of the blow-lamp is that it is easy to scorch the wood beneath when you are going over a tricky bit of moulding or re-doing a particular patch to get the wood clean as a whistle. Another snag is that it is difficult to get the wood quite bare and smooth, usually some old paint or primer remains as a fine crust. Both scorch-marks and crust can be removed by sanding vigorously, starting with a fairly coarse grade of paper and moving on to finer ones as the surface improves. Where the wood is to be repainted, you needn't sand the scorch-marks right off, of course, but where you want the wood left stripped it may mean quite a lot of extra work to get rid of them completely. In some cases you might think it best to burn off most of the paint and use a commercial stripper to clean off the remainder. With large pieces of furniture, a blow-lamp used in conjunction with stripper or caustic is often the quickest method of getting down to the nitty-gritty. The above-mentioned varnish-stain finish seems impervious to blow-lamps; if anything, the heat and scraping seem to drive it deeper into the wood. So use caustic when this appears.

A blow-lamp is used with scrapers, to peel off the blistered, softened paint. These come in different shapes for different requirements – a broad, flat blade for scraping flat surfaces, a heart-shaped one for curved mouldings, and a triangular one for narrow ridges and, sides of doors. Get all three; it costs a bit more, but you save time and scorch-marks. If you decide on a paraffin-fuelled blow-lamp, ask the shop-assistant to show you how to fill and light it and clean the parts which are likely to get clogged. The flame can be adjusted by pumping, from a great roaring blue tongue of fire to a narrow streak. When burning off, hold the flame a few inches away from the paintwork, playing it over an area about the size of a postcard. When the paint looks like toasted cheese, scrape off cleanly, following the grain of the wood where possible. As a safety measure, tie your hair up, and make sure any aerosol containers and inflammable liquids are out of range.

Caustic

Caustic is the he-man of paint removers. Given time it will shift anything. The easiest way to use it is to mix up a great bath of the stuff and dump the object in it, but this is beyond the scope of most householders. It has the disadvantage, too, that prolonged dunking tends to dissolve glue as well, which means the piece of furniture needs to be reassembled and glued. Pouring caustic over a piece of painted wood and scrubbing away works just as well and does less damage to the piece but is more laborious. Caustic is best for large pieces because it is not only powerful but cheap, compared with the commercial strippers. You need an awful lot of commercial stripper to dissolve several coats of old paint on something as big as a dresser, and even if you buy the cheaper kind sold to the trade it will add many pounds to the price of the dresser itself. The chief snags with caustic are: it makes a disgusting mess, it needs to be used with caution, and any piece stripped with it will need quite lengthy refinishing, because the caustic, plus wetting and scrubbing, roughens up the surface of the wood quite a bit.

First, the dangers. Caustic doesn't go through clothing and skin like vitriol, but it will burn in time, so wear protective clothing – Wellingtons, overall, rubber gloves – and keep your face and eyes out of the way when sloshing it about. Tie your hair back, too. Caustic is sold in tins labelled caustic soda by most ironmongers and household stores. Mix it with water in the proportions of 1 tin of caustic to 1 quart of water. Put the water into a bucket (an old enamelled one, a china slop-pail, or a metal bucket; *not* a plastic pail) and then slowly shake the caustic into the water, not the other way around. The reason for this is that adding water to caustic sends up much more powerful fumes, and there's more danger of splashing highly concentrated stuff about. Leave the mixture for a few minutes till it stops bubbling and fuming. It works best on a horizontal surface where it can lie and burn away undisturbed. So unscrew any doors and lay them flat, stand drawers on end, and tackle a large piece one surface at a time. Pour on enough caustic to cover the surface, leave for a few seconds and then rub away at the paintwork with an old long-handled brush or oven mop – the foam-rubber sort. After a bit, you will see the caustic turning the colour of the dissolving paint. Pour a little more on and leave for a while. It may take a couple of hours of this treatment to clear the wood completely. Rubbing round the mouldings and cracks with a wire brush may help dislodge paint which has stuck there. After a while the wood is so bedabbled in caustic and dissolved paint that it's quite difficult to see whether it is clean underneath. Take heart, a lot more paint will come away as you wash and scrub the piece clean. To do this, pour over buckets of clean water, and scrub with a large scrubbing brush till nothing but wood shows. Finish with a final swabbing of water to which a little vinegar has been added to neutralize any remaining caustic. Leave the piece to dry out slowly, preferably out of doors, under cover. If you rush it into a heated atmosphere immediately, the chances are it will warp as it dries out.

When dry, your piece will look depressing, so expect that. Caustic darkens wood, for one thing, and the surface will be woolly. The answer is, as usual, sanding. If you can borrow one of the power-driven sanding tools it will save time and energy. Otherwise, go over it by hand, starting with medium-grade paper and working up to really fine paper for a silky finish. Always sand with the grain of the wood; if you don't you will scratch the surface and then *that* has to be sanded off. If the wood is too dark, mop with domestic bleach, used full strength. Or use the oxalic acid and hypo bleach mentioned further on in this chapter, which is stronger. A wipe over with a permanganate solution during or after bleaching will bring up the figuring on pine, and give it a pretty grey-brown tone instead of the usual yellowish one. (A lot of stripped pine sold commercially is treated like this and waxed with white wax to keep the silvery look.)

Stripping pine often reveals blemishes you hadn't expected, knots painted over with red lead knotting, holes filled with a pasty white filler, cracks. Cracks should be filled with plastic wood first, and sanded smooth. The best and easiest camouflage for all these blemishes, I find, is to paint them over with artists' oil colours, keyed to the colour of the wood itself. Use several colours to get a good match, applied separately and smudged in with your fingertips. Raw sienna, ochre, burnt-umber and a little white seem to make a good pine colour. Use colour straight from the tube. Leave to dry for several days. Wax or shellac for protection. Use colourless shellac. Stripped wood of any kind, in a hot, centrally heated house, is best given a coat or two of colourless shellac all over to insulate it to some extent from the drying heat, otherwise it can crack alarmingly. This goes for doors and woodwork as well as furniture. Shellac all the bits you can't normally see, as well as the ones you can, to prevent warping. Cut the shine of shellac by rubbing very lightly with the finest wire wool. With time it will sink into the wood grain and improve its looks.

Lye

An American book I read somewhere suggested using a mix of lye, cornflour and water to make the strongest paint stripper ever; it can only be left on wood seven minutes or you will find brown burn-marks on the wood. I haven't tried this, but some reader faced with an intractable case might like to. Lye is commonly available in America (James Baldwin says Negroes used lye dips to straighten their hair). Try chemists over here. It needs to be handled with as much caution as caustic. Add the cornflour to the water, then the lye. The idea of the cornflour is that the heat of the lye cooks it, forming a clinging, glutinous substance instead of a liquid which runs off.

Commercial strippers

These are ideal for small or fiddly stripping jobs you want to do indoors. Spread plenty of polythene or newspaper on the floor as there will be a lot of mess. I find one application of the stripper dissolves one coat of paint, except where the paint is new and soft. (A paint surface put on a century ago is so hard and dry it's like a stove-enamelled finish.) Use a scraper or an old kitchen knife to scrape off the first layers of paint, and pads of fine wire wool for the final cleaning-up operations. Commercial strippers seem to have a bleaching effect and this, together with the wire-wool burnishing, makes most wood come up delightfully smooth, bright and shiny. If you get stripper on your skin, wash off with lots of cold water. You should wear rubber gloves in any case.

When cleaning paint off anything a hundred years old or more, go carefully at first because you may well uncover the original paintwork complete with decorative flourishes like painted lines, flower motifs, bamboo stripes. Unless it is in appalling condition, or hideous anyway, this is usually worth preserving, and restoring if necessary (see antiquing and painting), because it adds to the character and value of your piece. Also it is devilishly hard to remove. If you do hit something interesting proceed with care, applying the stripper with a soft brush and working it gently till the top layer of paint softens, then wipe off with rags or tissues. If you work very deftly and quickly, you can often wipe off the solvent and old paint just before it starts getting to grips with the painted finish you want to preserve. The protective varnish and/or glaze will probably go, but that can be restored quite easily. Even if some of the decoration unavoidably dissolves, you may be able to preserve enough to guide you when restoring the piece. The fact that these commercial strippers (Nitromors, Polystrippa, Blackfriars, etc.) can be controlled to some extent is what makes them so suitable for jobs like these, as well as for cleaning old frames where layers of paint may be sitting on top of fine old water-gilding.

The cheapest way to buy these strippers is by the gallon-can. As with olive oil, buying lots of little bottles works out much more expensive. If you live in London, Gedge and Co. (Suppliers' Index) sell a cheaper paint remover made up for the trade. The name is Perfecta.

Removing varnish and restoring finishes

Most varnished finishes will come off with the help of one of the commercial strippers and wire wool, but there is no harm trying one or two cheaper solvents to see if they work. Ammonia, applied full strength with wire wool and rubbed vigorously, will remove some varnished finishes. Shellac is the chief ingredient of French polish, and it dissolves in meths, so to remove French polish rub away with wire wool charged with meths. Much Victorian and later furniture was given a cheap and nasty version of the laborious old french-polish finish used by eighteenth-century cabinet-makers (it took weeks to perfect and you wouldn't have known it was there) which looks like treacle smeared over the wood. Cleaning the whole lot off and refinishing with oil, wax, or shellac, or all three, improves the look of the piece enormously, though it will take a little time to raise a shine.

Furniture of earlier date was usually finished to a high standard, but unless it has been very well looked after the finish will have deteriorated with time and use. I bought an old – eighteenth- or early nineteenth-century – mahogany table cheaply recently because it looked such a mess. Reeded legs and sides were black with dirt and grease, while the top was piebald with evil-looking black blotches and ghostly white rings. The legs and sides were easily dealt with by a meths and wire-wool rub, to the point where the light mahogany was revealed but some of the old French-polish finish retained, adding colour and richness. I gave the table top a similar, light meths rub to clean it and give the treatments a chance to penetrate. The black marks, caused by water seeping under the old finish, disappeared with bleaching. For this, use a saturate oxalic acid solution (buy the crystals at a chemist), made by dissolving as many crystals in a cup of warm water as it will absorb. Paint this on, keeping to the stained areas, leaving for a few minutes, then rinse off with clean water. Leave the wood to dry before repeating the process, if needed. Lots of short applications are safer than one long one which could leave you with a drastically lighter patch. The front part of the top was open-pored and pitted where the old filler had worn away. I gave this bit three coats of shellac, rubbed down with fine wire wool in between to force it into the holes and act as a filler. Then I oiled the white rings with olive oil till the natural colour returned. I oiled the whole table to bring up the grain and colour, and finished off with wax as a protection. Wax seemed more suitable for this faded old mahogany than repeated oilings. With a little more polishing it will look much as it did a hundred years ago, plus the appeal of what the trade calls 'distressing' – i.e., the little dents and tiny flaws which give character and prevent it looking too perfect and unused.

When cleaning off French polish you may come across a mongrel piece, made of two or three different woods. Give the odd bits a going-over with wood dye or stain to match the rest, refinish in the same way, and you won't know the difference. This mixing of woods usually occurs with chairs, where a stronger wood was sometimes used for load bearing parts of the frame, and given a coat of dark polish to even it up.

Minor repairs

It is surprising how successfully one can patch up surface scars and blemishes on furniture using nothing more complicated than plastic wood and beeswax.

Beeswax is ideal for filling small holes in a highly polished surface – those disastrous holes left by a screw that ran wild for instance. Buy a cake of natural beeswax from a chemist. Melt it in a small old saucepan over low heat till it liquefies, and mix in a dab of artists' oil paint – or powder paint – to colour it to match the wood you are repair-

*A typical junkyard chair –
this one, structurally sound,
cost £2 – shown before
and after loose covering in
thick, washable Indian
cotton. A generous seat-
cushion stuffed with the
innards of old sofa-pillows
(jumble sales) improves
the chair's looks and
comfort considerably – the
castors were removed to
counterbalance extra seat
height. A lighter-weight
cotton in a toning colour
might have been a better
choice for the piping which
looks a little clumsy in the
self fabric. I lined the seat
valance in unbleached
calico. Both calico and
cover material were
preshrunk in the washing
machine before making up*

The completed
locker-stitch rug
(see page 56)
showing the broken-
stripe design and
pleasant ribbed
effect of this quick,
easy rug-making
stitch. Overstitched
edges and fringed
ends give a
professional finish

Handsome cross-
stitch rug in four
colours (we used
peat brown, cream,
burnt orange and
pink) based on a
traditional Greek
design. Charts for
working central and
border motifs are
given on pages 67-8.
Readers should
consult this
photograph for the
number of repeats in
the border pattern
and the placing of
the central motifs

A miscellany of decorated objects in wood and tin to give you some idea of the range of effects possible with paint and varnish. The toys were home-made. The small boxes came, unpainted, from a craft shop. Other items turned up for a few pence in the local Oxfam shop. The lamp-base design was cribbed from an old pottery candlestick, and includes some gilding (see GILDING). The tea caddy (old toffee tin) was inspired by hand-painted china. Most of the other patterns derive from folk sources

Two quite different looks, both in the folk idiom: a) bold and stylized – a sturdy old blanket box gaily decorated in a 19th-century Bavarian design; b) flowing and floral – Victorian portmanteau in light deal given the Early American treatment in dull red, ochre and off-white on a slatey blue ground

This hooded sleeveless coat was made from a massive sheepskin tent coat I found in a jumble sale for 50p. I took the tent to pieces, and the shape of the pieces to some extent dictated the style of the new garment, which is lined in unbleached canvas and bound in green leather. The quilted leaf-shapes and pockets cover worn patches in the original garment (See SEWING FUR for instructions on cutting and remodelling sheepskin or fur)

Big and little versions of the traditional countryman's smock. We used natural coloured 'crash' worked in russet for the big smock; vivid blue linen worked in white for the child's version. The elaborate-looking embroidery is all based on a simple featherstitch, worked freehanded, though we have included patterns for you to copy or trace off if you prefer

A close-up of the wooden horse and rocking toy based on traditional designs. My husband did the carpentry, using the simplest tools (no power-driven appliances), and I put on the paint and finishes. We both enjoyed our respective tasks enormously – there is something magical in the stage-by-stage transformation of a block of rough deal into the bright and shiny finished toy

ing. A little red and brown for mahogany, a little brown and black for dark oak. Pour it out into a saucer to cool. When hard again, break off a narrow piece and melt it over the hole so that the wax drips in and fills it. Use a soldering iron, if you have one, to melt the wax, as it gives the right amount of concentrated heat in a small area. Smooth the wax filling over quickly with your finger or a knife blade and, when hard, level out any irregularities by going over it with a little piece of fine sandpaper or wire wool. Finally rub hard with a soft, lint-free rag.

Plastic wood is useful for filling in cracks, missing chunks, and for patching over those ugly gaps left by pieces of veneer dropping off. The correct way to replace missing veneer is with more veneer, using a carefully matched piece and glueing and cramping it into place. If the missing piece is more than a couple of square inches in size, or you are dealing with a fine antique, then it's worth going to so much trouble. But with the not particularly distinguished Victorian furniture which seems to shed veneer like cornflakes, I'm all for patching up straight away with plastic wood – it's cheap, effective and you won't be likely to rip off more sound veneer every time you dust and polish the piece. Plastic wood comes in various colours – buy it by the tin rather than tube. Natural is the easiest to get hold of, is fine for light-coloured woods and can be stained to match darker ones. Walnut, if you can get hold of it, is excellent for darker woods, with a little reddish mahogany stain added to counterfeit red-toned mahogany. It's always more naturalistic to use more than one colour when simulating wood – for instance a walnut patch should be reddened a little and then lightly streaked with dark brown to imitate reddish mahogany with a pronounced grain. You needn't go to the expense of buying two or three lots of stain – ordinary drawing inks, or oil paints rubbed in with the fingers, will colour it sufficiently. The edges of a plastic-wood patch are usually the giveaway part – colouring the patch a shade darker than the surrounding wood and feathering the colour irregularly over the join is the best camouflage. Actually, if you use plastic wood intelligently, sanding it very smooth and colouring it artfully, it makes a near invisible filling, with a much more woody texture than the fillings favoured by professional restorers, like beaumontage (stick shellac) and brummer stopping.

Incidentally, you may save yourself a lot of minor repair jobs if you avoid taking a new purchase which has been kept for any length of time in a damp place straight into a dry, centrally heated atmosphere; veneered pieces especially. The rapid drying out seems to propagate cracks, and veneer chips off in handfuls while solid parts, like table tops, often dry out warped, weakening the whole piece. Let the piece dry out slowly in a shed or garage, or cool place, before taking it indoors.

Before using plastic wood, clean the wood carefully to remove dust, grease, old glue, etc. Roughen it a little with coarse sandpaper to give the plastic wood something to grip. Apply the plastic wood with your fingers or a knife blade, a thin layer at a time. It may seem slow, if you are building up a deep hole, but it's quicker in the end because a thin layer dries out in half an hour or so, whereas a lump might take all night. Fill holes 'proud', i.e., slightly above the level of the surrounding wood. Sand very thoroughly indeed, beginning with coarse, then medium, then very fine sandpaper. Getting the patch satin smooth and perfectly level is the whole art of restoring with plastic wood – if it isn't smooth it won't take colouring evenly, and any tiny surface hollows and furrows will show up in a good light. Take care when sanding to scratch the surrounding wood as little as possible – I tear off little pieces of paper and fold them into points, or wrap them round a pencil on tricky little repairs. As plastic wood dries it tends to shrink slightly, so you are liable to get a hairline crack round your mend. Fill this, with any other tiny imperfections which appear while sanding, before staining the patch. A good mend can't be detected when you run your fingers over it, or squint along it into the light, but it takes patience to get it that way. When you are satisfied with your patch, colour it with stain, inks or oil paints. Use your fingertips to rub the colour in, a fine brush to counterfeit dark lines of graining. When quite dry, it's a good idea to brush a coat or two of shellac over the patch, rubbing that down lightly when dry with fine wire wool – the shellac gives a little shine and extra smoothness, as well as protecting the finish. Then wax or polish the entire surface.

A large raised blister on the veneer is treated by slitting the surface with a razor blade just sufficiently to slide a little Scotch glue or wood-adhesive underneath on a flexible blade. Then press the blister flat, cover with greaseproof paper or polythene and lay a heavy weight on top till the glue has dried.

Bits of inlay or marquetry which have lifted a little, through damp having softened the glue, can often be coaxed back into place by steaming with an ordinary domestic iron just enough to melt the glue a little. (One reason cabinet-makers always recommend using animal glues rather than modern adhesives for repairing furniture is that they can be reactivated in precisely this way, where synthetics need to be scraped off and a new lot squeezed in.) To do this, first clean off any polish, wax or varnish round the lifted area because this will check the action of the damp heat. Use a little stripper and wire wool. Then lay a damp cloth over the spot and hold a hot iron over it for a few seconds. When the inlay seems to be responding, lay a piece of greaseproof paper over the place and weight it with a heavy book and some weights till dry and flat. If the piece refuses to go back, this probably means too much dirt has got in underneath. The only solution is to steam the whole piece till it can be lifted out, then to clean the back of the inlay and the bed it was stuck into. Pads of cloth wrung out in very hot water and laid over the old glue will soften it enough to remove by scraping with a blunt-ended knife blade, and a little final sanding will smooth the pieces down. Reglue both parts and stick back in place, with a few bands of gummed strip to hold them tight, and some kind of weight on top.

Small missing bits of marquetry can be replaced with a little wax melted into the hole. Use ordinary beeswax in either the natural honey colour or white.

Woodworm

It is sometimes hard to resist buying something really pretty, like an old woodcarving or carved frame, knowing perfectly well that it is riddled with woodworm. Even where you are positive the worm has done its work and moved on, it might be a good idea to strengthen the piece by filling up the network of holes. The easiest way to do this is to dip the piece into melted paraffin wax which will run into the holes. Take it out and wipe off excess wax before it sets. Liquid epoxy resin injected into the holes with a hypodermic will make for a much stronger filling. Wipe off any resin that leaks over the piece with a cloth damped with meths. If there are so many holes the resin filler is going to show up, colour it with a little oil paint. When you are not certain the worm is dead, or departed, the piece should be hurriedly treated with Rentokil before the little creatures attack something else. This can be done by squirting Rentokil into all the visible holes, repeating the process after a few days if you think it is necessary. But try Rentokil on a small corner of the piece first – it does darken the colour of some woods very noticeably. The old way of killing worm was to soak the piece in paraffin. If you try this make sure the piece dries out thoroughly before bringing it into the house, and keep it away from flames.

Ink stains

Some old table tops and desks are marred by ink stains. These can be removed by bleaching. Wipe a little vinegar over the stain, then wipe over with a weak (10 per cent) solution of Milton. This will gradually bleach the ink. It is best done in two or three separate applications, checking to see how things are going. When the stain has faded, rinse with clean water and, when dry, oil the patch to bring back the colour (warm oil speeds this up) and finish off with wax to resurface.

Refinishing wood

In its simplest form, finishing simply means working up a shine on new wood or wood that has been stripped down to the natural surface, which tends to be somewhat pale in colour and open in texture. Plain rubbing, with the hands or a soft cloth, would bring up a shine in a year or two, but this is a rather too leisurely approach for most people, though connoisseurs of patina claim that the wholly natural finish obtained is the softest and silkiest of all. Rubbing plus oil and/or wax builds up a shining surface much more quickly while, at the same time, filling in the grain to a certain extent, enriching the natural colour and figuring, and giving the wood some protection against spills, stains and wear and tear. These are the two oldest and simplest finishes for a nice piece of wood, and the most popular today because they don't mask the wood's own character and texture. Some cabinet-makers swear by the one, some by the other. It seems to me that they each have special qualities which mark wax out as more suitable for some types of wood, and oil for others.

Then, there are what one might call the artificial finishes, which spread an instant high shine over any wood surface. These include shellac, varnish, French polish and the polyurethane sealers. Amateurishly used; i.e., just brushed on top, these are like a bad make-up which hides without flattering. Used properly, i.e., rubbed down with wire wool or glass-paper till the finish is forced down into the grain, preserving the texture of the wood, they can be very useful for improving the look of coarse-textured or insipidly coloured stuff like blockboard. They are often used in conjunction with special finishes, to protect and seal them in, and I shall be mentioning them later.

Oil

Oil gets down deeper into the wood fibres than wax, and it is a natural lubricant which feeds and preserves as well as bringing out the colour and marking. It takes much longer to build up a shine than wax but, by way of compensation, the accumulated layers of dried oil make a tough protective coating which stands up very well to spilled water, stains and heat. Linseed oil, boiled not raw, which is very sticky, is the most frequently used for the purpose. Its drawback is that it has quite a pronounced colour of its own, and this darkens and hots up the orange tones in pale woods – pine especially – too much for most tastes. On dark woods, mahogany in particular, this doesn't matter – linseed oil gives mahogany a superb auburn colour in time. Given its protective qualities, a linseed-oil treatment would be the perfect finish for a mahogany dining table or occasional table which is likely to get water and alcohol spilt on it quite often.

You can still use the oiled finish for lighter-coloured woods if you substitute olive oil for linseed; more expensive, of course, but a little goes a long way and it won't alter the colour. The cabinet-maker who recommended it to me assured me that olive oil is more lubricating, too, and imparts a softer lustre. The point about oiling is that it needs to be done frequently at first – a wipe over once a month isn't going to make any appreciable difference. Once a good shine appears you can space subsequent oilings out every few weeks till, finally, all your piece will need to look burnished and splendid is frequent polishing and a drop more oil very occasionally.

The directions given here are for a linseed-oil finish. If you are using olive oil omit the turps, but otherwise proceed in exactly the same way.

In a double boiler warm a mixture of linseed oil and real turps (from artists' supply shops) in proportions of two parts oil to one of turps.

Warm oil penetrates faster and brings out the colour better. Smear the warm oil over the surface with a soft rag. Then rub it in with your palms till the wood has soaked up as much as it will absorb. Wipe off the surplus. Leave for twenty-four hours, or forty-eight hours in cold weather, for the oil to dry. Then repeat the treatment. From four to twelve applications may be needed, depending on the degree of shine and depth of colour you want. When oiling a table top, incidentally, you should oil the underside as well to prevent any danger of warping caused by damp getting at the unprotected surface and making it swell. It doesn't have to be repeated so often, or polished.

Where the wood surfaces are very coarse-grained, as in some poor-quality mahogany, you can fill the grain, as well as working up a speedier shine, by adding some waterproof varnish to the above oil-and-turps mixture. Two parts oil, one part turps and one part waterproof varnish (don't get it in a dark colour or it will darken the wood noticeably) wiped on and rubbed in the same way. If the surface looks too hard and shiny for you, soften by rubbing down gently with finest wire wool or a felt pad moistened with water and sprinkled with Vim.

Waxing

The experts seem agreed that natural beeswax is best for this, and there does seem to be an affinity between its honeyed appearance and woods like pine and elm. Wax is excellent for refinishing stripped pine; you get an almost instant glow and shine. It needs a lot of hard rubbing though, otherwise the surface is tacky and shows every mark.

For a professional waxed finish mix roughly equal quantities of natural beeswax with real turps in the top of a double boiler and heat till the wax melts. Let it harden again slightly – it should look like crumbly cheese – and then scoop some up on a soft cloth and rub it over the wood, as evenly and thinly as possible. You don't want the stuff building up in crevices and corners. When dry, polish with a series of soft lint-free rags. Work across the grain with short, quick strokes and then along the grain with long, even strokes. As the rags get hard and stiff discard them. Rub till your arms ache. The first coat of wax should largely disappear into the grain of the wood. When you have got your breath back, repeat the whole process. Polish till all tackiness disappears. Do this three or four times, till you have developed that mellow sheen characteristic of waxing. Finish by brushing long and lovingly with a very soft brush, and your piece will glow like a thoroughbred's rump.

One of the nicest looking tables I have ever eaten off proved to be a standard old-fashioned deal kitchen table which years of faithful waxing and polishing had given an extraordinary surface, amber-coloured, like a pool in a peat bog.

NOTE: For a protective finish which will not darken the blondness of natural, or stripped and sanded, pine or deal, use bleached beeswax melted in a little real turps. Bleached beeswax can be obtained from any good chemist. Add approximately 1 tablespoon turps to 1 cake of wax. This treatment gives a soft sheen, a tone or so darker than the untreated wood but with no yellowing. It is good for deal kitchen tables which you can't get around to scrubbing every other day, as it will stand up to a fair number of spills without marking. Wax gives a surprisingly tough finish. Scrubbing with a stiff brush and ordinary scouring powder will remove accumulated or ingrained dirt without stripping off the wax, which is actually forced deeper into the grain of the wood. It can then be buffed up successfully with a clean rag. From time to time, if the surface begins to look patchy, scrub it clean, leave to dry thoroughly and then re-wax. A scouring powder containing bleach leaves the wood a tone or so paler, if that is the effect you are after.

Bleaching

Bleaching with oxalic acid and photographer's hypo will lighten a dark wood to mid-brown, mahogany to a pinky biege (*see* blonding), and gives stripped pine and deal a greyish driftwood colour.

Get the oxalic acid and sodium hyposulphate from any good chemist. Oxalic acid is poisonous, so don't leave it around for children to experiment with. The action of the oxalic acid combining with hypo gives off slight fumes, so try and do the job out of doors or keep doors and windows open. Mix the solutions with hot water, but use them cold. Borax in water is used as a neutralizer, and a permanganate solution helps the greying-down of softwoods.

You need 3 ounces of oxalic acid crystals dissolved in 1 quart of water, and 3 ounces of sodium hyposulphate (photographer's hypo) dissolved in 1 quart of water.

The wood should be quite bare, stripped of old polish or varnish. Sponge on the oxalic acid solution with a plastic sponge and leave to partly dry. Then sponge with the hypo. If the wood is not light enough when dry, repeat the process. If you wipe a permanganate solution over at this stage it will emphasize the greyish tone more than if used after the wood has been rinsed. Don't make it too strong – start with a light purple and see how it looks when dry. When the bleaching seems to have done the trick, flush the wood with a solution of 1 ounce of borax in 1 quart of water, then rinse with clear water. Leave to dry thoroughly. Sanding will improve the surface, which will have been roughened by all the wetting. Don't rub the bleached piece with linseed oil or one of the orange-coloured wax polishes, or you will start undoing the good work. Use olive oil, or one of the pale waxes. To seal the finish in, give the piece a coat of white shellac and rub down with glasspaper.

N.B. A quick bleaching – ten to fifteen minutes – clears all the stains off a scrubbed deal table and gives it the colour of new chamois leather.

Blonding

As the name suggests, this finish is used to turn a brunette piece into a dizzy blonde. It is often used to lighten dark mahogany pieces which can look rather looming and sombre in a small flat or room. As well as the bleach mixture (*see* above) you will need white shellac and natural wood filler. Any good trade shop will stock these.

First, strip off any old varnish or polish then bleach the surface, as above, till you have lightened the colour considerably, and rinse well to remove any chemical deposit. Leave the wood to dry out completely – at least forty-eight hours. Rub down with fine sandpaper to smooth out the roughened surface and refine the pores. Give the whole piece a thin coat of white shellac – thin it down with meths or denatured alcohol. Leave overnight and then rub down with glasspaper. Now apply the wood filler. The idea of this is to force the light paste down into the pores where it remains as pale flecks to help on the blond look. Spread a thin, even layer of the filler over the wood, forcing it down into the grain with a soft cloth, taking care not to let granules of filler harden till they scratch the wood. Wipe off any excess filler. Now give another thin coat of shellac, rubbing down with glasspaper when dry. Finally, one last coat of shellac, which should be rubbed down with fine wire wool when quite hard – after twenty-four hours. Finish with wax.

GREY OR ASHEN OAK. There is a fashion currently, among people rich or lucky enough to own oak-panelled rooms, for bleaching the dark oak down and treating it to produce what one interior decorator I met called 'a delicious Ryvita colour'. (The same man supervised the lightening and brightening of all the panelling at Chequers.) I don't suppose many of my readers live in panelled halls, but the finish itself might be worth trying on some of that 1920s mock-Jacobean furniture which can still be bought quite cheaply. The stuff I have seen was oak, solidly made and quite pleasing in general design but made oppressively dark and gloomy by a thick, treacly french polish and stain which was presumably intended to give it a look of time-darkened antiquity. The same pieces, stripped of their original finish and bleached, would look far more attractive and fit well into a modern setting. There are signs that the trade is catching onto this idea so don't wait too long to try it out or you may find the mock-Jacobean stuff has soared in price. The commonest examples of this style are sideboards, with barley sugar legs, panelled doors and a bit of carving here and there, also straightback chairs, sometimes with rush seats. But the range is wide, including refectory tables, gate-leg tables, massive carvers, corner cupboards and chests.

Meths and/or one of the commercial strippers should get the old black finish off. Before bleaching, you might consider sanding off the harder edges a little, carving included. This is a favourite faker's trick for ageing pieces; in this case it would soften the hard outlines and give them a slightly weathered look in keeping with the pale finish.

For the finish, first sand the whole piece over with fine sandpaper. Then bleach, using the oxalic-hypo treatment described above, leaving the solution on for an hour or so, till the wood is considerably lightened. Wash off with clean water and leave to dry. For a sandy-toned finish, leave the wood as it is but, for a silvery finish, brush on silver grey aniline wood dye, about $\frac{1}{2}$ an ounce dissolved in 1 quart of tepid water. Leave to dry thoroughly. Now lead-based flat white paint is rubbed on and off so as to leave only a faint white clouding, most of it in the graining. If you favour a Ryvita effect, mix a very little burnt umber into the white paint. The paint should be brushed on with a large paint brush and wiped off with a pad of clean rag. Stand back to see the sort of effect you are getting – it should be subtle and smoky. Now give the whole piece a coat of thin white shellac and leave to dry thoroughly. When dry, rub down with fine sandpaper or wire wool to break up the surface shine.

One or two more coats of shellac, rubbed down in the same way, will fill the grain quite a bit and improve the appearance. This sort of bleached oak shouldn't have anything like a shine on it, but if you like you could finish with a little white wax for a subdued glow.

PICKLED PINE. This finish is almost identical to the one above, except that you need fewer coats of shellac and preliminary bleaching should be lightly done as pine is a light-coloured wood to start with. Some people prefer the silvery finish given by the grey stain, others like the effect of the natural wood colour wiped over with the white and umber paint mixture.

I wouldn't use either on a really nicely grained piece of pine with a good colour of its own. (The term pine, as you have probably discovered, is applied very loosely to a wide range of soft conifer wood ranging in colour from a deep gold with distinct graining to a raw-looking whitish fir, probably inadequately seasoned like so much wood sold today.) But they can be used to improve the look of some of the new, knotty pine or deal furniture which looks so shabby once the initial factory finish – usually a few coats of sealer or varnish – has begun to wear off and get grimy. (*See* refinishing new furniture, below, for more details.)

Dyeing or staining

Dyeing is a much quicker way of adding colour to wood than painting and it can look very attractive with the wood texture and graining showing through the colour. The effect is unpretentious and rustic, which may be why William Morris chose to stain the rush-seated chairs produced by his workshop a dark green. Following through the rustic idea, dyed wood would make a good background for painted folk motifs (*see* painting wood). The most suitable wood for dyeing is a pale, close-grained one without pronounced figuring.

Wood dyes and stains come in all the woody colours, of course, and of these the experts prefer water stain, which is more penetrating and gives a better colour, though the wood needs sanding down afterwards to smooth down the roughened surface. There is a range of brightly coloured dyes, too, which penetrate well and give their own semi-lacquered finish. Most paint shops stock these. They are fine if you want a very bright colour.

For a wider colour range you can use ordinary Dylon dyes, but they should have several coats of shellac or varnish on top to protect the coloured finish. Mix up a concentrated solution of the dye colour and rub it on with a soft rag, wearing plastic gloves. The wood you are dyeing should first be thoroughly cleaned of any old finish or the dye won't penetrate evenly. Leave to dry. If it isn't dark enough, repeat. Remember that the actual colour of the wood will affect some colours slightly – i.e., a faintly yellow wood will turn a blue dye greenish; a dark, or even mid-brown wood won't really dye successfully unless you bleach it well first. When the dyed wood is quite dry, give it two coats of colourless shellac or water-white varnish, then rub down lightly with fine wire wool. If you fancy painting roses or bands of daisies on the piece, do it now and then revarnish or shellac over the painting when dry to protect it.

New whitewood furniture should be carefully sanded down before dyeing because it usually has a coarse, gritty texture. Use fine sandpaper to start with, moving on to glasspaper or cabinet paper for a smooth finish. It would also soften the appearance of it to round the sharp edges while you are sanding. A really conscientious painter rounds the hard-angled edges of a new piece before painting, partly to improve its looks, partly to make it less painful to knock against, partly to avoid those chips which form on painted knife-edges. A detail, but it's the sum of little attentions like these which give a carefully hand-finished job its sleek and solid appearance.

Plywood and blockboard

These are often used today for doors, kitchen fitments and so on. They are occasionally finished with one of the polyurethane sealers, usually over an inadequately sanded surface, with the result that the wood soon feels tacky and gritty and picks up dirt which is almost impossible to scrub off. One tends to accept these flaws on the grounds that, well, this isn't *real* wood. Actually the fault lies in the finishing, rather than the wood. The surface skin of wood in both blockboard and plywood is thicker than many veneers. Proper finishing will improve their looks immensely, and make them much easier to care for.

If the wood has already been sealed, first wash the piece thoroughly to remove surface dirt, going over any really dingy patches with a Brillo pad. When dry, sand or wire-wool all surfaces thoroughly, which will force the seal into the wood and act as a foundation for your subsequent finish. Use a fine sandpaper and follow the grain. Keep going till the surface is smooth but with no shiny streaks of sealer visible when you squint along it. The surface can now be refinished in various ways, to bring up such colour and figuring as the wood may have, or with one of the wipe-on, wipe-off treatments already described which will add distinction to a really uninteresting wood as well as building up a smooth, hard surface.

If you want to play up the wood itself – and some blockboard is handsomely surfaced – oil it with boiled linseed oil or olive oil until the grain begins to show. It may take two or three applications. It will already have a much more woody appearance, but the texture of the surface is probably rather coarse. This can be improved without altering the wood colour by several coats of shellac – use golden or colourless shellac – sandpapered or wire-wooled in between so that they fill up the pores without being visible on the surface. (On a working surface or table top use colourless varnish, lacquer or seal, instead of shellac, because they are more resistant to water, alcohol and stains generally. Apply as directed on the tin and rub down faithfully in between coats as for shellac. What you are after is an invisible filler not a shiny surface coating.) Finish off with wax, rubbed on with soft wire wool, and then polish with a soft cloth.

Alternatively, you might try filler (see blonding) to refine the texture. Using a natural-coloured filler will leave the surface flecked and lighten the overall colour of the wood.

Or, change the colour altogether by pickling (see above) with or without the stain, or by simply dyeing the wood with coloured dyes (see dyeing wood) given the usual shellac or varnish protective finish and a final waxing.

Refinishing new furniture

Almost all modern furniture except the most expensive is poorly finished. This can mean several things – the wood has not been dried out long enough, it hasn't been sanded down to a superfine finish, or the final finish – varnish, seal, or whatever it may be – was slapped on top, probably with a spray gun, instead of being laboriously rubbed in. If you take the trouble to hand-finish it properly it will not only improve the look of the piece now, but ensure that it goes on getting handsomer with time, as it should.

First the piece must be sanded down with fine sandpaper, to cut through the factory finish. Then, if you have any doubts as to the rawness of the wood used, it is a good idea to leave it to dry out gradually at room temperature. Among other things, this will prevent it warping as time goes on. Inexpensive, deal, ready-to-assemble furniture often warps badly after a while, because the wood wasn't seasoned properly and because it was sealed on one surface only, which means the untreated surfaces expand when they get damp. This drying out could take as long as a month, which sounds alarming till you realize that properly seasoned wood has often been drying out over a period of several years. Leave it as long as you can, anyway, till the wood feels dry and hard. Then smooth it down carefully with sandpaper again and start oiling it, using boiled linseed oil or olive oil (see oiling). Continue till the natural graining shows up. Leave for twelve hours. Then the experts recommend a light application of button polish, to mellow the colour and texture. This is a little tricky to do if you have never used it before, so either practise on a spare bit of wood first till you get the hang of it, or skip the process entirely and, instead, use several coats of shellac, rubbed down in between.

The button polish should be applied with a soft pad of linen (old linen, free of lint) wrapped round a pad of wadding or cotton wool, well-charged with oil. The oil will smooth the polish over the wood. The more friction and heat generated the better the results. Apply the polish in smooth, sweeping strokes carried through from one end of the surface to the other, never pausing or altering pace in mid-stroke because this will cause crinkling or dimpling which can only be removed by stripping the stuff off and starting again. Don't use too much polish, you don't want to coat the piece thickly, just enough to bring the surface to life. This was the standard finish for most Early American furniture.

Painting woodwork

Painting woodwork is one aspect of redecorating where thoroughness pays off. A careful paint job hangs together and looks respectable for years where a skimped one begins chipping and flaking off almost at once, especially if you have small children or removals men rushing through the house. It takes so much time and energy to paint a room out even half well, you might as well give twice the time to it in the knowledge that it won't need to be touched again for a long while. In your own place, that is. In short-term accommodation I would go to the opposite extreme and give all the chocolate-brown or green paintwork several coats of white emulsion. It isn't intended for use on woodwork, I know, and it won't last the way oil-bound paints do, but it is cheap, quick to apply and dries with a nice matt surface. When it starts looking shabby, stick another coat on top.

In your own home the sensible course is to go about painting slowly and methodically, room by room, even if it means waiting a year or two to have the place just the way you want it. The best time to begin a marathon job like repainting stairs and banisters is when you have just got back from a holiday and are feeling full of bounce and good resolutions. Once you have started on a job try and stick with it, even if you only manage a few yards of wainscoting a day. It's hard to get back into the rhythm after you have knocked off for a few days and, by then, dust will have settled over it all, the brushes gone hard and a skin grown over the paint. (*See* below for how to prevent irritating developments like these.) I should warn you that having once painted something to the highest standards it's almost impossible to be happy with the old slap-dash approach – there is something about a sleek, immaculate bit of paintwork which kindles a spark of perfectionism in the soul.

Tools and materials

For cleaning up old paintwork you will need sugar-soap or washing soda or one of the proprietary cleaners and a large sponge. Making good (*see* below) involves a lot of sandpaper or wet-and-dry paper in coarse, medium and fine grades, Polyfilla and a flexible knife. Wet-and-dry paper can be used instead of sandpaper at any stage of finishing, in the appropriate grade. It is particularly effective, used in a fine grade (400), for rubbing down the final coats, as the water lubricates the cutting action of the abrasive and gives a particularly fine, close shave, so to speak. Plastic wood and Araldite are useful for some patching jobs, and Fine Surface Polyfilla slides obligingly into all the tiny cracks and dents which appear at the undercoating stage. Buy a large tin of undercoat. The Woolworth's brand is adequate. $\frac{1}{2}$ a litre covers approximately 6 square yards, using undercoat. The thicker top-coat paints, like egg-shell and gloss, go slightly further if brushed out well on a well-prepared surface. Save on the more expensive top-coat paint by using a split coat (*see* below) for the one before the last. Use whatever the makers stipulate for thinning paint – usually white spirit.

Good brushes are an intelligent investment unless you know you'll never be bothered with cleaning them properly, in which case get cheap ones from Woolworth's and chuck them away when you have finished. A good brush, which is one with a thick, silky crop of bristles set round a smallish central block (cheap brushes have more block and less bristle) speeds your work considerably. You don't need to keep stopping to pick bristles off the paint and you cover the same area faster and more smoothly. Buy your brushes from a decorators' merchants and get at least two – a 2–2$\frac{1}{2}$-inch-wide one for general purposes, and a $\frac{1}{2}$-inch one for glazing bars, cutting out round door frames and other finicky details.

LOOKING AFTER BRUSHES. A housepainter's tip is to soak new brushes in raw linseed oil for a day or two before use. This makes the bristles less absorbent, and strengthens them. To do this, wrap a piece of brown paper round the bristles, securing it with an elastic band, and stand the brush in a jam jar with a little oil in the bottom – enough to soak the wrapper. Before using, press out as much oil as possible against the sides of the jar, twirl the remainder off in a clean jar, dip into white spirit and brush dry on newspaper. If you are knocking off overnight, just stand the brush in cold water which will prevent the paint hardening. Brush the water off on paper before re-using. To clean brushes, brush surplus paint off on paper then work the bristles around in a jar of white spirit to remove as much paint as possible. Wash in a good lather of detergent and warm water, rinse thoroughly and dry hanging up – from a nail – or flat. Scrubbing the brush with an old sink-brush, from the handle to-wards the bristle tips, helps to loosen more paint when you are washing

it. A caked brush can be rescued by soaking in a commercial paint stripper for half an hour or so, and then scrubbing down and washing as
above.

PAINT. Stir all paint very thoroughly before using to blend all the
ingredients together – the sticky sediment on the bottom of the tin takes
a couple of minutes stirring to clear but as it contains most of the pigment
your paint won't be much good without it. Use an old brush for stirring
(a stiff brush called a sash tool is what housepainters use), or a stick, or an
old spoon. To prevent a skin forming run a film of linseed oil over the
paint before putting the lid back on. If it does form peel off what you can
and run the paint through an old stocking into another container. This
sieves off the debris beautifully. Store paint in a cool place. Don't use
paint years old because it tends to go 'fatty' with time which means it
won't dry out hard.

Making good

This is the housepainter's term for the tedious – or to some careful
natures, satisfying – preliminaries which should be gone through before
putting on paint. Briefly, the object is to get the surfaces to be painted as
near flawless as possible; smooth, flat, unblemished and grease-free. Not
only will the paint look better but it will last longer because dirt collects
in cracks and craters and trying to scrub it out wears the paint away.
Making good takes time, and is quite hard work, but it counts for more
in the final results than delicate brushwork or superfine paint. A conscientious housepainter spends almost as much time on this part of his
job as on putting on the paint itself.

SANDING. A really gritty, lumpy, cratered old paint surface, so thick it
blurs the mouldings on doors and wainscot, should really be burned off
with a blow-lamp to get good results (see stripping wood). Varnished
surfaces too – paint falls off these – should be stripped down with
Nitromors. If this really isn't feasible, you can do quite a lot to improve
matters with sandpaper and filler. Sand the entire surface down
fiercely with coarse then medium sandpaper to scratch off lumps and
level the paintwork off as much as possible and to provide a key for the
new paint to stick to. Sand an old gloss painted or varnished surface till

you have rubbed away most of the shine. One or, better still, two coats of aluminium wood primer will help paint adhere to a varnished surface. Paintwork in reasonably good shape should be washed down with soda or one of the cleaners to remove dirt and grease. When dry, go over it – if gloss or varnish – with medium paper to roughen the surface. Bare wood, stripped or new, should be sanded smooth with medium paper, coarse over splintery patches. Round off sharp edges on new wood fittings. Dust all sanded surfaces thoroughly.

FILLING. Fill cracks and craters in painted surfaces with a stiffish mix of Polyfilla and water. Apply it with a flexible knife, fill slightly proud – i.e. above the paint level – and sand smooth when quite dry. Cracks and holes in bare wood can be filled with plastic wood, applied a layer at a time and left to harden in between, or more rapidly with putty. Unless you are experienced in using putty, it is best to buy the ready-for-use kind; it's easy to add a bit too much linseed oil if you are mixing it up yourself, meaning it won't dry out properly and the paint won't stick to it. Smaller cracks can be dealt with at the undercoat stage with Polyfilla – the undercoat helps to bind the Polyfilla in position. Structural cracks, where two edges need bonding as well as filling, can be dealt with using Araldite mixed to a doughy consistency with a little sawdust or dry Polyfilla. Pack it into the crack and leave for a few hours, under pressure if the edges need to be held in position. After a few hours, scrape off excess Araldite with a razor blade, and leave to dry quite hard. Sand all fillers as smooth as possible, using medium then fine paper, and dust all the surfaces.

A second, finer focus, stage of filling comes after you have put on the first coat of primer or undercoat, when small nail-holes, cracks and pock marks fairly leap to the eye. Use either a thinnish mix of Polyfilla or the Fine Surface Polyfilla to deal with these. Again leave to dry hard and sand flat.

PAINTING. The two golden rules of painting are that several thin coats, well brushed out, are better than one or two thick ones, and that rubbing the paintwork down between coats with fine sandpaper gives a smoother and stronger finish because the layers of paint are welded together instead of just sitting on top of each other, and any brushmarks, grit or 'nibs' on the surface are flattened out as you go along.

The experts recommend four coats of paint for ordinary interior woodwork. First, the priming coat – primer on bare wood, undercoat on old paint. Then the body coat – undercoat. Next the split coat – half undercoat, half top coat. Lastly, the top coat, which can be flat, matt, eggshell or gloss. This is perhaps a counsel of perfection. Use your judgement as to how closely you stick to it. Over existing paintwork in quite good condition, two or three coats should be enough. Over poor paintwork, three coats plus the rubbing down in between will improve the surface considerably. Over bare wood, use the four coats stipulated. On an exterior surface, like a front door, a second layer of top coat is probably a good idea, making five coats in all.

Usually commonsense suggests the most efficient order in which to paint a surface, but you might find these tips useful. When painting a panelled door, paint the panels and mouldings first, using the side of the brush to work the paint into the mouldings. Start with the top panels, then the bottom ones, then paint the frame itself working from the top downwards. Finish the job in one session or you will get hard-edged lines where paint has dried. When painting windows, begin by painting the rebates – the part of the frame nearest the glass, then the crossbars, then the crossrails and hanging stile (the rest of the window itself in ordinary language) and finally the frame.

Painters recommend brushing the first coat on across the grain and the second with it to cut down brushmarks but, with sanding, this isn't such a problem. It isn't a bad idea, though, over bare wood to sand the priming coat across the grain – which forces it down into the wood and makes it act as a filler – and the second coat with the grain. Sand each coat of paint when it has dried hard – allow longer for drying in cold weather than the makers stipulate. Use fine sandpaper and cover the whole area steadily and gently till it feels smooth to your hand. Dust before repainting. Gloss and eggshell can be rubbed down with wet-and-dry paper in the fine grade (400) used in conjunction with water – go over the surface with a wet sponge – to lubricate the abrasive action and give a very fine finish. Warm the room up before painting with gloss or eggshell to help the paint flow smoothly.

Flat paint has a chalky finish; matt dries almost without shine but is a little tougher than flat. Eggshell dries with a faint sheen if you use one coat, a deeper sheen if you use two. Gloss has a decided shine. On the whole, matt or eggshell paint looks more elegant over general woodwork in a house. Gloss is the easiest finish to wash down which makes it an obvious choice for bathrooms, nurseries, kitchens and for exterior woodwork. Coach paint, as used on car bodywork, gives an exceptionally hard, durable gloss finish for interior and exterior use. It is brushed on in the ordinary way. Huge colour range, including white, comes cheaper by the gallon – phone round local coach works and car repair shops. Try rubbing down the final coat of gloss lightly, with powdered pumice or ordinary kitchen scouring powder, to dull the shine a little. Sprinkle a little powdered pumice or scouring powder onto a damp felt pad and gently rub over the paintwork with large sweeping strokes, damping the pad again now and then. Or, wet the surface with a sponge and then rub with pad and powder. The water lubricates the action of the scouring agent and prevents it 'cutting' too much. This trick gives a nice, soft finish to a newly painted front door or kitchen fitment where overall shine can be a bit overpowering.

MIXING YOUR OWN COLOURS. The section on decorative painting shows how to mix up a special colour you can't track down in any of the standard ranges. Remember that flat paint dries darker and gloss paint lighter in tone. When mixing up a dark top-coat colour, tint the undercoat to match or you may get a piebald look if the paint is scarred.

Decorative painting

The impulse to pick up a brush and embellish a newly painted chair or box with flowers, birds, patterns must be as old as . . . well, certainly as old as the pyramids. Examples of fine decorative painting have survived among the Pharaohs' tomb furniture. Every lively culture has evolved its own distinctive style, from the filigree sinuosities of medieval Persian and Arab work to the cheery, *gemütlich* hearts and flowers of nineteenth-century Tyrolean and Bavarian painted furniture. It is only over the past hundred years or so, due to the rise of mass production, that hand-decorated pieces have ceased to be produced in any great numbers in the Western world. If the supply has dried up the demand certainly has not, to judge by the prices fetched by old painted chests, cupboards, chairs and knick-knacks in antique shops and salerooms. It's easy to see why – they are charming, colourful, individual, and they instantly evoke a

Figure 82. *Brightly painted and decorated cupboard; German, mid nineteenth century*

comely, ordered way of life with kettles singing on the hob, tall clocks drowsily ticking, the mingled smells of rising dough, drying herbs, and wood smoke. Encapsulated nostalgia, and very nice too.

To paupers who long for a bit of this instant atmosphere and can't afford such things at current prices, my suggestion is – paint your own. It doesn't, or needn't, take long; the materials are cheap; and it is great fun – no, better than that, it's *enthralling* to do. The problem is to get started, to conquer one's diffidence before the creative leap (copying is a great help at this stage) and actually put hand, brush, eye and mind to work. Once you have begun, the problem, usually, is how to stop. Don't be put off by the fact that you haven't handled a paintbrush since your schooldays. If you don't aim too high at first, which means going for formalized patterns rather than painterly techniques like grisaille, there's no reason why you shouldn't produce a very attractive object first time off. Start with something like the Bavarian trinket box or canal-boat posy illustrated further on in this section, and in a surprisingly short time you will find your skill and confidence increased to the point where you are bursting to fling roses riotously over blanket boxes, bedheads, even that painted chest of drawers you never got around to stripping.

With all the wealth of decorative traditions to choose from, I have settled on two which I think readers will find most congenial, practicable and useful – the one folksy, exuberant and colourful, the other restrained, muted, what might loosely be called classical. The first derives from European folk traditions and is splendid for adding splashes of colour wherever you need them. The second borrows – modestly – from eighteenth-century designers like Robert Adam, and is excellent for fading out large or ungainly pieces or linking up the unrelated odds and ends of furniture paupers often have to make do with. And, of course if you do have a pretty Regency chair in need of restoration it should be useful there too.

To help you get started I have included, as well as the written know-how, a collection of traditional motifs and patterns in both styles with suggestions on how to use them effectively, and colour keys. Some finished examples are shown in black and white in the photo inset. For further ideas and inspiration, visit museums, small provincial ones as well as the more important ones, and don't only look at larger painted pieces because some very pretty, copyable decoration was often applied to small things like toys, tobacco jars, trays, tea caddies. Then there are antique shops and stately homes. Next to an actual piece, a large colour plate is the best thing for copying from; most libraries have a good selection of coffee-table books on period furniture, the applied arts and so on, all handsomely illustrated. Make lightning sketches of ideas that appeal to you, with colour notes to jog your memory or supply a motif or colour combination. After a while you will find yourself looking about with a fresh, alert eye, culling ideas from all sorts of unlikely sources – a Victorian manhole cover might suggest a design for a tray or box lid, a lichen-freckled rock give ideas for colour schemes, a Fair Isle pattern produce a range of motifs. Inevitably, too, you will find yourself turning from copying to creating your own designs, a frequently humbling but always stimulating experience.

What to paint

For a start; anything which would look better covered up: wood with ugly grain, a nasty colour or spongy texture, i.e. whitewood; some poorly finished modern softwood furniture; junk-shop finds which turn out not to be figured pine but a dingy relation when stripped. Also, pieces too big or dark for their setting. I'm sure no one needs reminding that this doesn't apply to fine old stuff, however huge or time-blackened. But massive chests of drawers, old office desks, towering wardrobes and cupboards can all be scaled down visually by painting them some subtle shade of grey, grey-green, wheat yellow, buff, and then further breaking up the surface by 'lining' in a contrasting colour and a rubbed-on antique glaze. Avoid sugary pastels with big pieces or the effect will by coyly elephantine. Avoid painting oak, too, because the pronounced grain obtrudes through any number of coats of filler and paint. No one would be so daft as to paint a nice bit of mahogany, but some of those cheap veneered pieces, usually chipped and cracked, are much improved by stripping off the old varnish, filling cracks and scars and then painting in a somewhat classical manner.

Preparing the ground

All the wisdom about preparing wood thoroughly and working up a smooth, tough paint-surface applies particularly to pieces on which you are about to lavish your creative skill. A perfect finish matters less with folk painting, perhaps, but the painted ground for your decoration must be tough enough to withstand a good deal of wear and tear otherwise you will see your handiwork eroded away before your eyes. Give the piece at least two coats of top coat before decorating and finish off with several coats of varnish, which can be rubbed down if you don't want a brilliant shine. Small cracks can be filled as you go along with Polyfilla, but deep or structural cracks – i.e. on the rounded lid of a wooden box – are best knitted together with Araldite worked to a paste with dry Polyfilla before any painting starts. A really fine finish is important for the eighteenth-century style – paint-drips, stray brush-hairs and gritty foreign bodies make it look gimcrack and tacky. A counsel of perfection was passed on to me by a friend who used to work for one of our leading decorators, painting and decorating facsimiles of eighteenth-century designs to exacting standards:

It was a very thorough business. If the piece was newly made we first put some sticky stuff called knotting on any knots in the wood, then a coat of lead-based primer. After that, any cracks or unevennesses were filled in with Alabastine or Polyfilla. When dry, it was rubbed down with fine sandpaper till smooth. This was then sealed with a coat of shellac. Then we used undercoat till the piece was well covered – two or three coats at least. We usually used flat white or egg-shell mixed with artists' oils for the top coats. Any picking out, lining or decorative details were usually done with a clear flat or eggshell varnish, thinned with turps and mixed with artists' oils to the required colour. Sometimes things were varnished with flat or eggshell – never shiny – varnish, or glazed, and rubbed down on the parts which would obviously be rubbed in wear. The rubbing down can either be done with a cloth swiftly after putting on the glaze or with fine wire wool when dry.

A bedroom chair painted to these specifications sells for a cool £75–£100 so the finish must be impeccable. Refurbishing junk allows a more relaxed approach. All the same, some points are worth copying. Lead-based primer is the ideal foundation for these jobs as it is thick enough to fill as well as cover. (*Warning:* not for toys or baby-furniture because the lead content is poisonous.) Shellac gives a superbly sleek surface for paint. Varnish plus colour is ideal for painting fine detail, like lining, as it flows more smoothly than thinned paint. Glazing is useful, not merely for ageing a painted piece, but for pulling together decoration and ground colour and giving a faint, flattering overall haze of colour, white, neutral, or strongly contrasting, depending on the effect you are after.

Mixing colours

Mixing your own top-coat colours using artists' oils mixed into flat white or eggshell is the easiest, indeed often the only, way to reproduce a particularly subtle, off-beat period colour. Artists' oils are not cheap but as you will need relatively little paint to coat the average piece of furniture – a bedroom chair for instance can be covered with about 3 tablespoons of paint – the extra cost will be quite small. If you want a dark or rich colour like fir green or terracotta, which would take a lot more oils to tint than a pastel colour, you can economize by choosing a commercial paint in flat or eggshell near to, but lighter than, the final shade you are after, and then it's a question of adding a squeeze of this and that rather than an entire tube. Knowing what to mix with what, to arrive at a particular shade, becomes instinctive after a while. If you aren't that confident yet, try experimenting with watercolours on a piece of paper to work out the formula you need. Check with someone in the shop where you buy the paint – if you show them your water-coloured sample they will usually be able to pick the right oil shades to match it. If this sounds daunting you can always play safe with what decorators call an 'interesting off-white' made by mixing a little raw umber, yellow ochre and a speck of black into white paint. This suits almost any furniture and colour scheme and you can decorate it in almost any shade you fancy.

For mixing, you need real turps, a couple of jam jars and an old paintbrush or stick or spoon plus the oil colours and paint. First put a good squeeze of the oils into a jam jar with a splash of turps and mix till the oil colour is completely dissolved. If you are blending two or more colours to arrive at your particular shade add a squeeze of these now and again; stir till dissolved. Now pour a little of the flat white or eggshell (well stirred up already) into the other jam jar and add the thinned colour little by little, stirring away till thoroughly mixed, which takes longer than you might imagine. If you need more tint, dissolve the oil colour separately as before, don't just squeeze it into the paint. You can mix up as much paint as you will need for the two or three top coats at one go, remembering to float a film of linseed oil on top to prevent it drying, but I prefer to mix them separately because I like the slight colour variations showing through when the final coats are rubbed down.

Materials

Folk painters worked in a variety of media, probably using what was cheapest or came most readily to hand. The more elaborate work was done in oils, but canal-boat painting was done with colours mixed into undercoat and some Early American pieces were painted using, of all things, buttermilk, as a medium. If they were alive now I am sure they would reach thankfully for modern acrylic or polymer paints, which dry so quickly you can complete a whole design in a few hours instead of waiting days for the separate stages to dry out, as one has to with oils. The colours are a little harder and less glowing than their oil-based counterparts, but this hardly matters with folk designs, which tend to be brilliant rather than subtle. You can do a lot to vary the effect of acrylics by thinning some colours almost to transparency with water, and using others quite thickly for a near impasto effect. These modern plastic-based paints need plenty of protective varnishing to stop them chipping and flaking off, so follow up the decoration with a coat of clear varnish and add a couple more when this dries. Varnishing brings out the colours, so you have the pleasure of seeing your work improve with each coat. Polyurethane varnish is appropriate to this sort of painting, where a certain bandbox shininess looks right, and it is very tough.

Buy a few colours to start off with – vermilion or crimson lake, Prussian or cobalt blue, yellow ochre, raw or burnt umber, black and white will give you a reasonable range. Red, yellow and blue in different permutations make orange, green and purple while mixing in white gives a range of pastels and a little umber darkens without muddying. A thin wash of umber is useful for shading. The chief snag with acrylics is that they dry so fast your blobs of paint, squeezed onto plate, palette or whatever, have dried hard by the time you return for a dab more. You can either buy a special retarder, or keep moistening the blobs with a few drops of water to keep them runny. Also, cap the paint-tubes swiftly or you will find yourself having to dig out a large plug of dried paint.

Good brushes are a great help in achieving smooth, fluent strokes, as I found after struggling away for some time with worn-down water-colour brushes. You don't need many – three in different sizes are enough

– but get the best you can afford and clean them thoroughly after use. Buy one very fine one, preferably a sable pencil, for fine detail, a size 4 sable or camelhair for petals, leaves, etc. and a nice bushy brush (mine is a sable 11) for broader work. Rinse the brushes out frequently in water to

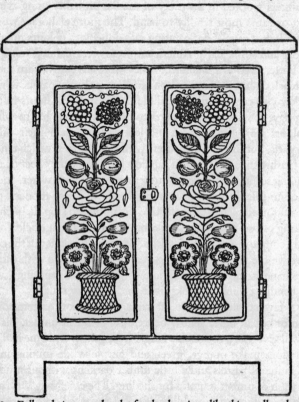

Figure 83. *Folksy designs can do a lot for chunky pieces like this small cupboard. In the original the flowers were buttonholed in red, the roses were a deep, unexpected blue, the grapes blue one side, pale yellow outlined in red the other*

Figure 84. *Two simple border patterns in two colours*

stop them caking, or soak in methylated spirits which dissolves acrylics efficiently. A film of linseed oil once in a while will help keep the brushes pliable. Use a standard brush – ½-inch is a handy size – for varnishing.

Folk decoration

For all its look of having been dashed off in a high-spirited moment, nearly all folk art is strongly imitative, carefully reproducing the colours and motifs traditional to a certain region, or even village. Innovators might add a curlicue here or a row of leaves there, but the basic shapes evolved slowly, if at all, which may explain their mysterious 'rightness'. Changing a colour or two or incorporating a motif of one's own often weakens the overall effect. This happens to be true, which is a useful alibi for a beginner slavishly copying some traditional design.

Although different regions and countries had their distinctive motifs and patterns – the Dutch naturally favoured tulips – it is the similarities running through folk art that one notices most; a general love of bright colour, flowers, birds, swags and curlicues, sentiment and symmetry. The European folk painters seem to have favoured dark, rich colours to set off their vivid painted decorations – dark green, red, Prussian blue. One popular combination was red and white roses with green leaves and daisy-chain borders on a deep blue ground. The crudeness of so much bright colour was softened by generous flicks of white, outlining flowers, leaves, as in canal-boat work. Early American folk artists, on the other hand, went in for sludgier colours – pea green, turkey red, ochre, warm brown – which they often got by adding raw umber to the basic shades. Colours on old pieces have mellowed and yellowed with time so you can suit yourself as to whether you copy the faded colours or think back to the original scheme. Less assertive colours might be easier to live with on a large piece like a dresser – a pretty one I saw was painted off-white, picked out in pink, with colourful Staffordshire figures, a very English form of folk art, reproduced on the doors.

Folk motifs

Most folk motifs are built up with the basic petal-shaped stroke, fat one end and tapering to a point. It's a good idea to practise these till you can dab them in quickly and confidently, controlling their size and direction without conscious effort. Apprentice pot-painters in the Staffordshire

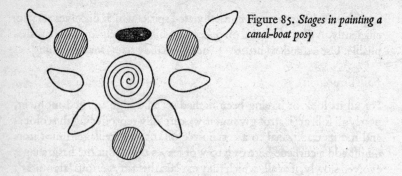

Figure 85. *Stages in painting a canal-boat posy*

Figure 86. *The posy dressing up a simple clog*

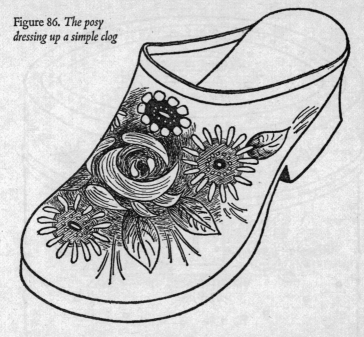

potteries spent their first weeks doing nothing else. Then practise daisy shapes – yellow blobs surrounded by short fat marguerite petals or longer pointed ones. With a fatter brush, add green leaves. Now try painting a complete canal-boat posy as shown in the step-by-step illustrations.

CANAL-BOAT POSY. This gives useful practice in handling brushes and making strokes of different sizes. It makes a pretty, versatile decoration.

Start by washing in a patch of raw umber about the size of the finished posy. Keep the paint very thin; it should show up as a shadow in the background. Now, using thicker paint, add blobs for the flowers, crimson for the rose, darkish brown for the daisies. Brush in green leaf-shapes as shown. When all this is dry, paint in all the various flower petals with quick, light strokes. With a bit of practice you will find the brush-strokes falling into a sort of rhythm, almost automatic. If you compare a daisy painted now with one of your first, careful efforts you will find it has gained new expressiveness and movement. This lively brushwork is crucial to decorative painting. For the rose, use a brush

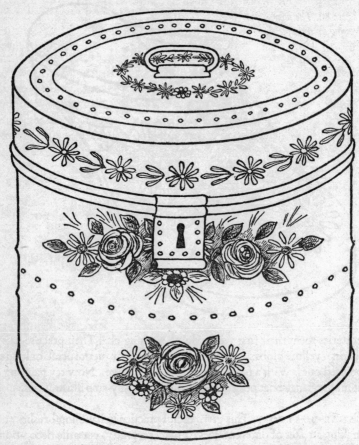

Figure 87. *Canal-boat posy decorating Victorian metal hatbox. Paint the box dark green or black, handle rim and lock red or yellow. Makes a capacious breadbin*

quite thickly charged with paint so that you can complete each petal in one stroke. Now add details like shading on the leaves, black dots in the daisy centres. Then the finishing touches – dark commas in the rose heart, white dots and highlights in daisy centres, pale green and yellow veining on leaves, white whiskers here and there to balance up the design, as shown. Varnish.

ROSES, FLORAL CENTREPIECES, BOUQUETS. It's only a step from the canal-boat posy to more elaborate motifs, many of them based on the same simple shapes. Some typical folk floral motifs are illustrated for you to copy or adapt. When working out a design begin by roughing it out on a piece of paper, playing around with the various elements till you have one that fits the space and looks right. Then block it out on the box, panel or whatever, with chalk (ideal for this job as it can be rubbed out and painted over). Just chalk in the shapes and general movement of the flowers and leaves, don't bother with fine detail because if you do you

Figure 88. *Variations on the tulip theme, all Pensylvanian Dutch. Paint them bright colours — think of parrot tulips*

Figure 89. *A cluster of roses for a wall panel, and an elongated spray for drawer fronts or hanging shelves*

will become mesmerized by the sketch to the point where your brushwork loses all spontaneity.

Clusters of more or less stylized roses in red, pink, yellows, with sprays of leaves, are one of the most popular of all folk motifs, found on anything from wall-panels to pin-boxes. It's not difficult to build up a cluster with the canal-boat rose as the basic unit, using different colours and tilting them in different directions to give movement and variety. Keep them massed close together for impact and balance the flowers with leaves. Large panels need a generous-sized cluster, while elongated surfaces like drawer fronts or cupboard doors need a spread-out arrangement of perhaps three or five roses with sprays of leaves each end (figure 89). The rose border (figure 90) looks pretty garlanding a round box-lid or mirror frame. The roses are as simplified as can be, but still recognizably roses. The pendant motif (figure 91) was often painted down the centre splat of a chair back, with a large cluster on the seat to balance the scheme.

Figure 90. *Simplified rose border. Pink roses, buds, green leaves, white and yellow flowers*

Figure 91. *Pendant motif using bellflower, roses and daisies and featuring typical white 'flicks' edging green leaves*

Symmetrical, rather stiff bunches of flowers, or flowers and fruit standing in urns or baskets, are another favourite and great fun to paint. Practise some more flower shapes for variety. Keep the treatment flat and decorative, not straining after botanical accuracy or realism. Stylized tulips (figure 88), lilies of the valley, half-open carnations (green calyx topped by coloured frill of petal), bunches of grapes, pears, apples, are all easy shapes to render. Use sprays of leaves, spiky, feathery or lushly green, to balance the flowers and fill spaces. Baskets and vases are painted as a child would see them, one-dimensional, with the detail carefully picked out in a darker shade. Flowers can be naturalistic or fantastic depending on the effect you want – the bouquets shown on the small cupboard doors (figure 83) featured sky-blue roses among more conventional flowers and fruit.

If a brightly coloured motif, (particularly one painted on a light background colour) looks garish you can tone it down by applying a wipe-on, wipe-off tinted wash or glaze. The glaze can be tinted any colour, depending on the effect you want. Raw umber and burnt sienna give a mellowed, 'antiqued' look, greenish in the case of the raw umber, golden with the burnt sienna. Black, used in minute quantities, ages paintwork dramatically and can look effective over darker colours. A white glaze was often used by French eighteenth-century cabinet-makers to give a pearly finish to soft, rich colours like Boucher blue, coral, pink. Sometimes a brightly coloured glaze or wash is useful for tying in painted decoration on a light inset panel to the overall colour of a piece. Thus, if you had a flower-painted white panel on the door of a red cupboard, washing over the panel in the same red will soften the colour contrasts and unify the appearance of the piece. Applying a wash doesn't take a minute. (A glaze, strictly speaking, uses oil colours in a linseed oil base, and I have dealt with this in the classical decorative painting section.) For a wash, mix a little raw umber, or burnt sienna with water and brush rapidly over the surface. Leave it on a minute or two and then gently wipe off with a rag or tissue. If you are nervous about the effect, use several thin washes rather than one strongly tinted one. The washed-on colour remains as a faint overall freckling in the surface irregularities of the paint. Using several different coloured washes, one over the other, produces subtle effects too. I have described earlier how picture framers use this trick to get a mellow, shaded, mysterious look on a painted frame.

LITTLE BOXES. Little boxes are quick and amusing to decorate, and make attractive presents. You can collect old scruffy ones (market stalls, Oxfam shops, junk shops, jumble sales) or buy unpainted ones in light thin wood very cheaply (Suppliers' Index). The old ones will probably need stripping down to the wood and a bit of sanding to smooth the surfaces, then a coat or two of undercoat, rubbed down when dry. Paint the inside too. The new wood boxes – identical to the ones folk painters have been using for centuries – need sanding lightly all over to smooth rough edges, then a coat of lead primer, followed by a coat of undercoat. Then give the box two coats of acrylic paint inside and out. Bright colours – red, blue, green – are traditional, with gaily painted patterns. But there's no need to be bound by tradition. One Early American painter made his name with a simple scheme of red and white roses and green leaves – painted in loose, sweeping strokes – on a black ground.

The pattern illustrated (*see* figure 92), for a round box, is nineteenth-century Bavarian. It's a good design for a beginner to try, as it is straightforward to paint, requiring only a sable pencil and a lot of patience, and looks highly accomplished and pretty when done. Mark out the out-

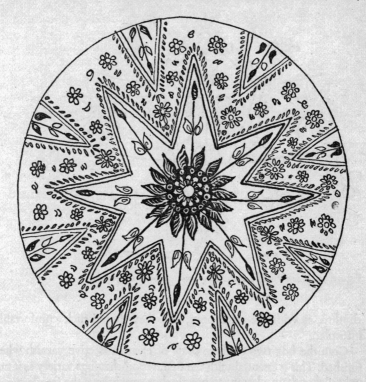

Figure 92. *Bavarian design for the lid of a round trinket box*

line of the star and kite-shaped motifs circling the box with chalk or pencil. Do them freehand, because none of these traditional patterns were geometrically accurate as you will see if you examine the star closely. Now fill in the star and lozenge shapes with French mustard yellow, and paint the rest of the box, including the part covered by the rim, bright vermilion. When this is dry, outline the shapes in a vivid greeny blue (add a speck of yellow to the blue) in a fairly thick line. Next, tackle the black motifs on the star and lozenges, using the sable pencil because these should look neat and crisply painted. Add pale blue wings half-way along the black spokes. You can suit yourself as to whether you do the flowers next or the white highlighting. When doing the white flicks right round the star and lozenges, don't strain to get them precisely the same length or parallel to each other – aim for an easy

Figure 93. *Side view of box showing how to extend the pattern*

rhythm, as with the canal posy, and they should flick comfortably into place.

Give the box two or three coats of clear protective varnish when finished. This is essential with the thin, wood-shavings variety as it not only makes them pleasant to handle, but strengthens the fragile wood and allows the top to slide smoothly over the bottom. Take a little trouble over the varnishing for a satiny texture. Use an absolutely clean brush, stand the box on a tray covered with newspaper and rig up a hood from a large plastic bag to prevent dust settling as it dries. Any varnish will do, as the boxes won't be handled overmuch. Clear picture varnish is all right if you use several coats. Polyurethane is very tough and dries fast.

As you become more skilful, you will want to try some more ambitious designs. Traditional ones include dragoons on horseback, tiny landscapes, unicorns, nosegays tied with ribbon. Look out books on European and American folk art. A nice idea for a wedding present would be a modernized version of the old 'bride box', which featured a *naif* portrait of the bridal couple in all their finery surrounded by flowers, butterflies and birds. The couple's initials and wedding date were often worked into the design. Alternatively you can inscribe these details, plus some suitable message or quote, in flowing copperplate on the inside of the lid. It takes very little time to 'personalize' these presents, as the Americans say, but it makes them twice as popular. Incidentally, if you have a reasonably neat-fingered child you might find a few of these little boxes – the new ones come in various shapes and sizes – would solve the problem of what to give grandparents, uncles and aunts for Christmas. Young children often have a startling ability to come up with fresh, attractive designs so encourage them to produce their own.

Chests, boxes, trunks

Large chests and boxes, even an old tin trunk, are perfect things to paint in the folk idiom; those nice flat surfaces 'compose' very satisfactorily, and the result is a handsome and very decorative piece of furniture – useful, too. This isn't a new discovery – beautifully painted and decorated dower chests, for storing all that hand-stitched linen, used to be standard bridal equipment. It is not difficult to find colour plates of antique chests to adapt or copy. Alternatively, you might like to try reproducing the two patterns shown here (see figures 94 and 95 and inset for close-ups of the finished boxes). The bold, stylized flower design is nineteenth-century Bavarian in interesting, off-beat blue and tawny colours. Strong, simple shapes make it easy and satisfying to paint. You can use a broad brush and really zip over the ground, so it is a good choice for a novice. The other, more elaborate, birds and flowers design is adapted from an old American painted chest. I transferred it to a portmanteau in light wood, with a domed lid, and it has been much admired. It is slower and rather more difficult to do, but a nice flexible design which can be adapted for panels of different shapes and sizes by adding a flower here or a whiskery motif there, with a leaf or two to balance up. My version uses the original colours, predominantly faded warm reds and yellows on an inky blue-black ground.

For those interested in painting up a box I thought I would give a breakdown of how these were done.

BAVARIAN-STYLE BLANKET-BOX. We used a somewhat dilapidated old deal blanket-box, with a little worm and one or two chunks missing. After treating the worm with Rentokil, the missing pieces were replaced

Colour key

☐ off white   ▨ red   ▨ seaweed brown   ⊡ pale pink

Outer scumbled band: mid blue and deep blue

Inner scumbled band, reading from centre: greeny grey, deep blue, ginger, tobacco brown

Figure 94. *Bold, easy-to-paint Bavarian design for a wooden box*

with wood roughly shaped, glued into place and then planed to match-up correctly. The old varnished finish was crumbling to powder so the box only needed a thorough sanding to be ready to paint. We gave it one coat of lead-based primer to improve the surface as well as provide a tough, durable base, then two coats of ordinary undercoat. Then the design was pencilled onto the lid in some detail. It is worth noting that bold patterns like this one need careful and accurate roughing out because mistakes leap out at you in a way they would not in a more intricate design. The red outlines were painted in first, then the centre panel was filled in with off-white and the flowers painted in – browny-green (seaweed colour) foliage and red, pink and tawny yellow for the stylized florets. Then the off-white band with the four bold spiked corners was painted, leaving only the striped, scumbled areas left to do. Scumbling gives a rich, self-striped effect like dragging (*see* dragged walls). Here it adds interest to what would otherwise be crude blocks of colour. To do it, first paint the blocks in flat colour as shown. Then, mixing up a darker tone of each colour and using a broad brush, draw the darker colour over the paler one, keeping the brushwork as streaky as possible and leaving the ends of each stroke ragged, so that the blocks of colour merge into each other. The same design was repeated on the front and sides with some modifications to suit the different shapes, and then the box was heavily varnished with polyurethane varnish – four coats – for protection, and rubbed down with fine wire wool to dull the pronounced shine to a faint sheen more in keeping with the design. The inside of the box was painted blue and varnished.

AMERICAN COLONIAL DESIGN. This box was in good condition apart from some bad cracks in the lid. These I glued with Araldite and filler to bind as well as fill – plastic wood or Polyfilla would have worked out in time because there is a certain amount of give in the curved top. Again, one coat of lead-based primer, followed by two of ordinary undercoat. I used artists' oils mixed into the same undercoat for the top coats, because I wanted a 'lean' rather than 'fatty' effect to make it look worn and weathered. But I think this was a mistake here, though it would be suitable for objects which don't get much wear. Undercoat

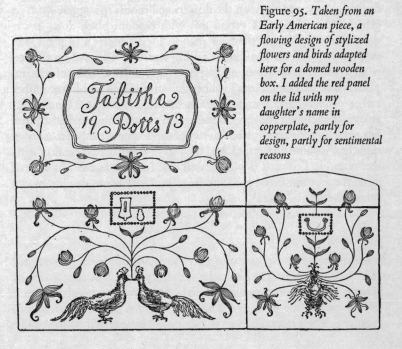

Figure 95. *Taken from an Early American piece, a flowing design of stylized flowers and birds adapted here for a domed wooden box. I added the red panel on the lid with my daughter's name in copperplate, partly for design, partly for sentimental reasons*

scuffs off at twice the rate of a good-quality top coat. I mixed cobalt, raw umber and a little black to get a dark air-force blue for the top coats, which I darkened further by giving the whole box a black wash, using acrylics this time. Then I roughed out the pattern with chalk, starting with the front panel. The actual decorating, using acrylics exclusively, took less time than the previous painting. The simplified tulip-shapes consist of yellowy crescents with faded red centres, the curving stems are white, leaves ochre, and whisker motifs tawny with a red line meandering through the curving feelers. All these are delicately striped with a pale (off-white) line, which breaks up the colour masses attractively. The birds were the most challenging bits, as I'm no ornithologist, but I settled for an impressionistic technique using a lot of seaweed brown, tawny yellow, raw umber and off-white, smearing it all artistically here and there with a fingertip. The design now looked very pretty as it was, but because I was after an antique look, all faded and weathered and worn, I went to some lengths to counterfeit this by rubbing on raw umber, burnt sienna (using it straight from the tube on a fingertip) here and there on the flowers and motifs to suggest worn or grime-darkened paint. I varied this with random black dots. It was quite fun to do, but in the final analysis I feel I prefer a brighter, less worked-over effect. The instant ageing was very effective on the red panel on the lid, however, adding interest to a flat expanse of red and plain white lettering. Here I rubbed in burnt sienna and burnt umber rather patchily (avoid uniformity in this sort of faking). Finally, for an overall mellow yellowing, I brushed on a coat of orange shellac (dries fast, which makes it useful for this sort of experiment), rubbed that down slightly with fine wire wool, and then gave the box two coats of eggshell varnish. I painted the inside dull red. Brass nailheads add a bit of interest to a plain metal lock and handles. These come cheaper by the pound (Suppliers' Index).

Spongeing

Spongeing is a quick, easy and effective way of decorating a painted piece in folksy style. The method is simplicity itself. You take a scrap of sponge – natural, preferably, since the holes are less regular – dip it lightly into a little paint in a saucer and dab the colour in random or regular patterns over the piece in question. The sponged colour can be boldly contrasting or just a few tones away from the base colour for a softer effect. Acrylic colours are excellent for spongeing since they dry so quickly there is less risk of smudging the pattern. Practise on a sheet of paper first to get an idea of the possible range of effects. A combination of a very light patterning – rather as though a tiny animal or bird had left painted footprints – combined with more densely sponged areas, outlined by coloured lines, looks attractive. You can further vary the effect by using the sponge dry for sharp imprints and damping it a little for blurry ones. Spongeing in two or three colours gives a richly coloured surface not unlike marbling. Dull blue, brownish red and burnt sienna or raw umber over a soft grey base coat is an attractive colour combination. Or, for a bolder impact, dark green spongeing over a cream base coat with faded red line-trim. Keep the lines quite broad or they won't register – $\frac{1}{4}$ of an inch or so. For a handsome tortoiseshell look which consorts well with brass handles, sponge an amber-yellow base coat with warm brown, a little Indian red and black, in that order. Finish any piece sponged with acrylics with a couple of coats of varnish to protect it.

Odds and ends

All these techniques can be used to make something presentable of cheap junk-shop finds – lamp bases, tin trays, canisters (*see* inset). None of the things shown cost more than a few pence. The lamp base was inspired by an attractive old pottery candlestick. One point to remember if you are painting metal – it's essential to remove any rust, otherwise the paint will just flake off. Use rust remover and wire-wool and scour till bright. Then give it a coat of metal primer. Use the same techniques with metal as for painting wood – undercoat, topcoats – but take more care with the rubbing down as metal throws brushmarks into stark relief, and finish up with several coats of polyurethane varnish to protect the article from water and continual handling. It's surprising what a fine (I was going to say factory but perhaps that isn't the appropriate word here) finish one can achieve with a little trouble on things most people would toss into the dustbin.

Classical painted decorations and antiquing

Painted decoration on the formal and elegant furniture of the eighteenth and early nineteenth centuries was intended as a subtle enrichment of the basic shapes, not a bright splash of colour as with folk painting. It is mannerly and restrained, using muted colours, with neat, precise handling of motifs which themselves tended to be stylized and demure. Compare the classical-style bellflower with a folk-art rose and you will see what I mean. The fashion for painted furniture seems to have spread to England from the Continent, where French cabinetmakers in particular excelled in making pretty and feminine pieces for the boudoirs of royal mistresses and other leaders of fashion. Robert Adam did more than anyone else to make painted furniture popular in England. He was an extraordinarily inventive designer and a brilliant colourist, and his flair for combining graceful shapes and sophisticated colours with elegant pastiche of classical motifs and 'ornaments' set the style for these pieces to this day. One good reason for the immediate popularity of this sort of furniture was its relative cheapness, despite all the skilled work that went into it, compared with furniture in exotic imported woods like kingwood, satinwood, tulipwood and later mahogany. Most of it was made from softwood or beech, which was easier to work and much cheaper. The Victorian passion for mahogany seems to have gradually ousted painted pieces but, by then, the Adam style had been copied by furniture makers up and down the country. The imitations are usually simpler, less ornamented, and slightly rustic-looking, which perhaps makes them more appealing to modern eyes than the Adam style at its most formal. It is these 'country cousin' versions of the eighteenth-century style which amateurs like ourselves can copy most successfully. They rely for their charm on interesting colours, a fine paint finish, a little simple decoration like painted lines, bambooing, and the odd motif, usually executed in an unobvious contrasting colour – brown, dark green, grey, lots of off-white, sludgy whites and sepia. Antiquing, in its simple form of washing a dark glaze over the paintwork to age and mellow it, makes any piece in this style look more distinguished.

The best way to get ideas for colour schemes is to study attractive old pieces carefully (or modern facsimiles, as they are often indistinguishable). Paler pastel shades with a tang to them were popular – sharp

Figure 96. *Eighteenth-century painted and gilded chair in the grand manner*

greeny-yellows, greyed pinks, pea green, cool buffs, a great deal of off-white. On pale ground-colours decoration would be in a darker contrast colour. An alternative is to paint the furniture a dark colour – lacquer red, black, dark green – and lighten the effect with decoration in the off-white, grey, sludge brown range. You could even introduce a touch of gold leaf (*see* gilding). If you have an instinct for colour – can you match colours from memory, for instance? – working out a colour combination which suits the furniture and goes with what you have in the room is interesting and fun to do. If not, you can't go wrong painting your pieces off-white and decorating them in one contrasting colour, which could be cherry pink, leaf green, snuff brown, grey.

I have included some motifs often used on period pieces which you can copy or adapt quite easily. As I found myself, it's one thing to look appreciatively at painted details and quite another to reproduce them from memory. A fraction out here and there makes a bellflower look like a tiny bunch of bananas. Artlessly simple borders suddenly proliferate dilemmas – how big were the berries, which way do the leaves point, what happens at the corners? You find yourself unable to draw, much less paint, an oval and there isn't an oval in the house you can copy. (I have included one as a pattern for this very reason.) As with folk decorating, I think it's a good idea to start by imitating the old models, which is a training in itself. They look simple, in fact they *are*, most of them, but they have evolved over centuries and it is surprisingly hard to improve on them.

A fine coloured line, or 'lining', is the simplest form of decoration and the most widely used to call attention discreetly to the basic shape and line of a piece of furniture: around drawers or a table- or desk-top, down either side of flat legs or chair backs, picking out an interesting detail like an arched panel or a Gothic cut-out. It can be a single line, or you can use two or three together for emphasis, but they should be fine – not more than $\frac{1}{8}$ inch across. Professionals paint them on freehand. This isn't as difficult as it sounds if you lay the piece flat so you are painting on a horizontal not vertical plane, and use your third and fourth fingers to steady your brushstroke. A hint of wobble doesn't matter, in fact it adds liveliness, but a noticeable swerve can be wiped off with a cloth moistened in turps. In the old days, men were employed to do nothing else but lining, striping or banding, as it was variously called, and there were virtuosi who could whip a perfect, steady line round an oval tray in one brushstroke. Inexperienced liners like oneself can usually manage a small surface, like a chair-back or seat quite successfully. For all lining use a fine sable pencil, and artists' oil-colour in the required shade mixed into flat or eggshell clear varnish. Varnish as a medium makes the colour

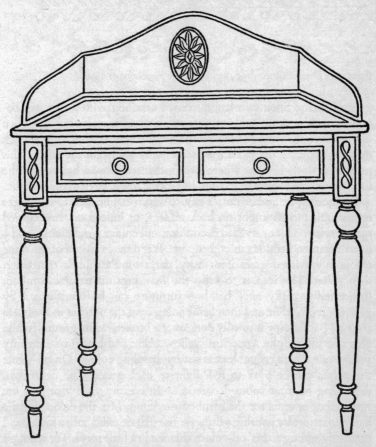

Figure 97. *Painted a quiet colour like pea green, buff, decorated with painted lines and a couple of simple motifs, a wooden Victorian washstand looks elegant enough to use as a small sideboard or drinks table. Paint wooden knobs to match, with coloured line trim – cheaper and just as nice as brass*

semi-transparent, which looks lighter and prettier, and it also flows on much more smoothly – a great help when you are trying to draw a fine even line with a brush. When lining on larger surfaces, like table-tops, masking tape is the answer. Use Sellotape, masking tape, or brown

Figure 98. *Diminutive border patterns. Draw a pencil line as a guide*

gummed strip. Stick two lengths down carefully with a tiny gap between, paint over the gap, and you will have a fine coloured line when you remove the tape. Make sure the inner edges are thoroughly stuck down though, or the paint may seep under and spoil the effect. This method is slow, because where two lines intersect you have to let the first dry before doing the second, but it cuts out a lot of nervous strain.

Bambooing is another simple device which can be used to dramatize chairs with turned knobs on back or legs, or indeed on any curved surface where a bit of stylized decoration and colour would look good – mirror frames, bedside tables, bedposts. It is done in stripes of the same colour in varying degrees of intensity; darkest in the middle, then paler, then palest. The idea is to echo the markings on natural bamboo. (Incidentally, really tatty bamboo furniture can be transformed by painting it off-white and then bambooing over the notches in a suitable colour.) Bambooing is usually done over a broken-white ground (white plus raw umber plus a speck of yellow ochre and black) or a creamy yellow one which resembles the natural bamboo colour. On off-white the stripes can be pink to red, light to dark green, blue or brown, depending on your room decoration. On creamy yellow or buff use raw umber or sepia for the bamboo markings. Mix the colour for the bamboo stripes by pouring a little varnish (flat or matt) into a saucer and gradually adding artists' oil-colour thinned in a little turps. Try it out on a piece of paper, and keep the paper to guide you when mixing the second stripe colour. Mix up the palest tint of the colour first. With this, using a soft fat brush, paint a ring round the leg or back (*see* figure 99) about I inch wide. It doesn't have to be mathematically correct, but try to make the ends meet up accurately. Paint similar rings wherever you feel they should go, either to pick out turned decoration, or to balance the design. On the chair here, bamboo rings have been painted round the smooth chair-back pieces as well as the notched foot-rails. Paint smaller rings round small turned knobs as in the chair-back. It is best to start by

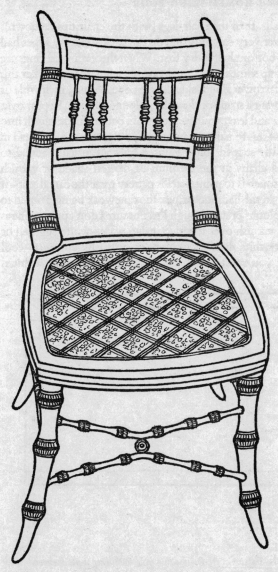

Figure 99. *Bambooing and line decoration on a painted chair. The caned seat has been painted in a trellis pattern in the same colours. Any chair with some turned work on back or legs can be given the bamboo treatment*

ringing the foot-rails, then the chair-legs (with the chair upside down), and then turn it over very carefully and do the back – clumsy types had better wait till the bottom half is dry first. When the varnished rings are perfectly dry, mix up some more tinted varnish, a few shades darker this time, and paint a narrower ring inside the first one, about ½ inch wide or slightly wider, leaving a stripe of the paler colour each side. Repeat over the rest of the chair and leave to dry. Now mix colour full strength into the varnish, and use this to paint a narrow stripe right round and dead in the middle of all the striped rings. Painted lines are usually added to bamboo-decorated chairs in the medium or darkest shade of varnish used. A decorator touch is to paint a trellis pattern over the caned seat – if it *has* a caned seat – in the bamboo stripes, the canework being painted to match the chair. It looks pretty though I'm not sure I don't prefer cane as it is. To finish off, varnish over the piece using water-white eggshell or flat varnish (water-white denotes a colourless varnish) and wire-wool very lightly or, if you want to age the piece instantly, apply a tinted

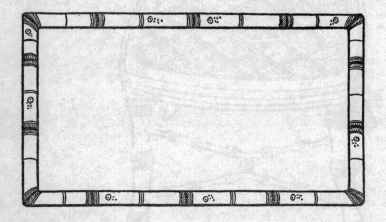

Figure 100. *Bambooing used to doll up a plain curved moulding round a wall mirror. Add little painted bullseyes as shown, with a cluster of freckles, painted in the bamboo colours*

glaze first. This is the simplest way of 'antiquing' a piece, and it ties painted decoration into the ground colour very effectively. It can (of course) be used on any painted piece.

Antique glaze

To make a glaze mix 3 tablespoons of real turps, 1 tablespoon of refined linseed oil and 1 tablespoon of artists' oil-colour – raw umber over broken-white and light-coloured paintwork, raw sienna for a much warmer tone over light to medium colours, and black for a sobering glaze over bright to dark shades. Paint work must be quite dry and hard before glazing, otherwise the turps might soften and smudge it. Paint the glaze on generously with a large soft brush (housepainter size) over one surface at a time. Almost immediately, start wiping the glaze off with a lint-free cloth (old bits of sheet) using a circular movement and working from the centre of the panel outwards to the edges. The centre of the panel, or arm or whatever, should be the lightest bit, to simulate natural wear-and-tear. Then pat with clean rag or tissues and finally smooth out colour with a clean brush, repeating the movement from the centre outwards each time. What happens is that the glaze seeps into all the hairline cracks and irregularities in the surface of even the most careful painting and remains there, as well as spreading a thin shadow of colour overall. These are the standard antiquing glazes. Eighteenth-century French cabinet-makers often used a white glaze over coloured paintwork for a pretty, opalescent effect. Apply it the same way, substituting white undercoat for artists' oils. For a dramatically aged look, you can try leaving the glaze on longer before rubbing off. And you can have fun experimenting with different tints one over the other – dark green glaze over apple green paint, blue over brown, grey over pink. Glazing gives some protection to paintwork in itself, but if the piece is likely to get a lot of wear – a chair for instance – a coat of varnish overall is probably a good idea.

Rubbed-down colours

If the shadowed, shot-silk look of colour over colour appeals to you, you can achieve it by applying top coats in two shades of one colour or in contrasting colours, and rubbing the top one down with wire wool when both coats are dry, so that the colour beneath shows through

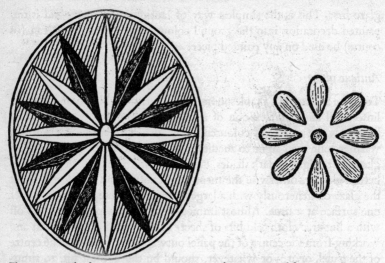

Figure 101. *The daisy or rosette turns up everywhere on painted furniture, sometimes artlessly simple or stylized as the centrepiece of an oval medallion*

faintly here and there. The possibilities of this technique are limitless, and one can get mysterious shaded colour effects obtainable no other way. It works best, I think, if you use the lightest colour as a final coat and rub down till the deeper and richer shades glow through – if you use the finest wire wool, you can't go wrong with the rubbing down, but do it in daylight so that you can check your progress accurately. This finish is so decorative in itself that very little further decoration seems necessary – some painted lines, or a little gilding if you feel up to it (*see* gilding) is enough. Try rubbing down buttercup yellow over saffron yellow, or forget-me-not blue over greeny blue, or saffron over orange-yellow, or red over Indian or Venetian red. Rarefy the colour still further by using a light glaze overall.

Motifs

The bellflower and its variants was a motif much used by Robert Adam, and it isn't too difficult to copy successfully, using a fine, tapering, soft brush. It looks very pretty painted down the front of a flat tapering chair- or table-leg, the flowers diminishing in size as the leg narrows, and often ending in a few 'pearls', graduated this time. The bellflower is nearly

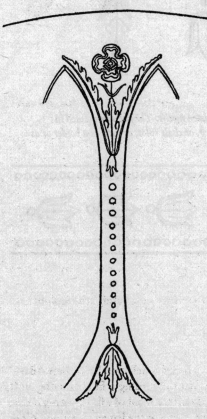

Figure 102. *Another variant on the stylized flower: here a Tudor rose is combined with oak leaves and 'pearls' on the back splat of an eighteenth-century chair. The original colouring was in shades of off-white, grey, wheat yellow, all shaded in sludgy brown, on a black ground*

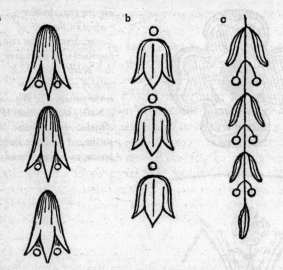

Figure 103. *Bellflower, husk and mistletoe motifs. They can be painted in diminishing size down a flat, tapered leg, or chair splat, or used as a border or as festoons and swags, caught up by bows*

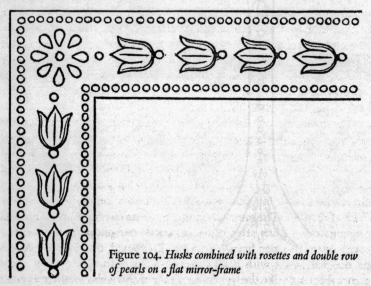

Figure 104. *Husks combined with rosettes and double row of pearls on a flat mirror-frame*

always painted in off-white, shaded usually with a warmer brownish colour. On Adam furniture the background would often be black, or a dark colour, and the delicate, pearly look of the bellflowers would be picked up in a double border of 'pearl' dots in off-white. Shading is done after the basic shape is dry, and remember that a tinted glaze will do some of the shading for you, so don't make it too pronounced. The husk motif is a little more solid than the bellflower and makes a charming continuous pattern round a flat mirror frame. Again, keep to the off-white to creamy yellow colour range – these motifs are intended to be delicate and unemphatic; they should lighten the overall look of a piece without hitting you in the eye. Rosettes break up the pattern a little and act as dividers, and should be painted in the same colours. A few minutes' careful study of an eighteenth-century piece – preferably *after* you have tried your hand at a sample of motif painting, so you know what the problems are – is worth pages of written instructions. The mistletoe motif (my own, probably botanically inaccurate, name for it) introduces a little more colour, because the leaves are painted a sludgy green, shaded in brown-green, while the berries are off-white highlighted with a touch of yellow. This also makes a pretty pendant decoration down the front of a flat, tapering leg, or a narrow panel down the side of a cupboard. On a very light pastel background, these motifs might look better painted in tones of a muted but darker colour, like sepia, or grey. One particularly attractive and light-hearted suite of painted Adam furniture I saw, designed for use in a summer house, was decorated with rosettes, satyr heads and husk borders entirely in shades of grey – palest silver to battleship – on a ground of sugar-almond pink, also faintly greyed, probably with a very thin black glaze.

The anthemion and palmette motifs (*see* figure 105) were frequently worked into a continuous border – the inventive way the old designers endlessly recombined the same stock of motifs in a fresh and interesting way is a mark of their genius – but they are bold and interesting enough to stand alone, filling a small recessed panel, or a painted oval, or weighting the bottom of long narrow panels of decoration on a cupboard or chest of drawers. The same goes for the rosette (*see* figure 102) in all its permutations. When attempting any more complicated motif, either rough out a specimen first on a piece of cardboard, or trace the outlines on the paintwork with coloured-crayon, or both. Continuous symmetrical patterns like the 'guilloche' (a bit of this is shown on the wash-

Figure 105. *The anthemion and its near relation the palmette. Not difficult to copy and useful for the centre of a chair-back or filling a small recessed panel as in figure 106*

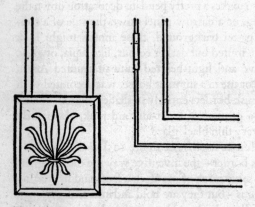

Figure 106

stand panels, *see* figure 97) are not strictly in period, but they are easy to do (use a large coin or button to trace off intersecting circles) and useful for filling small panels in a formalized way. It would take more space than this book allows to give a really wide range of possible motifs for painting. I suggest you take a notebook with you next time you go round a museum or stately home, and sketch ideas which appeal to you. They needn't be painted of course – most of the motifs shown here were carved, moulded, inlaid and treated in a variety of different ways in furniture of this period. Those copiously illustrated art and coffee-table books of which most libraries keep a good selection are another excellent source of ideas – better, really, because you can copy decorative motifs at your leisure. A larger and rather more complicated motif, like the flowering lyre illustrated (*see* figure 107), takes some time to copy accurately but is worth the trouble as it would make a very attractive decoration painted on the back of a chair or the centre of a long narrow table top. On a light background, paint it in shades of sepia or green; on a dark colour, in shades of off-white and burnt sienna.

Ornaments like satyr heads, grotesques, and classical faces (usually women's) might be painted at a key point in a formalized scheme of decoration, the top of chair legs, or the curved centre back of a chair splat. They were often executed in grisaille, which is a tricky technique

Figure 107. *An elegant flowering-lyre motif shown here combined with rosettes and acanthus leaves in an old mirror. Paint it in the back of a chair or in the centre of a long, shallow drawer, or on a box lid*

using shades of grey – or sepia – only, to suggest three-dimensional modelling. There were also many medallions showing impressionistically painted classical figures in flowing draperies. If you feel competent to tackle one of these more ambitious motifs, and they do look splendid done well, your best bet is to work from a large colour plate, copying slavishly, till you have mastered the technique.

If I have laid more emphasis on copying than following your inspiration it is because, as I have already said, you learn a great deal by trying to reproduce a motif accurately, and because the classical or traditional motifs are not easily improved upon. They are perennials unlike, say, the vagaries of Art Nouveau which look right one year and dated the next. You can find stylized daisies or rosettes on Egyptian tomb-furniture 3,000 years old and on cosmetic jars minted yesterday, and they look right for both. Once you have gained experience in using and adapting the reliable techniques outlined above, you will probably find yourself itching to modify them and try out more adventurous colour combinations and patterns of your own. This type of decoration needn't be – though it usually was – muted and restrained; it can look gaudy and gay as a peacock. A trip round the Brighton Pavilion will suggest brilliant colours and designs, many of them inspired by the then fashionable oriental lacquered wares. It's probably a good idea to try out your more daring ideas on a small scale – Dryad Handicrafts (Supplier's Index) sell small wooden boxes which are excellent for experimenting on – give the best ones away as presents. Old trays, cleaned down and carefully repainted, are naturals for decoration. Even old tea caddies, toffee tins and canisters, if they are in reasonable condition and nicely shaped, can be turned into attractive objects – the French had a name for painted tinware, *tôle*, and some of it is very covetable, and expensive. For designs, study any little period knick-knacks, painted boxes, trays, needlework boxes, tea caddies. Metal seems to look better painted in a dark, rich colour – pale colours show up minute imperfections in the painting and look slightly gritty, because rubbing down works less well on a non-porous material. Tin can look pretty left in its natural state, decorated in colours applied direct to the metal, and varnished several times over.

Marbling wood

Marble is very beautiful and its richly variegated colouring and formations have inspired many imitations. My own favourite is the stylized marbled paper widely used in bookbinding during the nineteenth century. If you like old books you must have known that flash of delight on opening a sober leather binding and coming upon one of these exquisite papers where wave pursues wave of colour across the page.

I had hopes when I began researching this book that I might track down some wonderfully simple old formula for marbling paper so that we could all henceforth dwell in marbled halls. But I found that while do-it-yourself marbling equipment exists (Dryad Handicrafts [Suppliers' Index] supply it) the results are only a pale ghost of the nineteenth-century papers. The beauty of the old methods, it seems, derives as much from the composition of the colours they used as from the actual technique, not vastly complicated by modern standards. Basically, marbling is done by floating colours on a denser substance like gum tragacanth, combing them into the characteristic patterns, laying a piece of paper prepared with size on top and removing it with marbling attached. The Turks are said to have discovered the technique some centuries ago – hence the name 'Turkish stone' given to one characteristic pattern. I have seen modern papers which attempt to reproduce the old hand-combed effects by mechanical printing processes, but even the best of these look more like multi-coloured salami than marble. I've no doubt some enterprising person will revive the old techniques before long, and do very nicely out of printing expensive marbled papers for de-luxe editions. In the meantime, marbled papers seem to have gone the way of many other old and pretty things.

Another way of getting a marbled effect, crude by comparison but effective in the right place and fun to do, is by floating artists' oil-colours, considerably thinned in turpentine, on a trough of plain water. This looks best on small objects like turned-wood lamp-bases (which one can buy cheaply from shops which specialize in lampshade frames, etc.), picture frames and wooden boxes. The object should be prepared by painting or staining it (see dyeing wood) in an appropriate colour, something fairly dark and not too bright for preference. Work out your marbled colour-scheme, drop blobs of the thinned colours onto the water (a large baking tin can stand in as a trough), swirl them about with a stick till you have got an interesting pattern, and then quickly touch your lamp-base or box to the colours, turning it so that it gets a bit of pattern all over. With a little practice you will find you can transfer the colours where you want them. Leave to dry hard, and then varnish.

Finally we come to the marbling technique which is really a cunning forgery of the real thing – real marble, I mean – rendered in paints and glazes. This form of *trompe-l'oeil* marbling has been in use for a very long time wherever decorators and designers wanted the look of marble for a fraction the cost and weight of crystalline or granular limestone. Used on a large scale, on woodwork, pillars or panelling, marbling usually aims for an impressionist likeness with large, loose veining and not too much detail. Over smaller surfaces, like table tops, and panels on painted furniture, it is often so skilfully done that you almost have to touch it to realize that it *is* painted wood.

To do this type of marbling successfully – and I don't think it's beyond the reach of anyone with some experience of handling paints and glazes and a knack for sensitive copying – the first requisite for beginners is either a piece of real marble to copy, or a large piece of one of the marbled wallpapers made by most of the wallpaper manufacturers. If you are thinking of marbling a table top you need some idea of how the veining and groups of stone-like shapes would be disposed over an area of real marble of roughly the same size. Trying to enlarge a small section over a larger area means you tend to repeat the same pattern over and over again, which isn't the way of real marble. Having got a pattern to work from, the rest isn't too difficult. Here I shall only give the standard procedures for reproducing two popular types of marble – verd-antique and rouge roi.

First, some general information about equipment and preparation. Wood should be prepared for marbling by sanding, smoothing and filling (if necessary) to as perfect a surface as possible. New wood needs a coat or two of wood primer. Then two or three coats of undercoat in broken white – white with a little raw or burnt umber added. If you are aiming for the darkest type of verd-antique marble, you should use a dark undercoat, black in this instance. The undercoat should be left to dry hard. The colours used are artists' oil-colours, thinned in a medium made up of two parts real turpentine to one linseed oil and a little oil dryers. All these can be obtained from artists' supply shops. A selection of standard artists' brushes plus a bunch of feathers (goose-wing for preference), a small sponge and a few rags should see you all right as regards tools. Experts use a 'badger' and 'softener' about 3½ inches wide but amateurs can usually get by without specialist equipment which is chiefly designed to save the professional time.

Verd-antique

This is one of the most distinguished marbles, often used for the tops of antique console tables, especially where there is a lot of carving and gilding. It is predominantly green, with some black and white. The green varies from almost black to the colour of spinach soup diluted with cream. If you want to be pedantic, it belongs to the 'brecciated serpentine' type of marble.

All the steps below follow closely upon one another unless otherwise stated. Over your ground colour apply a transparent wash of mid-Brunswick green dirtied with a touch of black. Apply the first veins and streaks with the tips of a bunch of feathers dipped into mid-Brunswick green thinned to transparency with oil medium. Over this, apply a paler network of veins, using the green, lightened with a little white but still transparent. The idea is to break up and complicate the darker under-veining with lighter, more opaque colours, rather like small capilliaries branching off main veins. Leave some areas untouched, in the plain green background colour. Using a large soft brush 'soften' the veining here and there, so it doesn't look too sharply defined. Now, with an eye on your photo or piece of wallpaper or marble, add the pebbly shapes, which range in size and colour from near black or dark grey to transparent white. The largest are dark; the small groups usually white and set in a network of green veining. Use your imagination to achieve as much variation as possible in the shapes, sharpness and opacity of these stone shapes. Use washes of black, greenish black and grey, and sometimes use these together for a cloudy effect. When you have got the general effect of the marble right – veining, disposition of stone shapes, and colours – leave the paint to set (the dryers will speed this up) before adding the finer detail and final touches. Small white and black shapes should be painted in with a fine sable pencil. Vary the white by using it opaque, semi-transparent and transparent, and tinting it here and there with a little yellow ochre. Larger areas of darker colour can be enriched by glazing with thin washes of contrasting colour – green over black, grey over green. Touch in fine veining with a sable pencil and pale green. Add fine veining round and across the large stones. When quite dry, the marbling can be over-glazed with the medium lightly tinted with a little black and green to soften, unify and add depth to the colours.

Rouge roi

The colouring of this handsome marble is predominantly red-brown, as the name suggests, broken by irregular patches of bluish-grey and white, streaked with a few opaque white veins. In spite of the rich colouring it has an effect of transparency.

To prepare the surface for marbling, cover the white undercoat with a very thin blue-grey wash of the medium. Brush or sponge it on and then immediately break up the colour by stippling some areas with a brush and wiping others with a rag till only the faintest blue-grey tone is left. Leave to dry.

The reddish colour is made by mixing Venetian red and a little ochre with the medium to a transparent consistency. Colour in some of the larger reddish masses of the marble, applying the colour over the tinted parts, leaving some veins pure white and some grey patches untouched. Now vary the red patches, darkening some with a thin wash of burnt sienna, others with Indian red and a spot of black. All the colours will still be quite fluid at this stage; now you want to break up the uniformity of the red areas to uncover some of the greyish ground-colour. To create a stony look take a piece of crumpled paper, dip it in turps and then in a little blue-black colour, and use it to stipple the red areas here and there to create a great variety of tints. If the turps seems to be running amok, check it by dabbing the surface lightly with a rag. Use a brush to break up the red patches further, very lightly. Now the plain grey patches must be varied, covering some with a thin white wash, others with a darker grey one. Outline the larger grey patches with grey or white. White veining can be strengthened with dilute white, broken with a touch of ochre here and there. When the marbling is quite dry, the whole thing can be pulled together by a very dilute blue-black glaze. Any fine lines can be added with a sable pencil in Indian red.

VARNISHING. Marbling definitely needs to be varnished, both for protection and to simulate the dull gleam of polished stone. Use the very best and palest – i.e. water coloured – varnish. There is a brand called Marble White, which you might be able to track down if you have a shop in your area which supplies the trade. Otherwise ask for water-white varnish. A good tip is to coat the surface with gloss varnish first and then, when this is quite hard, with eggshell varnish. The eggshell varnish should be rubbed down with powdered pumice (you can use Vim instead) to a dull sheen. The gloss varnish beneath gives the marbling depth.

Section 3

Pretty Things

In this section I have tried to collect together a catholic selection of pretty and/or useful things which are cheap and fun to make. Ranging from Victorian pincushions to punched tinware, and taking in such diverse items as tie-and-dye, and Jumping Jacks. Not many things to wear, because fashions change at such dizzying speed, but I have included some I thought would look as good in ten years time as now – a child's pinafore and a traditional country labourer's smock pattern for an adult and adapted for a young child. There is also advice on remodelling fur coats and sewing leather, which you may not have attempted before. A section on trimmings seemed a good idea – a couple of yards of deep hand-knotted wool fringe does a lot for a long skirt or a big cape collar, and silk cord and tassels make all the difference to cushions and curtain tie-backs. And there are some suggestions for patchwork quilting and canvas work.

Presents are always a problem when you're hard up, and it's depressing to come empty-handed to the feast. So I have included some ideas – silhouette pictures, attractively papered box files, keepsake pebbles – which don't cost much or take long to make, but would make imaginative and pretty presents. For children, there's a collection of toys, mostly derived from Victorian times, which seems to me the golden age of toys. Some physical strength is needed to make the wooden toys, unless you have a power tool to do the basic shaping for you. My husband made the two photographed, with no more experience than some carpentry lessons at school. It took some groaning and cursing to get them just right, but on the whole he enjoyed himself. There's something magical about whittling and shaping a block of wood, paring it gradually away till at last the perfect shape is revealed – definitely a compulsive activity, so be prepared for woodshavings and sawdust everywhere.

If you like making pretty things you should learn to hoard, if you haven't already. Odd scraps of beautiful old materials, old lace, buttons, trimmings, bead fringe, little bits of leather, old gloves, felt, printed papers, little boxes – the bigger your stock of all these unconsidered trifles, the more variety and charm you can introduce into the things you make. It may be years before you hit on the perfect use for that one yellow kid glove (pair of doll's shoes perhaps?) or scrap of tarnished gold lace (costumed picture?), but it is worth keeping one trunk, cupboard or chest to cram your bits and pieces into till the day comes. Stage designers usually have cupboards, even rooms, full of stuff like this. It's not just that decorative scraps and morsels bought from street-market stalls, Oxfam shops, jumble sales, secondhand clothes shops are cheaper, but that the old ones have more style, and were made of better materials than anything sold over the counter today. A patchwork made of tiny scraps of old materials may take a devil of a long time to complete, because you are waiting for a bit of pink or brown to complete a design, but it always looks nicer than one made from specially bought remnants of new fabric. And it is extraordinary, if you keep your eyes open, how much you can still find in the way of decorative bits and pieces in spite of the growing number of dealers interested. My local Oxfam shop has a box full of scraps, mostly worthless, but delving in sometimes produces odd lengths of Victorian silk and satin, faded old silk ribbons with pinked edges, yards of hand-embroidered broderie anglaise, bead fringe, lace, innumerable odd gloves. I have seen pretty patchwork cushion-covers made entirely from old silk ties, paisley designs mixed with geometric and polka dots. (Unpick the tie and use the wrong side of the material, which is the same in design, but much cleaner.) Old lampshade frames, in reasonable condition, and old cushions, down ones particularly, are worth collecting.

The very symbol of neediness, in my mother's eyes, is turning old woollen clothes inside out and remaking them. Actually, it's not as daft as it might sound (to a non-pauper) because secondhand stalls abound in sensible country lady tweeds of excellent quality and generous cut which look a lot better cut up and remade than most cheap fabrics sold by the yard. You do have to cut your coat to suit your cloth, of course, but there's a lot of material in those big shapeless coats and genteelly flared skirts. I made a pair of fringed culottes from an immense flared plaid skirt which have been much admired. Some people shudder at the idea of wearing old clothes, however clean and respectable. If that is one of your phobias it can't be helped, but it seems a pity when an outlay of

25p or so, and a little ingenuity, can produce an odd skirt or waistcoat in the sort of material one cannot normally afford.

SARTORIAL

Sewing fur

Nothing gives such an instant feeling of luxury as a fur. Old fur coats are not as easy to come by as they were, but if you look hard in the likeliest places – secondhand shops, Oxfam establishments, antique markets, even cards in tobacconist windows – you may still find one in reasonably good condition for a few pounds. The cut and fit probably won't be up to much but this doesn't matter because you can remake, or remodel it as the furriers say, very successfully. Avoid furs with bald spots in the middle of the front or back (unless you think you can contrive some small garment, like a jerkin, from the good bits) but worn patches round the neck and pockets and fronts can all be trimmed away. The easiest skins for beginners to sew are the ones made up of large skins with a tough hide – sheepskin and ponyskin for instance, not strictly fur at all. The sheepskin sleeveless coat photographed was made from a fluffy garment I found in a church bazaar two years ago, for 50p. Furs made up of scores of tiny skins machined together are trickier to alter for several reasons – you have to make sure the pile runs the same way, the skins are often fragile and one's handstitching doesn't look quite as neat as the original machining. I have chopped up moleskin coats and made skirts and waistcoats, so it can be done, but it is fiddly.

One pleasant thing about buying old fur coats is that it allays conscience pangs over the slaughter of wild animals – the deed was done a long time ago.

Having got your fur home, the first step is to clean it. Sprinkle light coloured furs with fuller's earth, or talc, roll up loosely and leave overnight in a warm place, like an airing cupboard. Dark coloured furs are cleaned the same way with bran, warmed a little in the oven and rubbed in. The next day, shake the fur and brush it the way of the hairs with a soft brush.

If your fur happens to be a good fit and the styling is all right, you may only need to make a few alterations. Worn patches round the front edges can sometimes be disguised by sewing a leather strip over the top, as I did with the sheepskin coat. Or, if it was designed to wrap over at the front, you might be able to cut the worn parts back so that the coat fits edge to edge. To do this unpick the lining round the inside facings, open out the facings and cut along the seam from the back with a sharp Stanley knife. Then trim away the worn parts, making sure you don't remove so much that the fronts won't meet. You will probably have to cut down the facings too, to fit. Stitch back as described below. If odd parts need to be completely replaced, like the collar, and you don't feel a collarless coat is the answer, you could shorten the coat all round and use the bits to make a new collar, taking the old collar as a pattern. (Try and match the way the skins lie.)

But, as a rule, an old fur looks better completely remade. To do this, take out the lining and interlinings with a sharp pair of scissors – unpick them, don't cut them out. Then, with a Stanley knife, cut the fur into its basic parts – back, fronts, sleeves, facings, collar – by cutting along the main seams from the inside. Try not to press too hard, or you will cut away a lot of fur. Coats often have slit or slash pockets and it's best to leave these for the time being. Then lay all your pieces out on the floor,

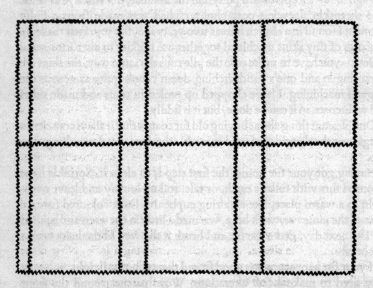

Figure 108. *Some furs (mole, squirrel, rabbit) are made up of a mosaic of small skins*

to get an idea of the basic shapes and sizes, which you need to work out in order to convert them. A straight sack-like coat won't convert into a flared shape – the fronts might be wide enough but the back hardly ever is. When you have decided on a suitable style, get yourself a paper pattern. Choose one with a clean, lively shape, not too many seams and as few inset bits – yokes, gussets – as possible. If you already have a pattern you like, that's better still because you will know beforehand what needs to be done to make it fit. Fitting is a problem with fur because you can't pin or tack the pieces together. Sellotaping or stapling along the seams from the back isn't very strong, but it will give you some idea. It's worth doing because there is nothing so maddening as unpicking a seam you have just laboriously stitched up. Long-haired furs, incidentally, need the simplest shapes of all – boxy collarless jackets are probably the best bet.

Now lay your pattern pieces out on the fur to see how they fit. Try and keep the fur pieces the same way round as they were in the original coat, otherwise you will get the hairs running in a different direction, which changes the colour – as with velvet. Similarly, if you have to add bits on here and there make sure the fur runs the same way and keep your joins as much like the original ones as possible. With sheepskin this doesn't matter so much, though you want to match the joined-on piece carefully. Fur is sewn edge to edge so you should trim off all the seam allowance round the pattern, and cut out the V-shaped darts. Now mark the pattern onto the fur on the skin side with chalk or crayon, or red biro if the skin is a light colour. Sellotape it down if it moves about. Cut round the chalked line with the Stanley knife – you can use a razor blade, but a Stanley knife is easier to control. Again, don't use too much pressure in case you slice off the fur on the other side – you don't want bald seams. To get rid of slit pockets, carefully unpick the old pocket and any facings and sew up the slit as described below. If the fur is very worn here, you may be able to stick a patch pocket on top, or alternatively, you might be able to take in a dart which will trim off the worn bits. (But only if your pattern is for a fitted coat.) When your coat is cut out, Sellotape the pieces together to give you an idea of how well it fits. The shoulders may be too wide, or the sleeves might need narrowing a little. Now is the time to make any necessary alterations. Trim off bits as necessary, but go carefully. Better to take off two narrow strips than one piece so much too wide it spoils the coat.

Figure 109. *When joining pieces on, to widen a hem for instance, do not cut straight across the original mosaic, as in (a), because the fur will not blend properly across the seam and it will show. For a professional looking seam follow the contour of the skins as in (b)*

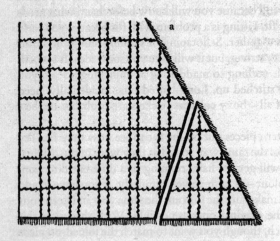

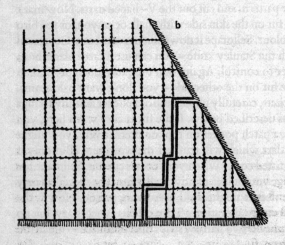

When it fits to your satisfaction, remove all the Sellotape. To sew the fur you need glovers' needles (fine grade for delicate skins, thicker for stout ones like sheepskin). These are essential, as the triangular shape prevents the skins tearing and splitting as you sew. Any good haberdasher's or draper's shop stocks them. I use button thread, which works quite well. And a thimble protects your finger, even if you have never worn one before, and gives you more push when stitching tough skins. To stitch up a seam, bring the two edges together, skin side uppermost, and oversew firmly but not too tightly, with fairly close even stitches. I usually do a double row, from top to bottom and then back up again, like cross-stitch. But don't pull the stitches too tight, or you will get a ridge inside when the seam is opened out flat. There should be just enough give in the stitches to let the seam lie quite flat. Stitch any darts up the same way. To strengthen the main seams of the coat, you can glue $\frac{1}{2}$ or $\frac{3}{4}$-inch cotton tape over them, on the skin side of course. Copydex is probably the best adhesive for this as it has a bit of give in it – leatherworkers usually use animal glue, for the same reason, but this is not easy to get hold of.

Interfacings should also be glued in place. Use a fairly soft, lightweight material for interfacings and cut them 1 inch wider than facings. Ordinary calico would do; you don't want to stiffen the facings so much as prevent too much stretching in use. Facings down the fronts, round the neckline and cuffs, are stitched on in the same way. Keep pushing the fur down inside as you go. A leather binding, like the one I used on the coat photographed, looks good on a sporty sort of fur coat, and gives a good strong edge. You can use a soft calf or suede in a toning or contrasting colour. Another possibility is a knitted rib binding, as on a cardigan. Leather bindings are hard on the fingers because you have to push your needle through a double thickness of leather as well as the fur, but if you do have a leather binding you may be able to dispense with facings, bringing the lining up to the edge of the coat instead. I did this with the sheepskin coat, which is lined edge to edge with canvas bought from a marine store. It was quite a good choice for this particular coat, as it gives it lots of swing, but it does get filthy very quickly, being white. I wouldn't recommend it for anything more fitted, which needs a slippery lining or it will creep about over your clothes.

Fastenings are a problem with fur coats. Buttonholes are out of the question. You can have fur buttons, with loops – a bit dowagerish. Or, for invisible fastenings, you could use the giant hooks and eyes sold for the purpose, covered with thread. I solved the problem with the sheepskin by using brass clips and loops, and stitching leather leaf-shaped pieces over the top to hide the fixings. The leaves looked unexpectedly decorative, with a quilted effect because of the sheepskin padding them out, so I seized on this and added a few larger leaves at strategic points – over the old slit pockets and on the shoulders. The idea behind this wasn't purely decorative – as the pieces were stitched right through to the canvas they helped to anchor the heavy lining to the fur, as well as strengthening seams which would get a lot of wear. Another way of strengthening seams on something like a man's jerkin, which will get some bashing in use, is to sew a strip of leather along them on the out-side, with ordinary running stitches along both sides of the strip. It looks handsome, but takes time.

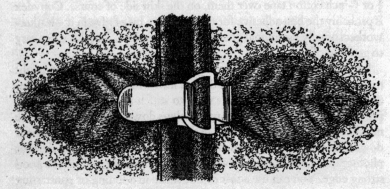

Figure 110. *Leather leaf-shapes used to anchor brass loop and clip*

Softer furs don't lend themselves so well to these butch trimmings. Best stick to fur facings for these. The lining should be a good-quality crêpe or satin. You might be able to use the old lining, after putting it through a coin-op cleaner. Cut the lining according to your pattern, *not* cutting the seam allowance away this time. Machine up as usual. Press the seams open. An interlining is a bore to make, but the advantage of it on a fur coat is that once the interlining – use that soft, fleecy stuff sold for coat interlining – is caught down to the coat here and there along the main seams, you can catch the hem down to the interlining rather than to the skin itself. The most elegant way to finish a lining is to sew a narrow binding of the lining material, cut on the cross, round the edges, except for the hem, which is turned up separately, and not stitched down to the coat hem. To fix lining in place, turn the coat inside out, pin to the interfacing and then sew it to the facings with large stitches. As with all linings, you want to make sure it is easy enough not to pull your coat out of shape. To turn up the coat hem, stitch a band of wide cotton tape the width of the hem, laying it on top of the fur and sewing it down with running stitch. Then, catch the top edge of the tape down to the coat itself, using large hemming stitches which should not be pulled too tight. When possible, stitch through seams, interlinings, rather than the actual skins. The lining hem is usually anchored to the coat hem by a buttonholed bar at each side seam.

Sewing leather

Anyone who has learnt to make good-looking, well-fitting clothes for themselves in conventional fabrics can confidently turn to dressmaking with leather. Leather isn't cheap to buy, but if you are prepared to take some trouble over the making, you can produce clothes with a real *couture* look about them for a relatively small outlay. The only serious difficulty when sewing leather clothes is that you can't tack them for fitting in the usual way, because pins and needles mark the hides. Paper clips and Sellotape will hold the garment together roughly, but the best solution is to use a pattern pre-tested for fit – either a pattern you have used before, or a new one which you try out first using calico or some other cheap material to make what the *couturiers* call a 'toile'. Any adjustments needed are made on the toile and then the toile itself can be used as a pattern for cutting the leather. Always use a reliable paper pattern when making leather clothes because the stuff is too expensive to experiment with. Alternatively, take to pieces a favourite pair of pants, or waistcoat which is getting shabby, and use these as a pattern.

BUYING LEATHER. Many of the big stores now sell leather for home dressmaking. You can also buy it at most craft shops, though these do not always stock large skins (*see also* Suppliers' Index).

There is a wide choice available in leather – everything from the softest chamois, which makes up into marvellously supple shirts, to heavy brushed suedes and pigskins for tough coats and jackets. You can buy antiqued calfskins; suedes so fine they drape almost like satin; snakeskin and shiny patent-finish skins for trimmings. Soft suedes and chamois are the easiest to sew and handle – you can have gathers, tucks, bound buttonholes in skins as soft as these. Crisp, lightweight calfskin is good for sharply tailored clothes, jackets, skirts, coats. The heavier skins are more difficult to handle easily, and it takes a lot of care to avoid lumpy seams – wherever thick fabrics would present problems a sturdy hide presents rather more. The difficulties aren't insuperable though, and these skins look really handsome made up into coats, pants, anything which needs strength and body to it.

It is useful when buying leather to make up a pattern, to have a rough idea of how to convert yardage into square feet, which is how most leather is sold. One yard of 54-inch fabric equals 13 square feet, so consult the yardage requirements in a 54-inch fabric on the back of your pattern and multiply by 13. Because hides are irregularly shaped and some parts of the skins may not be suitable for the main pattern pieces, it's wise to add on a bit extra to allow for this – about $\frac{1}{3}$ of the total already worked out.

Examine the skins you are buying individually for faults like weak spots, holes and discolorations. These are usually round the outside of the skin, but it is as well to check.

PATTERNS. The pattern firms have begun issuing patterns specially for leather clothes, but a lot of their standard patterns can be used equally well if you choose something suited to the handling qualities, weight and style of your skins. Avoid 'dressmaker' styles, soft-looking clothes with gathers, fine detailing, tricky collars, yokes, etc., unless you are very experienced – only the finest suedes are suitable for these anyway. Go for patterns which owe their shape and fit to well-placed seams rather than darts. Seams can be made a decorative feature by top stitching or lapping, and this makes the garment stronger at the same time. Darts are difficult to do successfully – it's hard to taper them off neatly, and ridges tend to show on the right side. You can save on leather by adding strategic seams of your own. Pants, long skirts, coats, all of which use long unbroken lengths of material, can be made up in sections instead – seams at the knee and/or across the thigh with pants, seams across long skirts or coats. The strongest part of a skin is down the middle, which corresponds to the animal's back, and your main pattern-pieces should be cut from this part of the skins, so avoid patterns which use a lot of flare or fullness like swing-back coats.

MATERIALS. You need some extra equipment for sewing leather. Sharp scissors, chalk for marking out patterns, and Sellotape and paper clips for holding the pieces together for fitting. Use medium to heavy sewing-machine needles – size 11 for fine suedes, 14 for soft calfskin, 16 for heavier skins. For handsewing, use medium-sized glover's needles, which are three-sided and designed to pierce leather without tearing. The right thread for machining is important – use a good-quality pure silk or one of the new polyester threads because stretch and strength are needed. Some sort of mallet – a steak tenderizer perhaps – padded round the head with several layers of flannel is useful for flattening seams. Use an adhesive like Copydex for sticking seams down. Paper comes in handy too – brown paper for pressing and tissue paper for stitching through along a seam where the machine's feed–teeth might mark the skin. A leather punch or awl is useful for punching neat holes for thonging, or eyelets, or just to make decorative patterns. Leather is stretchy, and interlining round collars and cuffs, down the fronts, and at other strain points, gives a leather garment a much crisper shape and prevents it drooping with wear. Use Vilene, or light tailors' canvas for heavier skins. Skirts should be lined to prevent sagging.

CUTTING OUT. Lay all the skins out flat on a large table and try out the pattern pieces to get the most economical arrangement. With napped

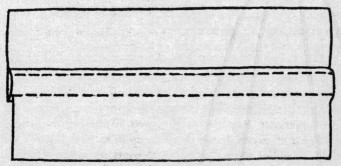

Figure 111. *Lapped topstitched seams look handsome, are much tougher and save leather*

suedes make sure the nap runs the same way on all the pieces – test by running your hand over it. Keep main pattern pieces to the middle of the skins; smaller pieces like pockets, collars, facings, round the edges. As I mentioned earlier, use a pattern previously made up in fabric, so you know what needs altering to make it fit perfectly. (A 'toile' would be excessive in the case of a simple straightforward garment like a flared skirt or a jerkin, but for anything more elaborate like a full-length coat, it's a sensible idea. You don't want to make mistakes with an expensive garment.) Where every inch counts, there are various ways of making your leather stretch farther. Cut seam allowances down to $\frac{1}{2}$ inch, since

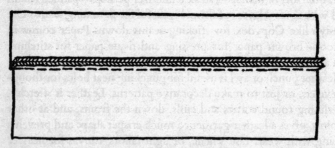

Figure 112. *Most economical of all – seams edge-stitched on* right *side of garment*

Figure 113. *Edge-stitched seams used to emphasize structure of a gored skirt*

leather doesn't fray. Top-stitched, lapped seams (*see* figure 111) look good and are twice as strong as the conventional type. Cut seam allowances further still by using an edge-to-edge seam on the *right side* of the garment, like the decorative seams you find on some handstitched gloves (*see* figures 112 and 113). The seam allowance can be as little as $\frac{1}{8}$ inch, provided the leather is fairly tough, and it is a pleasant way of emphasizing the basic structure of a skirt or coat. On heavy brushed suedes and the like, use narrow lapped seams wherever possible to reduce bulk and streamline the shape, and capitalize on leather's non-fraying qualities by top-stitching raw edges together down facings, round collars, cuffs, pockets, etc., instead of stitching on the wrong side and turning as one has to do with fabrics. Stitch a thin interlining between all these top-stitched raw edges to prevent the leather stretching too much. Any crosswise seams you have added to the pattern to stretch the leather farther should be marked and cut on the pattern-pieces beforehand, and the separate sections clearly marked so you know what all these odd-shaped bits mean.

Fix pattern-pieces to the leather with small strips of Sellotape placed crosswise. Check that you haven't missed anything out. Cut round with sharp shears.

FITTING. Little fitting should be needed if you have tested the pattern beforehand. Lapped seams can be taped down with Sellotape; the usual kind of seam held together with paper clips or stapled if you have a small stapler. Use clips or staples for set-in sleeves, which are usually the trickiest part of a garment to get just right. Staple inside the seam allowance so the holes won't show when the garment is stitched up.

MACHINING. Use longer stitches than if you were sewing fabric. Ten stitches to the inch with fine skins, eight for heavier ones. Experiment on odd scraps of leather to see how the machine behaves. You will probably have to reduce pressure on the machine foot to accommodate two thicknesses of leather. Machine slowly at a regular pace. Don't let the needle rush away unchecked because too many stitches on one spot can tear leather. Don't pull on the threads when finishing off a seam for the same reason. If the skins are delicate and liable to mark, stitch a layer of tissue in with the seam, the paper underneath the layers of leather. With shiny, slippery skins where the machine has difficulty gripping, try sewing between two thicknesses of tissue or dusting the surface with talcum powder. Machining the heavier leathers is hard work for the machine so oil it and clean it before using, making sure you get rid of any excess oil before sewing the leather. Don't try and take sudden bumps – where several thicknesses overlap – in a hurry because you will probably break the needle. Guide the machine over these a stitch at a time.

SEAMS. Plain seams, machined right sides together, are opened out flat. Stick the edges down with a little Copydex and gently bang with a padded mallet to flatten still further. On fine skins, press gently on the wrong side over brown paper with a warm iron. Do the same with darts. Nick curving seams at intervals to make them lie flat. Pare away the thicknesses of leather in bulky, hidden seams – such as collars, facings – just as you would for fabric, except that leather should be skived, properly speaking. To do this, use a sharp knife, lay the leather down on something which won't scratch and pare the excess away on a slant. This reduces the bulk considerably. This is not necessary with fine skins, which are trimmed with scissors the usual way.

HEMS. With thick hides the hems can be left unturned, just as they are. With lighter calfskins and suedes, turn back the hem allowance and stick down with Copydex.

FASTENINGS. These present no problem with light suedes and malleable calfskins, where bound buttonholes are quite easy to make. You can make stitched buttonholes, using buttonhole twist, on heavy skins but it might be safer to think of some other means of fastening. Use a heavy metal zip and make a decorative feature of it. Instead of hiding it in a seam, cut back the seam allowance round the zip and machine the raw edges down flat either side so that the zip shows as a flash of metal. Buy the hammer-on type of snap fastening from one of the big stores specializing in trimmings. These come in various sizes and patterns, and are not difficult to attach to clothes except where you are trying to fix them through two layers of a thick skin, where it may be necessary to punch holes before inserting the snaps. As a change from straightforward snap fastenings you could use tab fastenings, held down by snaps at one or both ends. Lacing is another possibility, which looks good on Davy Crockett type clothes in heavy suedes. For lacing you need an eyeletting tool and brass eyelets (craft shops, big stores). Use $\frac{1}{4}$-inch leather thongs or thin cord for laces. Lacing looks better and lies flatter, especially down a pants fly-seam, if you machine a flap of leather to one side of the laced fastening, as one does when inserting a zip.

Trimmings

SADDLE STITCHING. Handsewn decorative stitching in a contrasting coloured thread round pockets, facings, collars gives class to most leather clothes. Use a strong glover's needle and linen thread or buttonhole twist. Wax the thread on a lump of beeswax to make it run smoothly and prevent knots. Sew with quite large stitches – $\frac{1}{4}$-inch – on the right side, setting them close together by taking a small stitch on the back. Wear a thimble to help push the needle through thick, stiff skins. Don't try to take up more than one stitch at a time but push the needle through from one side to the other – this stitching takes time, so don't embark on a whole coat unless you have time and patience and strong fingers.

FRINGEING. Fringe is a natural for heavy suedes. You can have fringeing as deep and thick as you like – 5-inch fringes down outside pant-legs and sleeve seams look marvellous in motion. The easiest fringeing to do is by adding on a few inches when cutting out a hem, or round a collar, and cutting back to the depth of fringe wanted with a sharp knife. Machine round above a fringed hem done this way to prevent the leather tearing up. A separate strip of fringe machined on is stronger and looks handsomer, especially when doubled so that it forms loops. To make looped fringe fold a long strip of leather twice the depth of the fringe wanted plus 1 inch for the heading, and cut from the folded side to within $\frac{1}{2}$ inch of the other two edges. You can cut the loops any width you like, from spaghetti-fine to noodle-wide. To sew on, lay the heading flat round a skirt hem and machine down with two rows of stop stitching, or insert it into a seam (as with pant-legs) by sandwiching it, fringes to the inside, between the two pieces of leather to be seamed. The fringe heading should come to the edge of the garment seams. Staple the thicknesses together to keep them under control while machining. Single fringe is made in the same way except that the band for fringeing is not doubled.

BINDING. Binding the edges of a garment with the same, or contrasting leather, looks good and gives a strong, firm finish. On soft skins bind with a strip twice the desired width plus $\frac{1}{4}$ inch, and stitch on by machine as for bias binding with the difference that the fold-back edge of the leather strip is not turned under for hemming. The raw edge can be hemmed down by hand using glover's needle and buttonhole twist on the wrong side, or machined down flat so that the line of machining comes a fraction below the binding on the right side. On heavier skins the easiest method is to simply fold the strip round the raw edges and machine both sides in place at once.

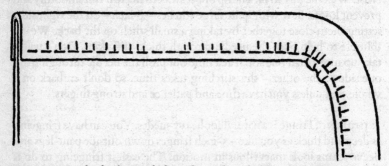

Figure 114. *Leather binding stitched round raw edges of a heavy leather garment. Staple binding strip down here and there, removing the staples as you machine*

PUNCHING. Punching decorative patterns of holes is easy with a leather punch which can be set to produce holes of different sizes. Don't punch the garment proper too recklessly though, as too many holes will weaken it. One way round this problem is to back the punched areas with a contrast piece of leather which shows through the holes. Whole yokes, patch pockets, etc., worked like this look very dashing. Best to punch the pieces and back them (use a little adhesive on the punched side to stick to the backing) before making up. Alternatively, punch long strips of

Figure 115. *Punch holes in a strip of matching or contrasting leather, and pink the edges for a decorative trimming*

matching or contrast leather about 1-1½ inches wide, cut with pinking shears, to make a trimming which looks like leather lace and can be sewn in bands round skirts, sleeves, or down jacket-fronts. A few brass eye-letted holes, done purely for decoration, look flashy round pockets, yokes. Leave them as they are or thread strips or thongs of leather through them, like ribbon insertion.

APPLIQUÉ. Appliquéed shapes – figurative or abstract – are easy and amusing to do with leather, as there are no fraying edges to cope with. Cut shapes from scraps of leather, mixing skins and colours as you like, and try out the effect by sticking them down with Sellotape before trying the garment on. Stick to the garment with Copydex, and top-stitch by hand or machine round the edges. Buttonholing instead of top-stitching gives a pleasantly primitive look.

OTHER SUGGESTIONS. Braid, webbing, bead embroidery, bands of snakeskin (unpick old skin bags bought in jumble sales for a cheap source).

Smocks for all seasons

The countryman's smock (*see* inset) of sturdy, sober linen or twill, richly embroidered, was a fine combination of the practical and decorative. Smocks have a long history. They were worn in Shake-speare's day, and the last recorded instance of smock-wearing was well into this century. Traditionally, smocks were embroidered in symbols connected with the various rural trades – shepherd, woodsman, butcher, gardener – and different counties had their favourite colour schemes, so that a keen-eyed employer at one of the hiring fairs would have been able to tell at a glance what you did and where you came from.

A modern countryman would hardly be seen dead in a smock, how-ever picturesque, but they look very fetching on pretty girls, make excellent maternity garments and, on small, active children (*see* Kate Greenaway), they look particularly beguiling, as well as being com-fortable and hard-wearing.

I have included a pattern for a child's smock because Alice Armes' standard work (Dryad Press) doesn't deal with small-scale garments, and a child's version takes half the time to work. The only part of smock-making which presents any real difficulty is the smocking itself, which needs to be accurately gathered up and stitched to hang properly. The embroidery looks elaborate because it is so thickly applied, but the basic stitches are the simplest – featherstitch, chain – and it is pleasant work to do sitting in the sun or in front of the box.

For a child's smock, choose one of the really tough, hard-wearing materials – holland, button twill, linen, even unbleached calico. A well-made smock in a strong material should last through quite a succession of wearers. For an adult, one can afford to be impractical – a smock worked in white on a soft, black, pure silk, for instance, would look suavely elegant and not a bit rustic. The *sine qua non* of smock-making is that the thread used for smocking and embroidery must match the actual stuff – linen on linen, silk on silk, cotton for cotton. As to colours, you can suit yourself. Traditionally white on white was usual, though some counties preferred white on blue, brown on olive green, white on black. The two smocks shown in our photograph, both of them beauti-fully worked by my mother, used strongly contrasting colours – the child's version is vivid blue linen worked in white, while the adult's is embroidered in russet on a natural coloured 'crash', a linen and cotton mixture with a homespun look and pleasantly springy texture.

Child's smock

The pattern given is for a four-year-old child, but a three-year-old can wear it as a long smock and an older child could wear it as a hip-length top over jeans, so your painstaking work won't have to be put away after one season. You need just 2 yards of 36-inch-wide material. Linen, denim and flannel are all suitable. You can transfer the shapes to squared paper but since they are mostly simple rectangles it would be quicker to work out the measurements on the fabric using pins or chalk. Use the pattern layout as shown. Try and get your pattern pieces exactly aligned on the cross weave of the material before cutting – to do this draw a thread on the cutting line between two sections. This will make the gathering up for the smocking easier to do.

Begin with the smocking, as this takes longest, and you can relax and enjoy the rest when it is done. Mark out the boundaries of the smocked areas front and back with coloured thread. There is an embroidered

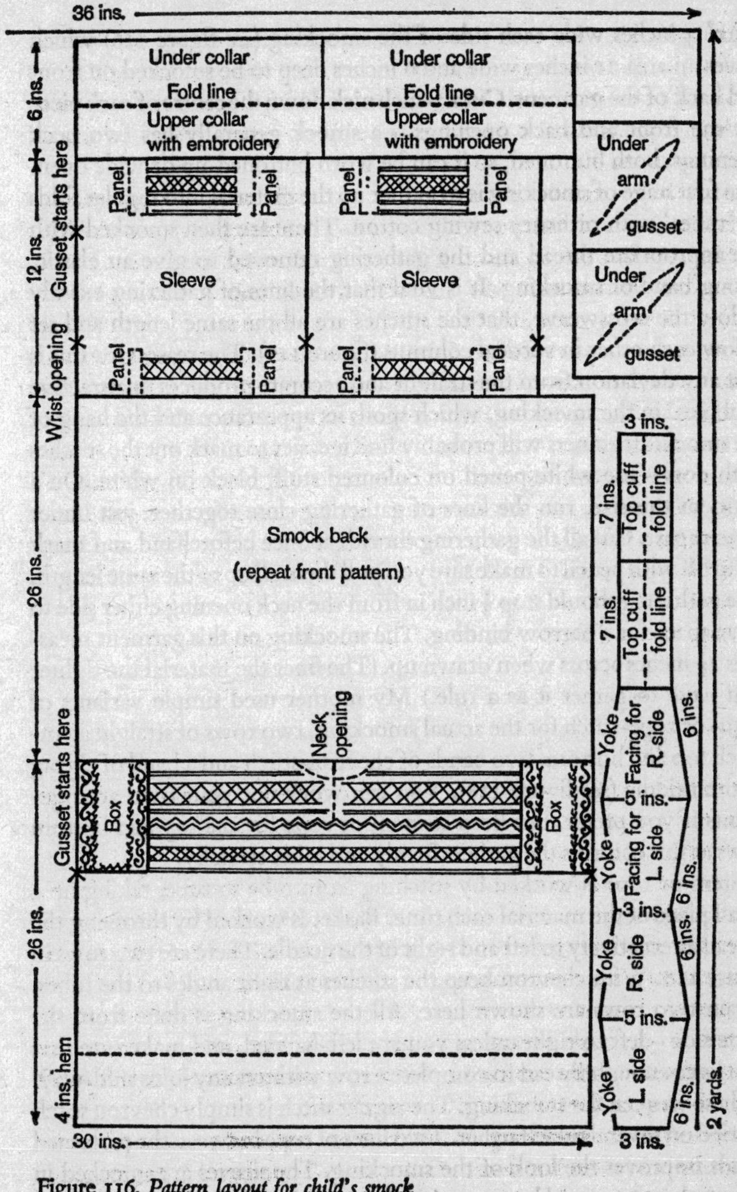

Figure 116. *Pattern layout for child's smock*

'box' 4 inches wide each side of the smocking (*see* figure 116) which leaves an area 21 inches wide and 6 inches deep to be smocked on front and back of the garment. Cut a 3-inch nick down the centre of each piece for the front and back openings – a smock generally has two neck openings, both buttoned, so it can be worn buttoned-up or wide open. The first stage of smocking is to gather up the material into regular folds or 'tubes' with ordinary sewing cotton. These are then smocked with the appropriate thread and the gathering removed to give an elastic, strong band of smocking. It is vital that the lines of gathering exactly follow the crossweave, that the stitches are all the same length and set below each other in vertical columns (figure 117). The reason for this is that any deviation from the straight and accurate produces unattractive 'bubbles' in the smocking, which spoils its appearance and the hang of the smock. Beginners will probably find it easier to mark out the stitches with dots – use white pencil on coloured stuff, black on white. On a garment this size, run the lines of gathering close together, just under ½ inch apart. Cut all the gathering threads at once beforehand and mark them off with pencil to make sure you pull them all up to the same length. The gathering should stop ½ inch in from the neck opening either side to leave space for a narrow binding. The smocking on this garment measures 4½ inches across when drawn up. (The finer the material the tighter you have to gather it as a rule.) My mother used simple variants of stem- or rope-stitch for the actual smocking, two rows of straight stem-stitch top and bottom, two bands of chevron-stitch and a band of zigzag in the middle (*see* figure 118). You can work out your own arrangements if you prefer, but keep to stem or rope for the top and bottom rows as this controls the gathers firmly and is less stretchy.

Stem or rope is worked by stitching from tube to tube, taking up a small piece of the material each time. Basket is worked by throwing the thread alternatively to left and right of the needle. There are two rows in figure 118. With chevron keep the stitches at right angles to the tubes. Again two rows are shown here. All the smocking is done from the same side – left to right unless you are left-handed, and make sure that you have enough thread to complete a row without any joins mid-way, as these weaken the smocking. The zigzag stitch is simply chevron stitch carried on several tubes farther. Two lines of rope between the patterned bands improves the look of the smocking. The sleeves are smocked in narrow bands top and bottom – (*see* figure 116). The top band below the

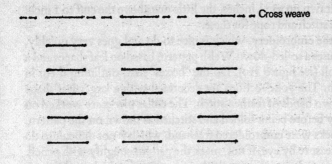

Cross weave

Figure 117. *Gathering stitches should be as evenly spaced as possible to draw up into regular 'tubes'. They must follow the cross-weave of the material*

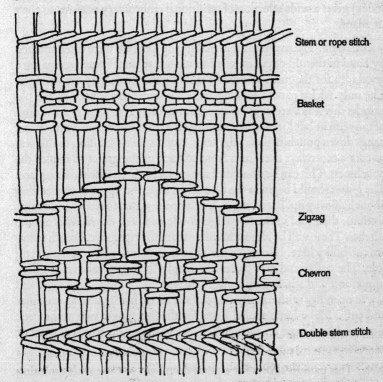

Stem or rope stitch

Basket

Zigzag

Chevron

Double stem stitch

Figure 118. *Different smocking stitches used on traditional smocks*

shoulder is drawn up to 1½ inches, the little one above the cuff to 1 inch. Use chevron stitch and rope for these.

Now for the embroidery, which is nice to do and goes very quickly. This smock uses a scaled-down Welsh pattern, based on leaf shapes and a running scroll (*see* figure 119). Do the 'boxes' first, outlining them in feather-stitch. The yoke sections are decorated with a larger leaf shape outlined in two bands of feather-stitch. The collar pieces are worked on one half only before being folded and stitched as shown on the pattern. The old smocks were embroidered freehand, which is not difficult to do if you can measure by eye. If not, mark the pattern roughly with pencil. It doesn't have to be accurate to the last fraction of an inch, and there is no reason why you shouldn't work out your own patterns instead of using the one given here. The excellent Dryad Press leaflet (Suppliers' Index) gives a wide selection of traditional embroidery patterns to copy or adapt.

MAKING UP. The main seams in making up a smock were often stitched by hand in the old days but you can use a machine. French seams are a good idea for the main seams of a child's garment as they are stronger. The only tricky part of making up is the underarm gusset. In the old smocks this was a rectangular insertion, which gives plenty of freedom of movement but looks a little clumsy on a child or woman's smock as it hangs down pouchily under the arms. My mother's solution to this was to take a crossways dart from front to back of the gusset to reduce the pouchiness. This can be done after the gusset has been stitched into place. The gusset should begin at the base of the box, the upper corner ending about half-way up. For strength, machine the gusset to sleeve and smock sections, then fold in the raw edges inside and hem down with minute stitches. These will be almost invisible from the right side. French seams are too bulky here. Hemstitch the yoke facings into place on the wrong side. The collar and cuff pieces are simply folded in half, embroidery uppermost and stitched into place without interlinings. Bind neck and sleeve openings with narrow strips of the fabric before sewing on collar and cuffs. Make buttonholed loops for the fastenings; two at the neck front and back, one on each cuff. You can use small, covered, pearl or brass buttons.

Note: This pattern allows for a good deep hem to cope with sprouting youngsters – at least 4 inches.

Box

Figure 119. *Patterns for embroidering on the boxes and yoke of child's smock. Collar pieces are embroidered with the box pattern minus one row of scrolls. Rows of scrolls should be worked on the sleeve panels*

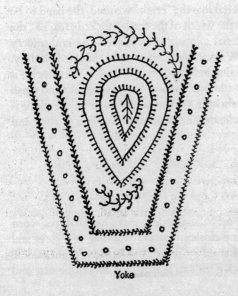

Yoke

Adult's smock

Using the child's smock layout as a guide, plus the traditional rule-of-thumb method, you should be able to plot the pattern-pieces for an adult's smock without much trouble. The traditional approach took the neck to hem measurement of the smock as the basic unit. Three times this length of cloth is needed. Fold the cloth into three equal lengths, two of which form the front and back of the smock. Fold the remaining piece into three again. Two of these form the sleeves, while the third piece makes the collar, cuffs, yoke pieces, gussets and neck bindings. For a woman's smock the sleeves should be narrower and somewhat shorter, and the yoke pieces wedge-shaped rather than rectangular to follow a more sloping feminine shoulder. (*See* figure 116.) The garment is not supposed to hug the shoulders like a tailored jacket so there is no need to be too precise in measuring and fitting. Apart from the bosom, which should cling quite close to the body, the general effect is easy and casual, like a man's shirt. Some points to note: the proportion of embroidery to smocking across front and back is not a hard and fast matter. On the photographed smock the 'boxes' are roughly the same width as the smocking; traditionally they were usually narrower and the smocked band wider – just over half the width of the smocking was standard. On a heavier material like the 'crash' we used, the band to be smocked is only three times the width of the final smocked area, i.e., the smocking reduces the material allowance by three. The embroidery pattern we used was the Warwickshire shepherds', adapted slightly. Allow a good-size neck opening before starting to gather and smock – if it's too big you can always add buttons and loops, but if it's too small there isn't much you can do about it. On our adult smock the smocking is built up of three bands of chevron alternating with rows of rope and basket stitch.

Easy-to-make pinny

Continental mothers are great believers in smocks or pinafores worn over a small child's ordinary clothes, to save washing of jerseys and those horrid indelible stains that always seem to collect bang in the middle of the front. The ideal in such garments is that they should be easy and

Figure 120 (a). *The embroidery on the adult smock. The clover motif is worked double on each collar piece and as a three-leaf clover on the yoke pieces. Fill the sleeve panels with scrolls as for child's smock*

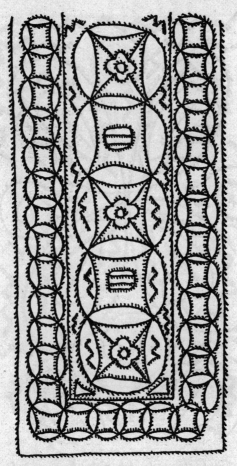

Figure 120 (b). *Box pattern for the adult smock*

quick, both to make and to wash and iron, and this idea – a French one –
is both. It is cut out of one continuous strip of cloth with a drawstring
neck and the whole garment – thanks to the ingenious crescent armhole – spreads out flat as a hanky to iron. It would look pretty made in
gingham, with bias-edged armholes and pockets (optional).

TO MAKE. Measure the child round the fattest part of waist or tum
and add on half to three quarters as much again, depending how full you
want the pinny to be. Measure length from neck to a couple of inches
above the knees. This gives you the length and width of your rectangle

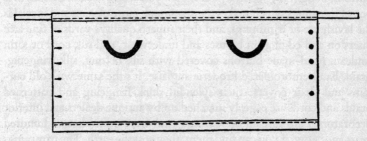

Figure 121. *Easy-to-make pinny*

(figure 121). Cut this out, adding 1 inch top and bottom for hems and the
same each end for buttons and buttonholes, or poppers. Fold your
rectangle as it will be when worn, i.e. with the back pieces turned in as
for hems and overlapping 1 inch at the back. Mark the side folds with
pins. Now measure the width of the child's shoulder from neck to
shoulder point. Mark this measurement on the side fold with pins too.
Open the material out and draw a half-circle outline for each armhole,
using your pins to guide you (*see* diagram). Use the edge of a saucer or a
large beer mug for the half circle. Cut round these crescents. Stitch contrast bias all round this cut. Turn back 1 inch at the neck and machine
along the edge to make a channel for your drawstring. Turn up the hem
by hand or machine. Fold the back edges in 1 inch or so, and either work
buttonholes up one side and sew buttons the other, or sew a few large
poppers on. Make a good long drawstring for the neck out of more bias,
folded in half and machined along. Thread through the neck channel.
It's a good idea to machine or handstitch the drawstring permanently in
place in the centre of the front, otherwise it will certainly get lost. Add

bias-edged pockets, embroidered initials, appliqué or anything else you fancy in the way of decoration. When the pinny is on and the neck drawn up, the crescent armholes stand up like little wings.

Trimmings

If, like me, you have a weak spot for really old clothes – my favourite jacket is a most beautifully shaped and tailored, black wool Victorian one with two rows of what I only recently discovered were real silver buttons, bought for 50p in a junk shop – you won't need to be told that one of the things which makes them so much more elegant and special is the lavish use of trimmings, and their superb quality: yards of fine lace insertion and edging on blouses and underwear, real silk cord or satin rouleau, hand-made buttons covered with silk netting, silk fringeing, braid, hand-embroidered broderie anglaise. It's the same with old curtains and chair covers; their splendid thick fringeing and patterned braids and cords are eagerly snatched up by antique dealers and interior decorators. I am sure all these little extras were quite cheap a hundred years ago; now, if you can find them, they cost the earth. The trimmings counter in the average department store has nothing that can compare for quality – nearly everything is made from shiny, cheap looking imitation silk in poor colours. In the soft furnishing section things are worse still – gimp, cord, fringe, tassels are so sleazy one usually ends up buying anything available in plain cotton, like rug fringe, which can be dyed and has a pleasant texture.

Until some bright manufacturer decides to improve the standard, the solution as usual is to make your own. In this section I shall be describing how to make some basic trimmings like knotted fringe, cord, tassels, frogs and chinese buttons. The hand-knotted fringe is particularly splendid, and a few yards of it would lift a cape or long skirt, or Victorian chair come to that, quite out of the ordinary.

Cord

Silk cord of the dressing-gown type – i.e. made of twisted strands – can be made to any thickness using skeins of embroidery silk. You would need an awful lot of silk to make a thick cord, which would work out expen-

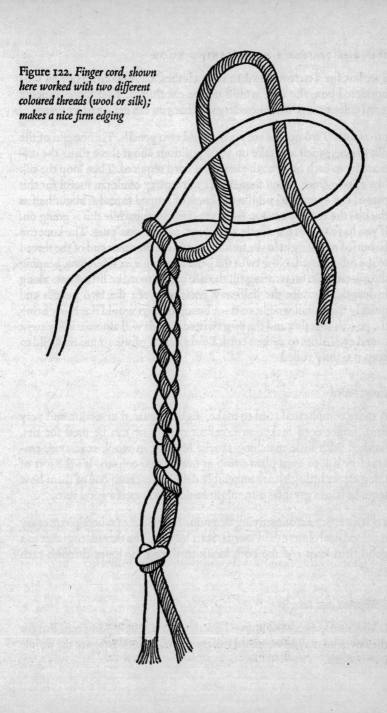

Figure 122. Finger cord, shown here worked with two different coloured threads (wool or silk); makes a nice firm edging

sive, but for a narrow cord to edge clothes, cushion covers or an embroidered box, the cost would not be exorbitant. And there is such a good colour range in embroidery silk that you can get a perfect match.

TO MAKE. Two people are needed, and two pencils. Tie one end of the silk to one pencil and take up your positions about three times the distance from each other as the length of cord required. Then loop the silk like a skein from pencil to pencil (a third party comes in useful for this part of the operation) till the thickness of looped thread is about half as thick as the cord you want. Keep the threads taut while this is going on. If you have to join the silk tie a reef knot, which won't slip. The knot can be buried out of sight in the finished cord. Tie the other end of the thread to the other pencil. Now twist the pencils in opposite directions, keeping the silk taut. Go on twisting till the silk begins to make little knots along its length. Measure the half-way point between the two pencils and quickly tie a small weight to it – a bunch of keys would do. Now bring the pencils together and the two twisted strands will automatically twist round each other to make a cord. Bind a length of silk round each end to keep it tightly rolled.

Finger cord

A more complicated cord to make, slightly squared in section and very firm, finger cord makes an excellent edging or can be used for ties, finished with little matching tassels. Make it in wool, macramé, embroidery silk or even plain string in one or two colours. It's the sort of thing clever little girls are incredibly deft at. Teaching one of them how to make it, as a great favour, might be doing yourself a good turn.

TO MAKE. See accompanying diagram. This is a case where pictures say it a good deal clearer than words. Start by tying the threads together in a good firm knot and use both hands to thread the loops through each other.

Pompoms and tassels

I think nearly everyone knows how to make a simple pompom. But for the few who may have missed this treat in childhood here are the simple instructions.

Figure 123. *Making pompoms:*
(a) *winding wool round two cardboard discs*
(b) *cutting round to release pompom*

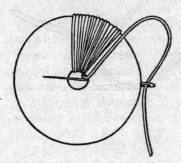
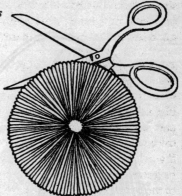

Cut two cardboard discs the diameter of the pompom you want. Make a hole through the centre of each card large enough to wind a considerable thickness of wool or silk through, but not so wide that the pompom is halved in size when you pull the threads up (*see* figure 123). Wool makes the nicest, fluffiest pompoms. Using a long strand of wool threaded on a blunt needle, a tapestry needle for preference, bind the wool over and over your cardboard ring till every bit of card is hidden and the wool bulges fatly. Join on extra lengths of wool by knotting at the circumference of the ring. The knots will be trimmed off. Now with a sharp pair of pointed scissors cut round the outside of the circle, making sure all the strands are cut through. Part the card rings a little and quickly tie two or three thicknesses of wool round the waist, drawing up tight and knotting securely. Now slip off the card rings. Clip the pompom to make it nice and round and teaze it out gently with a wire brush if you want it fluffier. The lengths of wool can be used to sew the pompom in place or if long enough crocheted into the ties traditional for knitted baby-clothes.

Tassels

These are made on the same principle as pompoms, using wool, silk, lurex, string or whatever you like. They look more elegant finished off

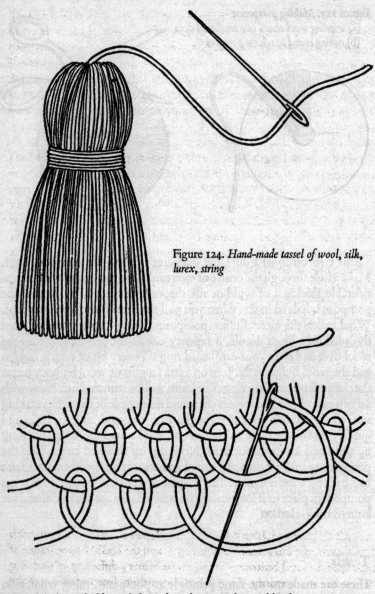

Figure 124. *Hand-made tassel of wool, silk, lurex, string*

Figure 125. *Detached buttonhole stitch used to cover the tassel head*

with a cap of detached buttonhole stitch in the same stuff (*see* figure 125). The instructions here are for making smallish tassels. If you wanted to make really large ones, for curtain tie-backs for instance, stitched onto cotton cord or ordinary rope, insert some sort of a core into the head of the tassel (a stiff cardboard ring the diameter of the tassel) to make it look thicker and lusher. Otherwise you will need an enormous amount of wool, string or whatever you are using to make a generous looking tassel.

TO MAKE. Cut a length of stiff card as wide as your tassel is to be long (*see* figure 124). Wind threads round and round till you think you have enough for a fat tassel. Slip a needle along under the threads at one end, threaded with a good strong thread, and knot both ends quite tightly together. Cut the threads at the opposite end of the card. Now take your needle again, threaded with stuff matching the tassel. Take the needle down through the tassel to where you want the 'waist' to come, pull the thread down after it, losing one end inside the head of the tassel. Bind the thread round a few times at waist height, not too tightly, and take the needle back up through the middle again, leaving the thread to sew the tassel on by. Now, for a superlative finish, pad the head of the tassel with a little cotton wool, pushing it up through the waist with a pencil. Starting at the top, work a cover of detached buttonhole stitch reaching down as far as the waisting threads. Attach the buttonholing to these here and there to prevent the cover slipping off, and finish off by drawing the needle back through the tassel.

Small covered buttons were often made in the same way a century or so ago. I remember a grey silk dress in a museum in Essex, with a row of little round buttons in the same silk, all covered in silk buttonholing to match.

Chinese or knot button

As small children in China we all had cheongsams – narrow gowns with slit sides and buttons across one shoulder – and the budlike appearance of these little knotted buttons and the extraordinary difficulty of undoing them is an early memory. The Chinese make them from a rouleau of the gown fabric, but they can also be made of a narrow, rounded braid.

Figure 126. *How to knot rouleau or braid for Chinese knot button*

Figure 127. *Clover-leaf loop used with knot button. The button itself is sewn to another clover-leaf loop opposite*

With their frogged clover-leaf attachments, they are a decorative trimming as well as a functional one.

TO MAKE. Cut a narrow bias strip (about 1 inch wide) for the rouleau and fold into a narrow roll, tucking in the raw edge, and hem down. The amount you need for each fastening depends on the size of the frogs; 8 inches per frog, plus 5 inches for the button will make frogs about 2 inches across. The frog is the double clover-leaf part, including the loop for sewing the button to or the one which fastens round it.

To make the button, study figure 126. Twist the rouleau as shown for the button. When you pull the ends tight it makes a button which only needs to be stitched at the base. To make frogged attachments, cut the remaining rouleau in half, one piece for each side. Loop each into a four-leaf clover shape, following the arrangement shown in figure 127, and tucking the raw ends under one of the junction points so that they do not show. Use a firmly stuffed pillow to pin the frog to while getting the shape right. Catch the lengths of rouleau together from the back with needle and thread, where they intersect. Sew a button securely to the end of a loop on one of the two frogs as shown. To sew onto clothes, pin frogs either side of the garment-opening as in figure 127 and catch three loops of each clover-leaf with small stitches as you would sew cord to a fabric, i.e. with a single line of stitching along the back of the rouleau. For a tight, edge-to-edge closing, cut off or omit the loop the button is stitched to and sew the button over the intersection point instead. The Chinese often coil the two ends of rouleau round on themselves, like earphone plaits, for a different decorative effect. For this, the rouleau should be ironed flat, coiled tight and stitched at the base so the coils stand up in relief.

Sprat's head

This stitched embellishment is both practical and decorative. Use it to strengthen pleats, darts and slot seams.

The sprat's head is worked in buttonhole twist over a $\frac{1}{2}$-inch equilateral triangle marked out in tacking cotton. Start by catching the thread in with a couple of tiny stitches in the middle of the triangle, then bring the needle out at the bottom left-hand corner (opposite side if you are left-handed). Take a tiny stitch across the apex of the triangle from right to left as shown, then take the needle down into the right-hand corner and bring out again at the left-hand corner just inside the first stitch. Repeat till the triangle is solidly filled in.

Ruched cord trimming

One cheap and effective trimming – good for edging cushions and chair covers and long skirts which need a bit of stiffening – is made by covering a length of ordinary cotton cord with a ruched sausage (if you follow

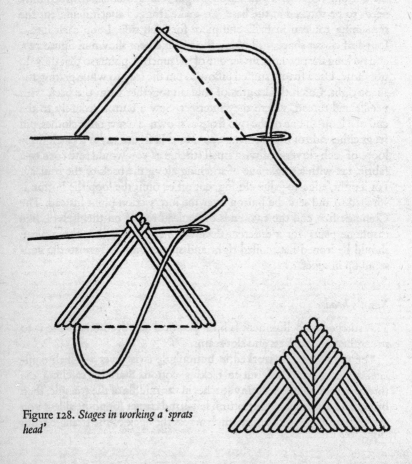

Figure 128. *Stages in working a 'sprats head'*

me) of fabric. The sausage should be cut on the straight (bias cut turns cord into piping) and a little wider than the cord to allow you to ruckle the covering material up with your hand after you have inserted the cord. Make the cover anything up to twice as long as the cord, depending how shirred and bulky you want the trim to look. It makes up particularly well in velvet and velveteen. Sew it on as you would a cord trimming.

Knotted fringe by the yard

Thick hand-knotted fringe knocks any machine-made equivalent for six. The single-tasselled sort would add tremendous panache to a tweed cape or long skirt. The one with stepped, double rows of tassels would make a knitted shawl look luxurious, or finish off the bottom of a Chesterfield sofa or Victorian chair in great style. On the whole, use wool fringe on woollen fabrics, cotton on cotton, but this is a rule made to be

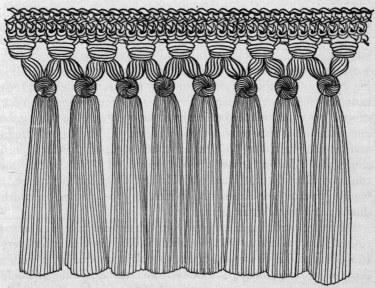

Figure 129. *First example of hand-knotted fringe, with one row of tassels*

broken. A dyed fringe of soft string would look pretty good trimming a velvet sofa.

Suitable yarns are: knitting wool from 3-ply to double knitting; various thicknesses of crochet cotton; vest cotton; fine soft string. A yarn which comes up very well is a lustred nylon or tricel and nylon knitting wool. It is on sale under various trade names, and is recognizable by its slight sheen. This yarn readily untwists and may cause difficulty in the crochet work, but it makes an attractive, soft, silky fringe.

TOOLS. Use a crochet hook suitable for the yarn selected. The shop where you buy the yarn should be able to help you find the correct hook. To keep the fringe taut while the tassels are being hooked through and knotted, and to keep the knots at regular intervals, use a stretcher made from a piece of wood 2 inches by 1 inch by about 30 inches. $1\frac{1}{2}$-inch nails should be knocked in to a depth of $\frac{1}{2}$ inch at $\frac{7}{8}$-inch intervals along the length of wood. This piece of wood may be either wedged in a vice or clamped to a table. If neither is available then it can be wedged in a drawer. You also need a piece of card to gauge the length of the tassels – $7\frac{1}{2}$ inches by approximately 24 inches.

QUANTITIES. For both of the following examples I used double knitting wool and a number 4 crochet hook. Quantities will vary according to the yarn you use, but for these examples it worked out at approximately 3 ounces of wool per yard of fringe, using ten strands per tassel. It is important to note that ten strands in every tassel is the minimum for a reasonably full fringe; more strands may be added for a more flamboyant effect. Finer yarns will need more strands in every tassel to achieve the same fullness. For a fringe with an overall depth of $5\frac{1}{2}$ inches (including a braid measuring 1 inch), you need a tassel length of $7\frac{1}{2}$ inches which allows you 2 inches for two rows of knots and $\frac{1}{2}$-inch wastage for trimming. Since the tassel is made by folding the yarn double, you need a winding card or gauge measuring $7\frac{1}{2}$ inches by about 24 inches, which should take a whole ounce of yarn.

The fringe can be made longer if you wish and can have many more rows of knots, as long as you remember to allow 1 inch extra for every row of knots. It is unwise to attempt to make a knotted fringe with a depth of less than 5 inches, because even the most nimble fingers would have difficulty knotting a free tassel of less than 4 inches. If you badly

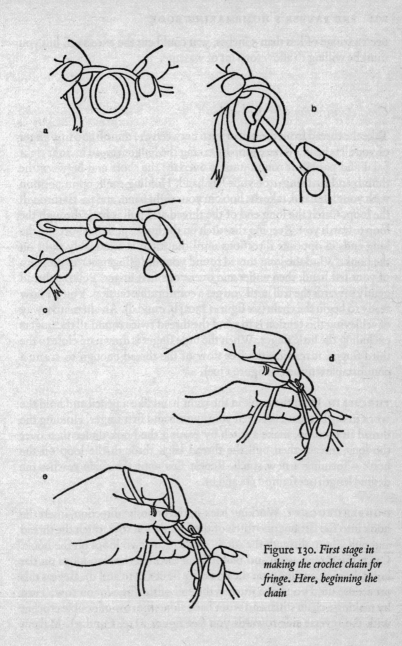

Figure 130. *First stage in making the crochet chain for fringe. Here, beginning the chain*

need a fringe of less than 5 inches, you could cut the excess off, but you must be willing to allow for a lot of wastage.

Crochet instructions for the braid

Take the thread from the ball of yarn between the thumb and first finger of your left hand. Make a loop by taking the longer thread in your right hand and passing it round until it overlaps the short end between the thumb and first finger of your left hand. Holding the loop in position with your left hand, take the hook in your right hand, and pass it through the loop. Catch the long end of the thread and pull it back through the loop towards you. Keeping the stitch on the hook, pull the short and the long ends in opposite directions until the stitch is reasonably tight on the hook. Wind the long thread round your little finger, across the palm of your left hand, then under and over your first finger. Pull the thread gently towards the ball until you get a comfortable tension. You are now ready to begin the chain (*see* figures 130a, b, c and d). An alternative way of achieving this tension is to wind the thread twice round all the fingers excluding the little finger. When the little finger is drawn up close to the third finger, it restricts the free flow of the thread enough to create a comfortable tension (*see* figure 130e).

THE CHAIN. Hold the hook in the right hand like a pencil and hold the work in the left hand between your thumb and first finger. Holding the thread in position, make a stitch by passing the hook under then over the long thread, then pull the thread back through the loop on the hook – forming a new stitch. Repeat this until the chain reaches the desired length (*see* figure 131a and b).

DOUBLE CROCHET. Working back in the opposite direction, insert the hook into the last but one stitch of the foundation row, catch the thread and pull a loop through the stitch, so there are two loops on the hook. Catch the thread again and pull it back through the two loops on the hook, leaving one loop on the hook (*see* figure 131c and d). Repeat this procedure until you have reached the end of the foundation row. Turn by making a chain stitch and work back along the row of double crochet with the reverse side towards you (*see* figure 131e, f and g). Make a

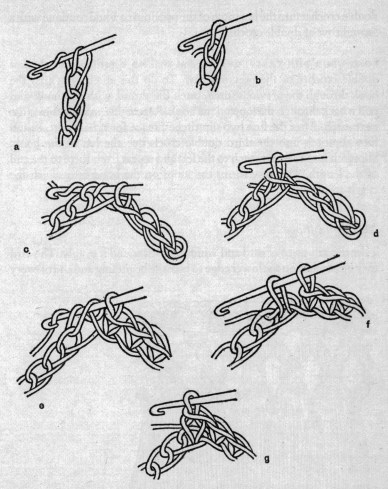

Figure 131. *Working crochet braid*

double crochet into the last stitch of the previous row and continue with a second row of double crochet.

LOOPS FOR THE TASSELS. Turn and make a slipstitch into the last double crochet of the previous row. To do this stitch, you pass the hook through the previous stitch, catch the thread with the hook and pull it back through the loop on the hook. Repeat this procedure into the next stitch. After the first two slipstitches, make four chain-stitches and then slipstitch into the third double crochet to the left of the hook. Slipstitch into the next stitch to the left and repeat from there to the end of the length. This row forms the loops on the braid into which the tassels are slotted.

Making the fringe

Take the stiff piece of card and wind the yarn round it evenly. The card may be notched on the lower edge to take the beginning and end of every

Figure 132. *Second example, showing two tiers of knotted tassels*

ball of yarn. Alternatively you could knot the ends together as long as the knots occur on the lower edge of the card. Steam-press the yarn on both sides of the card paying special attention to the top edge. Then cut along the lower edge with sharp scissors, cutting off any knots. This will produce a strand 15 inches long. Leave the strands hooked over the card until you are ready for them.

Take the stretcher (nailed wood) and clamp or wedge it firmly as I have described above. Slot the loops of the braid over the nails, but do not stretch it too much. You can miss the occasional nail out if necessary. The loops should face you. Bring the crochet hook from the back through the first loop of the braid. Take ten strands from the card and place them over the end of the hook – a large hook is useful here – using the pressed fold to indicate the half-way mark. Pull the hook back through the braid loop far enough to enable you to slot the two free ends of the tassel down through the ten-strand hooked loop. Pull the two free ends until the knot tightens. Make sure that the ends are even and then move on to the next tassel. Repeat this procedure until you reach the end of the fringe.

For the second row of knots, start on the left. Take ten strands of the first tassel and ten strands of the second tassel, leaving ten free at the edge. Twist and knot approximately $\frac{1}{2}$–$\frac{3}{4}$ inch below the first row of knots. Carry on knotting the two halves of the tassels like this to the end of the row. The first half of the first tassel and the second half of the last are left free. Trim the bottom edge of the fringe carefully.

If the fringe ends meet when you have stitched the braid onto a garment, you can knot the free halves of the end tassels together to make the pattern continuous. If you are sewing the fringe to something flat, knot the end tassels singly.

SECOND EXAMPLE. Follow the instructions for the first example until you have finished the second row of knots. Then, starting on the left, take five strands from the right-hand side of the first tassel and five strands from the left-hand side of the second tassel, twist and knot $\frac{1}{2}$–$\frac{3}{4}$ inch below the previous row. Take five strands from the right-hand side of the second tassel with five strands from the next to the right and make a knot. This should leave you with ten strands hanging free from the centre of each tassel. Continue knotting and dividing the tassels in this way to the end of the fringe.

You can trim all the fringe down to one level if you wish, but a nice feathery effect is produced by the two-level fringeing of this method. Trim the fringe in two layers by masking the longer fringe off with your winding card while you trim the top layer. Then remove the card and trim the longer fringe. If the fabric you are attaching the fringe to is washable, the fringe dries better if the whole item is drip-dried, as the weight of the water pulls the strands of the fringe straight.

NEEDLEWORK

Embroideries

Fine old pieces of embroidery, canvas-work (what we call tapestry) and needlework can be lovely things to look at; the problem is to find a way of keeping them on view which doesn't reduce them to shreds.

With a piece of Victorian tapestry or canvas-work in good condition, the usual answer is to make this up into a cushion cover. Back the work with fine cotton to prevent it stretching, stick down any loose threads with Copydex, and use a suitable scrap of velveteen for the reverse side of the cover. Silk cord, or fringe stitched round the outside edge, improves the look of the cushion and protects it from wear and tear. Pieces too small to make a cover on their own can be set in a fabric frame (figure 133). Worked borders can be used the other way round, framing a fabric inset, or stitched down the sides of a plain cover. Velveteen is the best material to use with Victorian tapestry-work, because it has the right plushy period look, but thick wool flannel in dark colours – if you can find such a thing – was quite often used with Berlin wool-work. Bare spots in the canvas, where the old stitching has worn away, can be reworked in matching wool or silk. Tapestry wools and embroidery silks come in a very good range of colours and can be bought at most needlework shops. Try and match the original stitch used – tent-stitch and cross-stitch were two of the most popular. (*See* figure 139 or, for more elaborate stitches, consult one of the many excellent books on embroidery.)

A really beautiful and fragile piece of embroidery is best framed and hung on the wall. Rather than wait till an old frame just the right size

Figure 133. *A small panel of embroidery or canvas-work can be set in a fabric frame to make a cushion cover. Mitre the corners. You could sew fine silk cord over the joins*

turns up, get an art shop to make one up for you. A plain narrow gilt moulding is one of the cheapest standard mouldings available, and looks well for this sort of job. If it strikes you as too shiny, you can dull the surface by rubbing very gently with fine wire wool and then coating the frame with a very dilute tinted glaze (*see* picture framing). If the embroidery is very fragile, strengthen it by stitching it to a fine net backing. Stretch the backing material over some sort of frame – the back of a picture frame might do – and tack down with tin tacks. Lay the needlework on top, catching it down at the corners first and then stitching down all round the edge with small running stitches. Don't pull them too tight, or the fabric may tear. Use a matching thread, one of the colourless nylon threads would be a good choice. An actual rent in the embroidery can then be very carefully repaired by stitching through the net backing, keeping the stitches tiny at the front and doing the heavy work

Figure 134. *Short lengths of worked borders – sometimes intended for use as bell pulls – can be extended by a central inset of velvet or corduroy. Finish with a piped or ruched edge*

Figure 135. *Long narrow strips of embroidery are best used framing a velveteen panel. A boxed shape looks nice*

at the back. A less painstaking way is to glue the embroidery down to a piece of backing fabric with Copydex. A piece of embroidery to be framed will look better mounted on a wooden stretcher which fits into the frame like an oil painting on canvas. Make your own with four narrow strips of wood (¾-inch section) screwed together, or with a piece of wooden board about ½-inch thick. Smooth the needlework on top, tacking first in the centre of each side, then at the four corners. Then tack down all round. If you don't think the work will be harmed by water, damp it and leave to dry to shrink it taut. Steaming for a few minutes over a boiling kettle might be an alternative with fabrics whose colourfastness you are not sure of.

To clean or not to clean? It is hard to resist the temptation to plunge any old piece of embroidery into a bowl of hot suds in the hope of seeing a complete transformation, colours bright as new, textures fresh as when they were first worked. It's a case of fools rushing in though, because the colours may run, weak spots become gaping holes and really fragile old materials like silk, satin and cotton disintegrate completely. Never wash anything embroidered in gold or silver thread. If you think the embroidery is sturdy enough to stand water, test it first for colour-fastness by damping a piece of cotton wool or white cotton and pressing it firmly to the back. If it comes away dirty but not coloured, make up a bowl of lukewarm water with a squeeze of liquid detergent and a pinch of salt added. V.I.P. treatment would be rainwater, or distilled water and pure detergent like Teepol. Lay the embroidery on a piece of old sheet or polythene and lower into the water, paddling up and down gently. Rinse in the same way, with several changes of water. Dry by laying out flat between two towels, or on a cloth between several sheets of news-paper which should be changed as they get soaked. Dry away from heat. Don't iron, because the heat and pressure will squash all the life out of a piece of embroidery or tapestry-work. Steaming and stretching is all it will need, if that.

If you have any doubts about washing, clean it by covering with a layer of magnesium carbonate (buy it from a chemist). Lay the fabric flat, sprinkle on the powder, brush in very gently with a baby brush and leave for a few hours. Then gently shake the powder out, and you will find much of the dirt and grease has been absorbed by it.

Covering a box

A good way of making use of an irregular fragment of embroidery, unsuitable for cushions or framing, is to use it to cover a box, an idea which came to me looking at those delightful stump-work boxes in museums, mostly worked by young girls in Stuart times. Don't try this

Figure 136. *Embroidered box piped with cord and closed with a Chinese knot button*

with a piece of embroidery so intrinsically valuable that even a scrap is worth preserving entire. I have used a piece of embroidered Chinese silk, and an odd fragment of Jacobean wool-work (left over from making bed-curtains) which turned up in an old wicker basket I bought at a sale. You make the box as well, so its size and shape can be determined by the shape and pattern of your embroidered piece. Cut paper patterns to the approximate shape and size and move them about on top till you have got the best bit of pattern for the top. You need one panel for the top and four small ones for the sides. The bottom can be covered with felt, or the lining material. Cut panels ½–¾ inch smaller than the fabric pieces (allow more turn-back on loosely woven materials and raised embroidery), out of something fairly sturdy like mounting card, heavy cardboard or hardboard, using a Stanley knife. Pad the panels slightly with a pad of cottonwool, or better still lambswool, slightly raised in the centre and thinned out towards the edges. Stretch a piece of fine cotton or scrap material over this, folding the edges over and glueing down on the back. Use Bostik or Copydex. This will hold the padding in place. The best way to assemble these boxes is to cover and line each panel separately, then stitch them all together, covering the seams with a fine silky cord, stitched on separately. They won't look so streamlined as if you machined up the seams and cover the box in one operation, but a hand-made look adds to their charm.

Cut your panels of embroidery, sticking down any bits of thread which threaten to unravel with a dab of Copydex or Bostik. Smooth the pieces over the padded panels, folding over and glueing as before. If the material is so thick that the mitred corners are lumpy, cut a little triangle away and stitch firmly. Now pad the back of each little panel to fill in the hollow in the middle between the stuck-down edges of embroidery. Cut pieces of some scrap material – curtain lining cotton is good and comes in pretty colours – to line each panel, including the bottom of the box, which should be padded to match the sides and top. Pin these in place, fold in edges, and stitch to the embroidery all round the outer edges of the panels, using neat oversewing stitches and matching thread. You now have five panels, six including the bottom, ready to stitch together into a box. Stitch the side panels together first, stitching from the outside. Then stitch sides to bottom. Sew fine cord (you can make your own if the selection available is unsuitable, *see* trimmings) all round over the stitching. To hinge the lining to the box either sew loops of lining fabric to the top and box inside, or stitch cord frogs (*see* trimmings) on the outside.

Canvas work

Embroidery on canvas, or canvas-work, which consumed so much of a Victorian lady's leisure time, seems to be in for a general revival. It is soothing to do, keeps the hands occupied (excellent if you are trying to give up smoking) and the results can be quite beautiful. You can either buy canvases printed and ready to work – these tend to be expensive, and the level of design banal at all but a few specialist shops – or make up your own, which is cheaper and offers more scope. To start you off I have included a few simple motifs from Victorian samplers which can all be worked quite easily by counting – if you have a poor head for

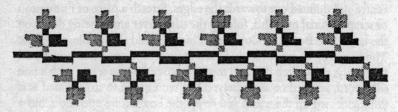

Figure 137. *Sprigged border taken from Victorian sampler*

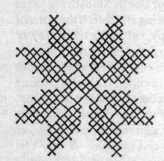

Figure 138. *Stylized rosette to be worked in cross-stitch as repeating motif*

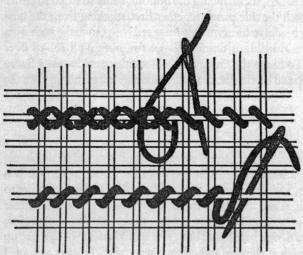

Figure 139. *Basic stitches shown worked on double-mesh canvas; cross-stitch above, tent-stitch below*

figures you could ink the general outlines as a guide. One tends to think of Victorian canvas-work in terms of florid Berlin wool bouquets and religious subjects, but they also did a lot of natty geometric patterns and simple repeating motifs, and these look particularly attractive in modern colours and rooms. Start with something small, like a belt or a small cushion-cover, which you are fairly certain to finish. Needlework shops stock an excellent range of wools and stranded cottons for canvas-work, as well as a range of canvases of varying-sized meshes. Ten holes to the inch is the standard one and, worked on it, these designs would come out the same size as in the patterns. To increase the scale of the patterns you could use a canvas with fewer holes to the inch, or count one square of the pattern equal to four stitches on your canvas. Consult the ladies behind the counter; they will be able to give you expert advice as to which canvas is best suited to the sort of thing you want to make and the pattern you have chosen.

Work these patterns in cross-stitch or tent-stitch (figure 139). The sprigged border (figure 137) and the rosette motif (figure 138) would both look very fine worked on a narrow strip of canvas and made up into a belt, or curtain tie-backs. The sprigged border could be worked entirely in shades of green or, more colourfully, as a bud-and-leaf motif, with one dark and one pale green leaf and red and pink buds alternately. The background could be black or off-white. The rosette would look sophisticated done in sober shades, cream rosettes at spaced intervals on a brown background, for instance. A problem when working something long and narrow like a belt is that most canvases are too narrow to encircle any but the proverbial 18-inch waist, which means you have to buy a yard, cut the belt piece out lengthwise, and use the leftover bit for something else. Always turn in a generous margin at both edges and ends of a tie or belt because most canvas frays as you handle it. Run a little Copydex all round to check the fraying. Embroidered belts can look marvellous and they last for years, so it is worthwhile going to a little trouble and expense. Back the embroidery and bind it with leather. The best way to fasten an embroidered belt is with a couple of leather straps and buckles, you could use sturdy watch-straps cut down to size or a dog collar, cut in half. Curtain tie-backs can be backed with fabric and bound with ribbon. A brass ring at each end anchors the tie-back to a hook screwed into the window frame at the appropriate level.

The tile pattern is a favourite of mine. Worked in bright clear colours

Figure 140. *Repeating geometric 'tile' pattern*

Figure 141. *Palm-leaf motif in four graduated shades of one colour*

Figure 142. *Suggested layout for palm-leaf motifs. Background worked in contrasting tent-stitch*

it makes a splendid cushion or stool cover. Increase the scale for these. Worked to the size shown here, using tent-stitch and subtle colours like cream, bronze and black, it would make handsome waistcoat fronts. Choose a pattern without darts so as not to break up the design. Trace the outline of pattern-pieces onto canvas with Indian ink as a guide for embroidering, but don't cut them out till you have worked them. Make sure the design matches up across the front and that the stripes are horizontal when worn. Line the fronts with cotton, make the back of soft leather or velvet and bind the edges all round to match the back. If it needs fastenings make loops along one side and covered buttons along the other.

The palm-leaf motif is more impressive when worked than the pattern suggests because of the shading. To bring this out, choose four shades of one colour – say crimson, red, pink and off-white – and use the darkest for the heart, shading out to the palest round the edges. In the Victorian example the motifs were set close together on a dark background (figure 142). This pattern would look good as a bag, or covering the seat of an antique chair.

Needlework shops stock a selection of bag frames and handles, all a bit ladylike for my taste. I don't think one can improve on that Victorian favourite, the carpet bag, which combined canvas-work (or carpet) and leather in a capacious, sturdy shape. Alas, there aren't many skilled cobblers around to knock a bag up for you out of your own embroidered panels, but it would be possible to make a modified version, using a zip closing. Use a fairly sturdy leather, but soft enough to machine. Line the bag with striped ticking as the Victorians did, and strengthen the handles by binding leather over rope. Four brass studs (craft shops) knocked into the bottom, one at each corner, will protect it from getting scuffed.

You can work canvas embroidery on a frame, or just hold it on your lap. I don't think it is worth getting a frame for the odd small piece, though it would be worth having for an elaborate piece of work. But you do need to know how to stretch your piece of embroidery into shape when finished. Never iron canvas-work – it flattens all the life out of it. Stretch by tacking the canvas down to a wooden board (bread-board covered with a bit of old cotton), starting with the middle of each side and pulling it into shape as you go. It probably won't look perfectly flat, but don't worry about that. Then damp the whole piece thoroughly and leave to dry. Remove the nails and the piece should be quite flat and back to its proper shape.

Florentine or Bargello-stitch belt

The current craze for Florentine- or Bargello-work is one of those un-accountable seismic upheavals in the world of fashion. One minute no one has ever heard of it, the next every needlework shop is packed with pamphlets telling you how to Bargello yourself cross-eyed. Its rise has been so sudden, it may disappear again with equal speed, but for all that it's a fine stitch and looks particularly well made up into belts, so no apologies for including a Bargello belt. Incidentally, I recently saw a

Colour key

- 0381 brown
- 078 crimson
- 493 pink
- 0387 natural
- 0306 yellow
- 0308 gold

Figure 143. *Chart for working Bargello belt (or border)*

small room in a Tudor house in Oxfordshire whose walls were entirely hung with Florentine-work in deep, rich colours and it was quite sumptuous, even though the tapestries were faded and moth-eaten. It dizzied the mind to think how long those Tudor ladies must have sat over their frames but the reason behind their labours was quite plain – it was the coldest, draughtiest house I have ever been into.

In the past, Bargello or Florentine embroidery was worked in wool on canvas using large stitches to cover big areas. For smaller articles, like this belt, use a special Eavenweave linen (like a fine-mesh canvas) or single canvas with 14 holes to the inch. Soft embroidery cotton is more suitable than wool for a belt as it will not rub up with wear and is a little less bulky. The motif is worked out here on a 2-inch square, which means you can make the belt as long or short as you need it. The same amount of yarn will cover a 38-inch belt as a 32-inch one.

MATERIALS: ⅛ yard of Penelope Evenweave linen, 21 threads to the inch; Tapestry needle; Clarks Soft Embroidery in six colours, two 10-yard skeins of each (we used 0381 Brown, 0387 Natural, 078 Crimson, 0306 Yellow, 493 Pink, 0308 Gold).

Figure 144. *How to work Florentine or Bargello stitch*

METHOD. Turn back the edges of the linenweave to prevent fraying, or run a little Copydex along them. The diagram shows the basic stitch, which is worked vertically from right to left. The design uses stitches covering two, four, and six threads. Don't pull the thread too tight when stitching. Basically, Florentine-stitch is a vertical one repeated over and over to create a wave-like effect, which can either be highly stylized or appear quite random. This pattern is made up of row upon row of regular wave-shapes. To finish off the belt either work a continuous band two or three threads wide in one of the colours right round the belt, turn the edges back and glue down before sticking or stitching a lining, or bind with a narrow strip of soft leather or fabric and have the buckle (unless you use an antique one) covered to match. Get eyelet holes made professionally or use a buckle which doesn't need a prong and eyelets to grip.

Patchwork

Nearly everyone gets bitten by the patchwork bug at some time or other. The idea of making something beautiful and useful from all those bits and pieces of material one accumulates is extraordinarily appealing. Unfortunately, one usually runs out of steam rather early on and then large fragments of uncompleted patchwork go to swell the mountain of unfinished masterpieces in drawers and trunks. There was an awesome amount of patient stitching in those delectable quilts our ancestors made on long winter evenings. Women today are too impatient, or busy, or perhaps they have other ways of passing long winter evenings. So I thought it would be better to include a patchwork design that can be stitched up by machine. Log Cabin was an obvious choice, as all the pieces are straight-sided, and the piecing is straightforward. It is a popular Early American design, and one of my own favourites. The American Museum near Bath has a beautiful example made up in those demurely figured calicos, chintzes and percales which add so much to the charm of nineteenth-century quilts.

The correct thing was to use the same material throughout in quilt-making, though mixtures of silk and velvet were admissible for the more sumptuous 'winter' quilt. There is good sense in this as an all-cotton quilt is washable, while a mixture of silk and wool might not have been.

Log Cabin was usually made up in half dark, half light patches, giving a stepped effect over a whole quilt. One block (one completed section of the pattern) on its own makes a very attractive cushion cover if you do not feel equal to making a whole quilt. A dozen blocks would make a child's cot quilt; three across, four down.

To make up, draw the pattern pieces on cardboard to use as templates. Cut out with a sharp knife. If you want to make the block bigger, add several more rectangles, increasing the length proportionately. When cutting the pieces allow a $\frac{1}{4}-\frac{1}{2}$-inch seam-allowance round each patch and make sure they are all cut exactly on the straight. You must make the

Figure 145. *Completed block of Log Cabin sewn up by machine*

same allowance on each patch, or you will get into a right old mess when sewing them together. Turn the seam-allowance under and iron down to give you sharp creases as a guide for machining. Sew the first three small squares together by hand and then transfer to the machine.

To make up into a cushion-cover, the pieced block only needs backing with light cotton before being made up in the usual way. If you want to make a light cot-cover, more decorative than warm, back the patchwork

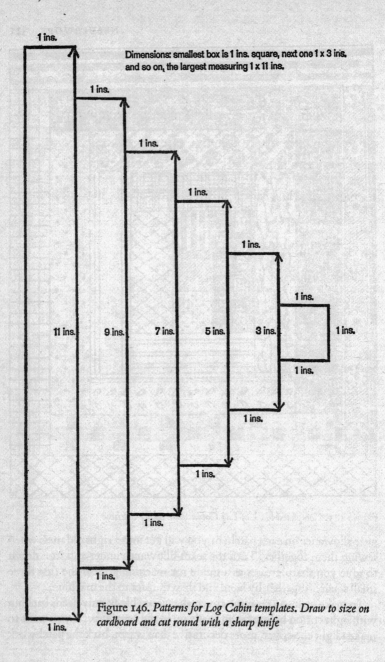

1 ins.

Dimensions: smallest box is 1 ins. square, next one 1 x 3 ins. and so on, the largest measuring 1 x 11 ins.

1 ins.

1 ins.

1 ins.

1 ins.

1 ins.

11 ins.   9 ins.   7 ins.   5 ins.   3 ins.   1 ins.

1 ins.

1 ins.

1 ins.

1 ins.

1 ins.

1 ins.

Figure 146. *Patterns for Log Cabin templates. Draw to size on cardboard and cut round with a sharp knife*

with strong cotton and perhaps an interlining of flannel (an old flannel sheet perhaps). Machine the blocks together along the outer-seam-allowances. Press them from the back over a damp cloth to flatten all the seams and smooth out any creases. Tack the backing and optional inter-lining in place to make sure the pieces stay properly aligned while finishing off. With an interlining it is advisable to machine-quilt the three thicknesses to make the coverlet more solid. Machine along the seams between the blocks, and round two or three squares in each block. Then, tack wide coloured bias, or a bias strip of one of the patching materials, round the coverlet. Machine, and then turn back and hem.

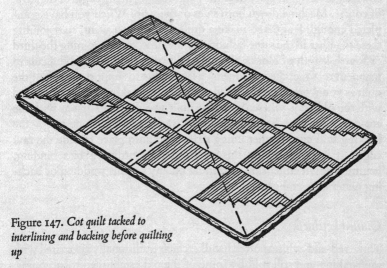

Figure 147. *Cot quilt tacked to interlining and backing before quilting up*

For a warmer, more luxurious cover, interline with cotton batting or with one of the Terylene waddings which are easy to wash and quick-drying. Traditionally, most quilts were padded with lambswool, which is deliciously warm, but unless you live near a sheep-farming centre it's almost impossible to get hold of now. The quilting would also have been done by hand; in the case of Log Cabin by simply stitching round each patch with tiny running stitches. However, it seems more consistent to quilt a machined patchwork by machine, as well as being much quicker. Tack the three thicknesses of patchwork, wadding and backing together carefully as shown in figure 147, and then machine in an unobtrusive shade of cotton down the main seams and round as many of the smaller rectangles as you feel equal to. The more closely quilted a cover like this is, of course, the better it looks and feels. Then bind the edges with bias or matching fabric as above.

If you were contemplating making a full-size quilt, the easiest way to cope with such a weight of material would be to machine-quilt each block separately, leaving the outer edges of each block unstitched. Then use narrow (1-inch) strips of contrasting or matching cotton, cut on the straight, to link the blocks together. Join lengthwise first, setting the blocks edge to edge, with the outer seam-allowance ironed flat this time, and tack the strips in place over the joins, folding in the edges of the strip, of course. Machine down both sides of the strip. When you have completed enough lengths to make a quilt the size you want, start joining these together in the same fashion. By the time you are joining the third or fourth length of blocks, the quilt will be very bulky and difficult to manoeuvre, so set the machine on a large table to support the rest of the quilt as you work. This is a speeded-up way of making a quilt compared with the old way, where the whole quilt was made up first as with the cot-cover and then hand-quilted on a frame, but it has one snag – the backing will need further lining strips sewn into place to hide the raw edges. It is easiest to do this by hand. Use ordinary bias binding, hemmed down either side, trimming off any surplus wadding or backing material as you go.

Quilted kerchiefs

Those red-and-white spotted handkerchiefs traditionally associated with snuff-taking and still sold by some of the old-established tobacconists, look very gay quilted up into cushion covers, or joined together to make a quilt for, say, a small boy's bed. They come in a wide variety of patterns, all basically geometric, which makes them easy to quilt by machine. Mix lots of patterns at random for a bed quilt, or combine two or three patterns in a regular sequence. Make up in one of the ways described for Log Cabin, either joining the kerchiefs directly together by machine and quilting as one piece, or quilting each square individually. White cotton is the usual thread used for quilts, whatever the colour, but red might break the patterns up less. Machine-quilt the patterns in any way you fancy. Edge the quilt with a white bias strip.

Lined baby-basket and holdall

I don't suppose an infant notices whether it sleeps in an orange-box or a nest of frills so long as its chief needs are attended to. But mothers, even the most anti-frill in the ordinary way, feel an impulse to surround a new baby with soft, pretty, beribboned things. One of the very nicest

Figure 148. *Moses basket with quilted lining for a pampered baby*

presents for a new baby and its mother would be a lined and quilted baby-basket together with a smaller, handled basket, trimmed to match, for carrying the inevitable collection of pins, powders, nappy liners and so forth from room to room. The baby-basket can be either the standard crib model, with or without a hood, to be found at most basketwork shops, or a Moses basket, like an outsize shopping-basket, with two handles and soft sides. These are light and useful for transporting small babies in. Check with the future parents to see which would be most useful. If they are already stocked up with cribs and carry cots, just give them the holdall, prettily lined, and stocked up with the usual baby necessities. It is surprising how much time and flap a simple gadget like this can save, even if it isn't your first baby.

On the other hand, if you are a prospective mother, and you can't rely on a kind relation or friend to provide you with either of these things, making them yourself would be a pleasant occupation for some of the long weeks of waiting.

Materials

For the baby-basket, you will need a wickerwork crib, or soft straw Moses basket with two handles; for the holdall, a shallow, *flat based* basket with a handle – the kind sold for picking flowers are a good shape. The next requirement is a cotton fabric for the lining to both baskets. Choose a washable, pretty cotton rather than nylon or Terylene; gingham in tiny checks, violet, perhaps, as a compromise between pink and blue, or a small floral print. The yardage needed depends on the size of your baskets – a crib will take quite a bit more than the other kind. Buy the baskets first and measure up to give you a rough idea. The lining, which will be machine-quilted onto wadding, should fit smoothly over the sides and base of the baskets, and is detachable for washing. Allow extra fabric for a self frill if you want to trim. Alternatively, buy broderie anglaise. Use Terylene or Courtelle wadding, which washes and dries easily and fast, for the quilting. Don't quilt the base of the crib or Moses basket. It is better to make a separate waterproof pad of two or three thicknesses of wadding sandwiched between plastic fabric. So buy enough wadding to quilt the sides of the baby-basket, to fill the waterproof pad and to quilt the holdall lining. You will also need plastic by the yard for the pad.

Figure 149. *Fabric, wadding and backing material quilted in a trellis pattern*

As further trimming, buy several yards of ribbon in a suitable colour –
you can really go to town on ribbon bows.

TO MAKE. It is a sensible precaution to wash the cotton lining fabric
before sewing it, to prevent it shrinking later. Iron it smooth when damp.
Cut a pattern from newspaper or large sheets of paper, Sellotaped where
they need to be joined. It is easier to machine-quilt smallish sections at a
time, so make the lining for the sides of the basket in two sections, seamed
together at head and foot. The lining should come to just below the
wickerwork rim of a crib, or the edge of the carrying basket. Add on
1 inch all round to allow for turn-backs and seams. Cut a pattern for the
base in the same way, with a 1-inch seam-allowance. Cut two pieces of
lining fabric and wadding for the sides of the basket, and a piece of lining
fabric only for the base. (When joined up the pieces will be something

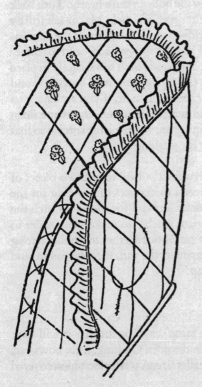

Figure 150. *Tacking self-frill in place round top of quilted lining*

like a large bag with quilted sides.) Tack the side sections to the wadding, criss-crossing the lines of tacking so as to hold the fabric and wadding together securely while you machine-quilt. Quilt each side-section separately using a strong matching thread, cotton or Polyester for choice. The lines of machine-quilting can go in any direction you fancy, in parallel rows round the basket sides or, perhaps prettier, in a diagonal trellis pattern (see figure 149). Right sides together, tack the sections together at each end. Then tack the lining for the base to the quilted sides, pinning it in place first to check that it is the right size. Try the lining in the basket to see whether it needs to be made any smaller to fit smoothly. Make any adjustments needed, then machine the pieces together.

FINISHING OFF. Press the seams at either end of the quilted sides open, and hem down either side. Oversew the bottom seam neatly. Turn back the top edge of the lining to the right depth and tack. Make a self frill by doubling a long strip of lining fabric – one and a half times the circumference of the basket in length, and about 3 inches wide – and machine-gather it along the raw edges. Tack and hand-stitch this securely in place round the top of the quilted lining (see figure 150). Add bows here and there. The lining can either be stitched in place or, if you are lining an openwork wicker basket, provided with ribbon ties. Use white linen thread if you can get it to sew the lining on, and use large stitches so that it won't take too long to remove it for washing.

WATERPROOF PAD. Use the pattern for the base to cut two pieces of plastic fabric for the cover, and several thicknesses of wadding for the pad itself. Don't allow the extra inch all round for the pad. Catch the layers of wadding together with giant stitches to make them easier to handle. Sew the two sections of plastic fabric together to handle, wrong side out, leaving a gap at one end to insert the pad. Ease the pad in, and then machine or handsew up the gap.

Holdall basket

The lining for this is made in the same way, except that it will look prettier if you quilt the base as well as the sides. Quilting, frills, bows, etc. should be scaled down to suit the smaller size. A small pincushion covered

Figure 151. *Holdall for baby things lined and quilted to match*

in the lining fabric is a thoughtful extra, particularly if you fasten it to the handle. Stuff the pincushion with kapok, sawdust or bran. Sew ribbon ties to the centre back and tie round the handle. Stick a good supply of nappy pins into the pincushion and stock the basket up with baby powder, lotion, shampoo, nappy liners and anything else you think might be useful. Provide a plastic soap-container for the baby soap.

IDEAS TO TRY

Keepsake pincushions

Heart-shaped pincushions made of patchworks of brightly coloured scraps, decorated with improving texts or tear-jerking mottoes made up of clusters of beads threaded on hat pins, sequins, are one of the quainter relics of the Victorian age. Old ones sell at stiff prices to American tourists. Pretty as these are, I often think they are not a patch on the ones made to celebrate a birth or christening. These were usually made of white satin or silk (a scrap of the mother's wedding dress?) now ivory-coloured with age, and decorated with patterns made entirely of pin heads. The combination of the darkly glinting steel pin designs with the soft pale silk is particularly successful.

Figure 152. *Victorian pincushion probably intended as a christening present. For display rather than use. The original was covered in ivory satin, with fine silk tassels and cord, and studded in hand-made pins with slightly faceted heads*

The originals of the two shown here are both in a museum. They are early Victorian. They would not be too difficult to copy, if you worked the design out first on tissue and pinned through it, and they would make charming and unusual christening presents. Of course, they are for decoration, not use.

To make one, hunt out a scrap of old silk, or satin if possible. It wouldn't have to be white, though this seems more suited to the occasion. Otherwise, buy a $\frac{1}{4}$ yard of the nicest silk you can afford. Cut the cover pieces (the originals of the two shown here were about 6×5 inches). Machine round. Make the pincushion itself in a different material, something strong and closely woven. Measure so that it will fit snugly into the satin slip-cover. Stuff the cushion very tightly with bran or sawdust.

Figure 153. *Another version with a flossy fringe edging held in place with – naturally – more pins*

Put on the satin cover and stitch the seam opening shut. Rough out the main outlines of the design onto a piece of white tissue paper cut to the size of the pin-cushion. Lay it on top of the cushion, pin down at the corners and then peg out the design, using steel, rustproof pins, through the paper into the cushion. Don't be mean with pins, they should be massed together for the motifs, and set almost side by side for lettering. The cushion should be finished off with some sort of decorative cord or fringe, sewn or pinned down over the seams. You could make a fine silk cord (*see* trimmings) and flossy tassels for the corners as in the 'God Bless The Babe' cushion. Or you could use a pretty piece of old lace, whipstitched in place and then studded with pin heads.

NOTE. Bran can be bought at any pet shop for a couple of pence. It is essential to use *rustproof* pins, or the cushion will be a sorry sight in no time. The rustproof kind are more expensive, but they have larger heads and look more like the hand-made steel pins used for the Victorian cushions.

Papered what-nots

Strictly speaking, what-nots are those little tiered shelves for displaying family bric-à-brac, but I've borrowed the term to describe all those dull but useful articles like waste bins, box files, folders, without which no desk is complete. Smartening up these utilitarian objects not only pleases the eye but encourages tidiness and takes some of the chill off the moment when one sits down to struggle with tax returns or a difficult letter. I know one shop which does a thriving trade in beribboned and charmingly papered what-nots. It is much cheaper to cover your own, using odd bits of leftover wallpaper, decoratively patterned papers sold by the sheet (look for the handsome Florentine papers – *see* Suppliers' Index), or plain cartridge paper hand-printed by yourself. Some fabrics can be used successfully too – velveteen, hessian, light close-woven cotton. These are perhaps less practical as they tend to pick up dirt. Buy the basic items – files, bins – from a stationers, or pick up secondhand ones in Oxfam shops and the like. It doesn't matter how hideous they are as long as they are in good shape. Papered what-nots, neatly covered and embellished with grosgrain ribbon, can make attractive presents.

Wastepaper bins

One of these per room is the minimum in a well-run household. Buy the cheapest tin or plastic variety from chain stores, market stalls, or stationers and cover them in a paper which matches each room so you know where to return them after emptying. The easiest shape to paper is a straight-sided cylinder with detachable base; many plastic and metal bins have sloped sides which are trickier to fit neatly.

There are dozens of adhesives on the market now, but I find old-fashioned decorator's glue size is cheap and efficient for this kind of work. Mix up a concentrated solution of size in a jam jar. Half-fill the jar with size, add enough cold water to soak it, then top up with boiling water, stirring very thoroughly to dissolve granules of size. It will set to a thick

Figure 154. *Prettily papered wastebin*

jelly when cold so, before use, stand the jar in boiling water to liquefy. Paint on warm with an old brush.

Covering a straight-sided cylinder with removable base is a rapid operation. Measure height and circumference of bin and add on 1 inch all round for folds and overlaps. Pencil the shape onto the wrong side of your paper. Cut out. Cut triangular nicks $\frac{1}{2}$ inch deep along top and bottom edges of the paper to help the paper fold smoothly and prevent ridges showing through the lining paper. Now cut the lining which should be the depth of the bin less $\frac{1}{2}$ inch and the circumference plus $\frac{1}{2}$ inch. Using the detachable base as template cut two circles to cover the base, one $\frac{3}{4}$ inch wider all round, the other $\frac{1}{4}$ inch smaller. Nick round the larger circle.

To glue brush a thin coat of size over both outer cover and bin. Make sure all edges are properly aligned. Lay the paper over the bin, starting at the middle of the sheet and smoothing outwards to press out creases and air bubbles. A soft rag pad will help here. If both surfaces are sized, the paper remains manoeuvrable longer. Size does not give impact adhesion but it sticks as it dries so don't expect to be able to peel off wrongly stuck paper after ten minutes. Bend nicked edges over top and bottom and glue down neatly. Make sure the overlap at the side is vertical; trim off with Stanley knife or scissors if not. Stick the larger circle over base, folding nicked edges carefully. Glue smaller circle on top. Covering the underside of the base may seem fussy, but it makes for a professional-looking job. Band the outside of the bin, top and bottom, with $\frac{3}{4}$-inch grosgrain ribbon, or jute webbing (depending on the materials used) stuck on with size. Leave size to dry out thoroughly – overnight. Finally, give the paper a protective finish with special paper varnish (artists' supply shops) or matt polyurethane. When using polyurethane check first on a scrap to see that the paper won't discolour or the colours bleed.

A sloping-sided bin with attached base is covered in much the same way except that cover and lining consist of two shaped sections rather than one continuous strip. Make a newspaper pattern to prevent mistakes with expensive paper. Fold the newspaper sheet back over top and bottom of bin to make creases as a guide for cutting. Cut sides straight for the time being. Now lay the roughly shaped piece in place over half the bin and mark with a pencil where side seams should come. Metal bins have

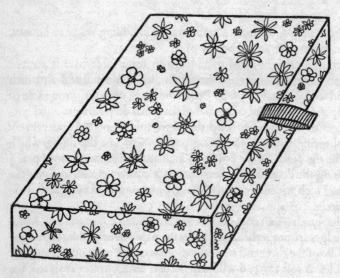

Figure 155. *Papered box file with ribbon tab*

a side seam so use this as a guide. Lay the pattern on your paper, wrong side up, and trace out shapes with pencil, allowing $\frac{3}{4}$ inch extra top and bottom and $\frac{1}{4}$ inch each side. Cut linings the same way, allowing $\frac{1}{4}$-inch overlaps at the side seams but trimming top and bottom edges off to fit inner measurements of bin. Cut two circles for papering the base, using the bin as a template. Glue the paper sections to the bin in the order given above, trimming the side seams if they overlap more than a fraction. Allow to dry thoroughly. Trim with braid or ribbon as above. Dry. Varnish.

NOTE. Some metal bins have a projecting rim. To cover this neatly glue the lining section on first, extending the top edge to fold outwards over the rim. Then glue outer cover paper on top to cover nicks and come flush to the rim. The more nicks you make on a curved glued edge the more neatly it fits.

Box file

Lay the file down on the wrong side of the paper and draw a pattern round it (figure 156). If the paper is very thick you might save time by making a newspaper pattern first. Score all the folds lightly on the wrong side with a paper knife drawn along a ruler edge to make them crease sharply. Nick the fold-back edges with a Stanley knife. Cut a slit in the box about 1 inch long to take a ribbon tab in the top of the lid. The tab slit should be set mid-way down the lid, about 1 inch back from the lift-up edge. Cut it parallel to the edge, not at right angles to it. Glue the cover to the file, smoothing all the surfaces from the centre outwards to squeeze out air bubbles, and folding all the nicked edges over. Cut a ribbon loop about 3 inches long and thread through the slot. Glue the ends down to the inside of the box and reinforce by gumming a square of paper on top. Now cut a lining from matching or contrasting paper. Cover the lid and the box part separately. Mark where the spring attachment comes on the appropriate section and cut a piece out so that the lining fits neatly round the attachment. Give the file a coat of clear paper varnish or matt polyurethane varnish inside and out to protect it from dust and fingermarks.

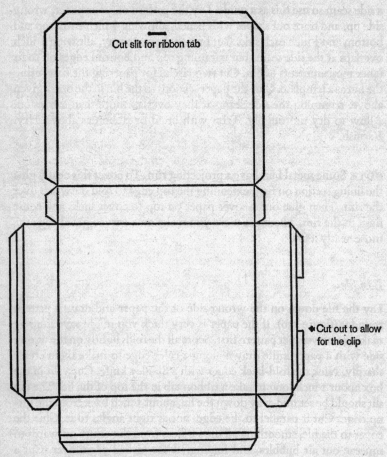

Cut slit for ribbon tab

◆ Cut out to allow
for the clip

Figure 156. *How to trace off a pattern for papering a box file. All the fold-back edges should be nicked so that they stick down neatly*

Spring folders

These can be covered to match. Choose one with rigid covers. Covering the spine and corners with adhesive carpet-tape looks nice, and strengthens the parts that get most handling. Paper front and back outer covers of the folder separately, nicking all edges that will be folded round to the inside. Now stick a length of tape down the spine so that about ¾ inch is folded under to the inside top and bottom. The tape should overlap the paper covers as with a book. Open the file flat and cut a lining from one continuous strip, marking and cutting out a piece to make it fit round the spring clip. The lining must come close up to the inside edges, covering the folded-back pieces. Fold a square of tape round a corner till you get the right size and shape to fit neatly with a mitred seam down the centre of the inner corner. Cut four pieces the same size and stick down over all four corners of the folder. Varnish as above.

Figure 157. *Spring folder covered to match*

Letter tray

Paper as for the box file, drawing a pattern in newspaper for outer cover and lining, nicking folded-back edges, scoring folds lightly. Glue and varnish as above.

Hand-printed paper

You can use any smooth but matt-surfaced paper. Buy it in large sheets from a stationers' or artists' supply shop. Use lino ink, or designers' gouache as a printing medium. The easiest kind of decorative printing to do yourself is stick printing – a slightly more elaborate version of cut-potato printing. There's no need to buy special tools – there are all sorts of odds and ends that can print nice patterns. Try cutting through a Brussels sprout and using the cut sides to print delicate rose shapes. Or, for a more abstract pattern, bunch four Drima cotton reels together with a rubber band and glue one end of the bunch to a small block of wood with Evo-stik, making sure the printing faces of the reels are all absolutely level. Use reels of different shapes and sizes to produce varied patterns. Spread the colour on something flat – a small sheet of glass – stamp the stick tool into the colour and then onto the paper. Keep to simple patterns, at any rate to begin with; a rich-coloured border with a central motif looks good (best to print the paper after the box has been covered in this case). You can mark guide lines very faintly in pencil. Varnish over the printing after the ink is quite dry.

Silhouettes

If you can't draw for toffee but the idea of making some sort of personal record of your family and friends appeals to you, why not try silhouettes? These little black-on-white profiles can capture an excellent likeness – a silhouette cut by Mrs Leigh Hunt of Lord Byron was acclaimed by all his friends as the 'best likeness of his Lordship ever made'. They are entertaining to do and, nicely framed, make charming things to hang on your walls or give away as presents. I have never known anyone who wasn't secretly gratified at having their features imperishably recorded. If you can obtain a good profile snap of them to work from, it can all come as a big surprise. One reason modern silhouettes make a poor showing compared with eighteenth- and nineteenth-century examples, is that our clothes and hairstyles are dull and shapeless compared with the fantastical wigs, beribboned caps and shepherdess hats ladies wore then, not to mention the ruffled fronts and queues and high collars in which the gentlemen caparisoned themselves. I don't see why one

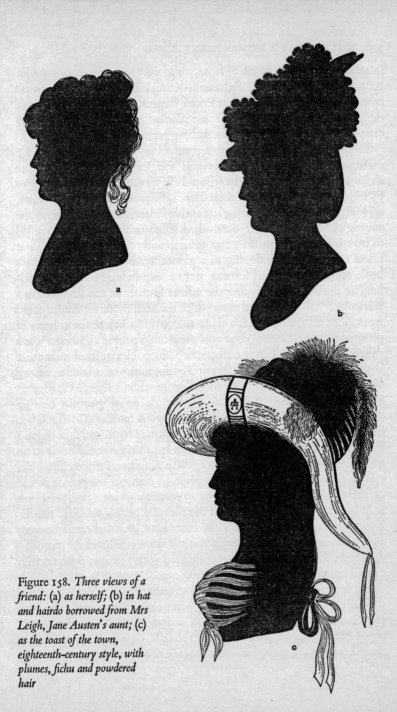

Figure 158. *Three views of a friend: (a) as herself; (b) in hat and hairdo borrowed from Mrs Leigh, Jane Austen's aunt; (c) as the toast of the town, eighteenth-century style, with plumes, fichu and powdered hair*

shouldn't introduce a touch of fantasy into silhouettes by showing your contemporary miss as an eighteenth-century belle, or a portly male relation handsomely got up à la Prince Regent. To give you an idea of the possibilities I am including some silhouettes of a friend with a fine classical profile dressed in various dashing period headgear.

Silhouette portraits have been around a very long time; you can see examples on Egyptian tomb-carvings and Etruscan vases. From the sixteenth century onwards the leisured classes often amused themselves by snipping out likenesses of their friends. But it was a book by Lavater, a Swiss pastor, published in the late eighteenth century, which made the cutting of 'shades', as they were called, a fashionable craze and soon led to troops of profile artists setting up shop and offering their services at prices ranging from a shilling to a guinea, frames included. Lavater's book claimed that facial features were a sure index of character. Silhouette portraits, by isolating the salient features of the sitter, were a particularly valuable record from which the keen character-reader could work. Like all systems which claim to provide a key to the enigma of personality and character – one's own and other people's – Lavater's was an instant success. All over Europe the fashionables quizzed each other knowingly with a copy of 'Essays on Physiognomy calculated to extend the Knowledge and Love of Mankind' close at hand. Queen Charlotte's son, the Duke of Kent, visited the famous physiognomist bearing compliments and the gift of a watch from his mother. Goethe saw a silhouette of Baroness von Stein, was enraptured by it, and thus began a love affair which lasted ten years. Nelson cut a very spirited shade of his friend, Admiral Collingwood. George III's daughter, Princess Elizabeth, was an ardent profilist and cut likenesses of many of the people in and around the court in her day. The album containing these is still preserved at Windsor. One can understand the pleasure people took in 'shades' before photography arrived. They must have been the contemporary equivalent of those instant snaps you get from machines on stations – they were the work of a minute compared with a proper portrait, they caught a good likeness, and they were cheap.

But to return to the present. If you just want to play at making profiles to while away a rainy day, all you will need is a quantity of squared paper, some tracing paper and carbon, Indian ink, and a candle. That is, if you propose to get your silhouettes the old way by interposing your sitter between a candle flame and a piece of paper pinned to the wall where you trace round the shadow with a black biro. It takes a little experiment to get this right; people *will* move their heads and candles will flicker. One of those lantern torches which throw a strong, concentrated beam might be better. Simpler still, you can use a clear profile snapshot if you have one available. If you are using the shadow-on-the-wall method, trace your profile off onto squared paper with a carbon, taking care to set the outline straight. Then reduce the size by reproducing the outline exactly on whatever scale you think appropriate. Draw it in with pencil first. When you have got it right go over the outline with Indian ink and a mapping pen, or fine nib. Paint the profile in carefully inside the outline with ink till quite black and, when dry, cut it out and mount on white card. If you are working from a snap, trace it off carefully. It might even be the right size, in which case all you need do is paint your tracing, and cut out and mount that. If it needs to be made smaller, repeat the method given above for shadow outlines.

If you find you have a knack for doing these silhouettes, and would like to do quite a few to give away, you will find a pantograph useful for doing a small scale copy quickly and accurately. This is a draughtsman's tool, and it is best to get a fairly good one which is easy to manipulate.

The old profile artists used many different ways of getting their silhouettes, some of which you might like to try. As well as simply inking a profile straight onto card, or sticking a cut-out onto card, they sometimes used the reverse procedure, in which the white card from which a profile had been carefully excised was stuck over black paper. This was known as 'hollow cut'. A hollow-cut profile, thought to be of Jane Austen, turned up pasted into an old edition of *Mansfield Park*. A great find this because only one other likeness of her, by sister Cassandra, survives. Another method was to paint the silhouette onto the back of a piece of plain, or domed, glass. This cast a slight shadow onto the white backing, adding to the interest of the picture. Or the silhouette might be set slightly above the white card, to cast a more pronounced shadow. Shades were often embellished with fine white shading about the hat, hair and clothes, though the face was always left plain black. The shading can either be added afterwards with white ink and a fine pen or sable pencil or, better still, because more delicate, by shading in the two-tone areas very carefully and cautiously with diluted ink, leaving the highlights white. If you pine for a touch of colour, you could follow the style of Buncombe, who painted a series of officers in full dress uniform (round about 1795, when they were very dressy) leaving the profiles black but shading the hair in with white and painting the costumes in the correct colours. Finally, you could dress the profile in scraps of material and beads.

Modern scrap screen

Judging by the number of mural collage efforts one sees, almost everyone must feel the urge sometime or other to play that old Victorian game of cutting out colourful scraps and sticking them together to form a satisfying pattern. The trouble is that today's source of scraps is invariably the glossies and Sunday supplements, and any attempt to varnish over these is disastrous – the paper goes semi-transparent and the print or whatever on the obverse side glares through the art-work. Varnish is essential to these collages I discovered when restoring a damaged Victorian scrap screen. It provides the unifying golden tone which blends the disparate coloured bits and pieces together and jells them into a picture. It also protects the scraps and keeps them firmly stuck in place. A designer friend suggested a simple solution – paint them over with Emulsion Glaze, which is a special protective finish with many of the properties of varnish (golden tone and slight sheen) but water-based, so that the paper returns when dry to its original state. It is often used to seal wallpapers in a steamy atmosphere like a bathroom. Ordinary do-it-yourself and decorating shops may not stock it: try decorators merchants (Suppliers' Index). Follow the maker's instructions, thinning it with more or less water depending on how glossy a finish you want.

If you want to make something portable and permanent of your collages, a large picture or screen is probably the answer. The Victorian screen I mended was constructed on simple lines, and wouldn't be difficult to copy. The three panels, hinged together, were basically light frames of ordinary deal 1 × 1 inch, with a couple of cross struts for strengthening (see figure 159). Over this, a covering of plain white cotton had been stretched taut and tacked down on both sides of the frame, much as a painter stretches and nails down a canvas. You could use ordinary unbleached calico, or a close woven muslin. This can be painted with a thin coat of glue size to stiffen it. The scraps are glued directly to the fabric panels. I used wallpaper paste, which doesn't show if splashed on the right side of the screen. Self-expression should be the keynote of a collage screen, and to hell with rules. However, I have noticed that the most attractive Victorian scrap screens seem to be composed rather like a bouquet of flowers, with the choicest blooms in the centre and the smaller ones radiating out and encircling them. To finish off the screen some flat wood beading of the sort often used to frame modern paintings should be tacked or screwed down to the panel frames all round. It can be painted, stained or simply oiled and waxed. The separate panels are then joined by hinges, two or three depending on the height of the screen. If you don't feel equal to decorating both sides of the screen the back can be covered with some suitable fabric or dark

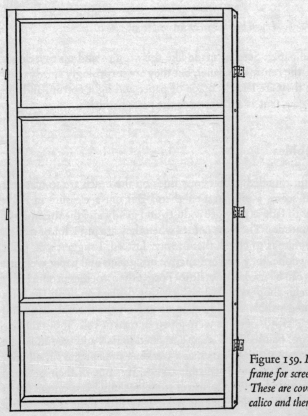

Figure 159. *Light wood frame for screen panels. These are covered with calico and then with scraps*

Figure 160. *Flat wood moulding tacked or screwed round panels*

patterned wallpaper. Screens made like this won't stand up to a direct kick through the centre of a panel, but they are surprisingly sturdy considering that they are largely made of paper and light cotton, and the fabric cover goes taut as a drum once the paste has dried.

Painted pebbles

Those smooth, rounded pebbles one finds on the beach are so nice just as they are it seems a pity to alter them. But one's pleasure in *objets trouvés* begins to fade as they grow dusty and grimy and the memory of that holiday recedes. The time comes when they are just a lot of stones, and your impulse is to chuck them away. Instead, I suggest you paint them – nicely done, they make attractive ornaments and paper weights. The big ones can be used as doorstops. Forget the atrocities produced by sea-side souvenir shops with 'views' garishly daubed on them. To look good, a painted pebble should retain or exploit the natural shape and texture. Some friends of mine were given an oval pebble, about the size of a duck's egg, painted with their entwined initials and wedding date framed in a spray of green leaves, as a wedding present and for all their home is full of much more valuable things, it is one of their personal treasures. A talented girl in Cornwall paints reclining cats on the flanks of suitably sinuous pebbles, making use of any little natural coloration

Figure 161. *A common old pebble off the beach grandly decorated with a painted acanthus wreath and initials to make an attractive memento for a wedding anniversary*

or shape in the stone itself. They look charming curled up on a window sill, or acting as a doorstop. There are lots of possibilities.

Paint them with artists' oils, mixed into clear varnish for translucent colours or undercoat for greater opacity. Some stones are so porous paint seeps into them. Coat these first with varnish, or shellac which is quicker drying. If you don't want the whole pebble to gleam, only varnish where your design is to come. When the decoration is dry, you can varnish over it to protect it, or simply wax it for a softer finish. Varnish does bring up the colours of pebbles so that they look almost as they did when wet from the sea.

Punched tin

Tin, which to us means tin cans and an overflowing dustbin, was a valued decorative material to earlier, less blasé societies. Pennsylvania Dutch punched tinware and New Mexican fantasies of shiny tin and mirror glass are some of the most attractive folk creations I know, and they made me look at the common tin with new eyes. As soon as I began experimenting with it I discovered what was presumably well-known to thrifty folk a hundred years ago, that, as metals go, tin is amazingly tractable. You can cut it with scissors, bend it, and punch designs on it which show up beautifully against the shiny surface. Decorative punching, where the pattern is embossed on the surface but does not cut right

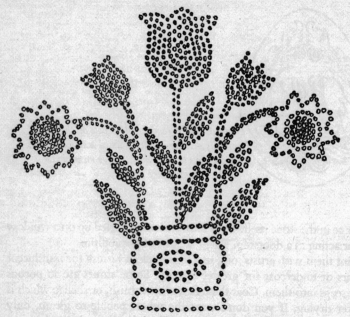

Figure 162. *Early American pattern for punching on tin*

Figure 163. *Another easy and decorative pattern, also Early American*

through the metal, makes pretty things of small cigarette or tobacco tins. Punching simple designs right through the metal makes original lampshades, like starry firmaments when lit up inside. Better still, but this requires a soldering iron and a little practice, you could make little candle lanterns to sparkle away on the dinner table, or stand around at parties. Anyone who discovers they have a real knack as a tinsmith might like to try making one of the traditional tin candle-sconces shown (figure 166). A mosaic of mirror glass let into the back adds to the brilliance.

For simple decorative punching all you need is a tack-hammer, nails, a wooden board to rest the work on, and a supply of small tins, preferably with flat lids. Unfortunately, most tobacco tins have a raised ridge round the edge, which means your pattern doesn't stand out in quite such sharp relief. But they still look attractive and a suitably embossed tin would make a useful little present for a pipe smoker or someone who rolls their own fags. First, you have to remove the maker's finish. Use one of the commercial strippers, leave it on for a good ten minutes and rub as much as possible off with rags. Wire wool tends to scratch the tin. Draw your pattern on the inside with a felt pen, and then scratch over it with the

Figure 164. *Candle-lantern design combines pinprick holes and slashes to let the light through*

nail – felt pen rubs off as you work. You can use the traditional American colonial designs shown here or invent your own, weaving in initials, hearts and flowers or whatever you fancy. The punching should be done with a light hand, as you don't want to pierce the metal – practise on another tin first. Using blunt points will raise a larger goosepimple on the tin than sharp ones, and you can use the contrast in the design. Some tin items look good painted in bright colours, finishing with several coats of varnish. For a different effect you could colour the finished item with several coats of tinted varnish, which allows the metal to show through. Or, on a really grand piece, combine punching with patterns applied in gold leaf, as the more elaborate Pennsylvania Dutch tinware does (see gilding frames). Varnish or shellac over for protection.

For lampshades you need a good large tin – an old paint-tin is excellent. Remove the finish, as before. Holes on a shade are punched right through, round nail-holes being combined with slashes to get varying patterns of light – a row of slashes lets out a good bit more light of course. Back the metal from inside with a curved log and punch quite sharply from the outside, using a round nail, to make a neat hole. Slashes – a couple of diagonal rows along top and bottom look good – are made with a strong penknife or chisel. For a hanging shade, remove the old paint-tin handle and make a ring attachment with stout wire passed through the holes and twisted – or soldered – at each end. For a table lampshade make a wire attachment the same way, except that the ring must be big enough to rest over a wire lampshade holder. Punched-tin lanterns and candle-holders were often painted matt black, probably to heighten the contrast when lit, and you could do this with a coat of blackboard paint over metal primer.

Candle lanterns and sconces need a soldering iron, plus soft solder, flux and a blow-lamp, preferably one that can be adjusted to make a small flame. The butane gas sort is best for this job, though a paraffin blow-lamp can be used too. Alternatively, a small electrically heated soldering iron is adequate for soldering tin.

The simplest candle holder has a conical hat soldered onto a simple cylinder which in turn rests on a flat tin saucer with a raised rim all round. An inner ring holding the lantern steady is a good idea too, though not necessary if you aren't going to carry it about. The top and sides of the lantern should be punched decoratively. The lantern lifts off the base to set the candle in place and clean off old wax. Use the top of one large tin

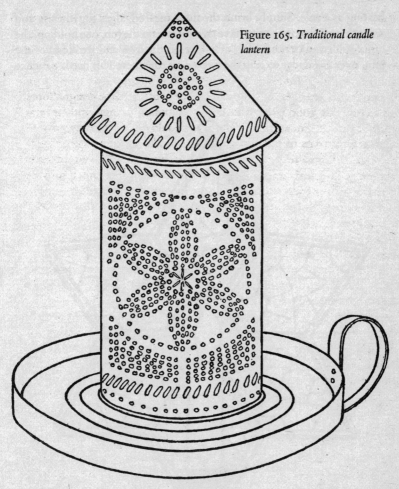

Figure 165. *Traditional candle lantern*

for the base, a narrow cylindrical tin for the lantern and a piece cut and bent to shape for the hat. Punch before soldering. To solder, first wire wool or lightly sand the edges to be joined till quite bright and free from grease. Smear with flux on a rag. The soldering iron should be cleaned with sandpaper, heated till hot, smeared with flux and then touched with solder to tin it before use. Small pieces of tin can be soldered without heating as a rule. Simply bring the flux-smeared edges together as you want them (I find it helps to have two people on the job, one holding, the other soldering), take a blob of solder on the iron and stroke over the join, over *and* under to grip the two edges together. This needs patience

Figure 166. *New Mexican wall-candle sconce which could be copied by anyone familiar with solder and its problems. The reflector is made in sections separated off by a ¼-inch fillet of tin and filled in with a mosaic of broken mirror bedded in tile cement or adhesive. The cracked reflection is prettier than one using whole mirrors*

because it may not stick straight away. You may need to apply quite a bit of solder along the join or seam. Also the join should be held in place for a minute or two to let the solder harden, especially if it is under any pressure. Larger pieces of tin have to be heated before and during the soldering process because at a certain point the area of metal – if unheated – draws the heat of the iron off instantaneously and the solder stays stuck to the tip of the iron. On the other hand, too fierce a heat will burn a hole in soft metal. Experiment with odd bits of tin, taking great care not to burn yourself. One method is to flux the edges to be joined, bring them together as you want them, using some sort of tongs or clamp to hold them together, then lay small pieces of solder along the join and play a small flame along till the metal and solder are heated to the point where they stick. Alternatively, heat your metal with the flame, after fluxing the join, and touch the soldering iron to the solder just above the desired join so that it runs in. There is a knack to soldering successfully, so persevere even if you don't get a good join the first time. Excess solder can be removed with a file or simply by sanding. Finish with fine paper to polish it up. Learning to solder efficiently does obviously open the way to making all sorts of interesting things – you might even manage a punched-tin coffeepot like the Pennsylvania Dutch ones.

The candle lantern needs soldering to join the sides together, to join the hat to the cylinder and to fix the raised rim round the edge of the base. Ideally, an inner ring should also be soldered in place. To hold the candle steady, punch a nail up through the middle of the base and solder it in place. Spike the candle onto this. The handle is held by two rivets. (For fixing these *see* jumping jacks, but back the metal with a piece of wood before hammering the rivet ends apart.)

For wall-candle-holders you need some sort of decorative-shaped back which will act as reflector, a small projecting sconce to take a candle and something to hang it by. Use rivets as well as solder to fix the sconce strongly to the back. Make the sconce part first with a rim to hold the candle securely. Hang it by a wire loop soldered in place, or better still run a straight piece of tin up the back to which the decorative reflector and sconce are riveted and punch a hole at the top to hang by. Soldering a narrow rim all round the reflector part, or bending the edges up and soldering where they meet, allows you to bed fragments of mirror in a mosaic on the back, as they do in New Mexico. Use tile cement or Araldite. A lot of trouble but fantastically pretty.

Tie-and-dye

Even if that endless stream of smudgy T-shirts several summers back thoroughly quenched your interest in tie-and-dye, I do urge you to give it just one try. Apart from the fact that you can get quite spectacular effects from the word go, it's enthralling to do – that moment when one snips the sodden bandages of string to unfold a great streaming, swirling, marbly mosaic of colour is as palpitating as a blasé adult can hope for between tea and supper on a cold winter afternoon. The preliminary tying up operation is a bit long-winded, but it contributes to the suspense. As unpredictableness is so essential to the pleasure of tie-dyeing, I suggest you never repeat the same method or colours twice – unless of course you want to recapture a particularly successful pattern for a specific purpose. Dye is cheap, the possible colour permutations almost unlimited, and two different fabrics given the same treatment will emerge quite astonishingly different. I think one of the reasons so much tie-and-dye looks a little dingy is that the materials used – cotton knit, for one – tend to be uninteresting in themselves, and the colours often look more like the remains of a Neapolitan ice than a Turner sunset. Try dyeing odd lengths of handsome fabric (scraps of silk, velvet, velveteen); use hot and strong colours and you will be agreeably surprised. I used an old piece of flimsy pure silk for my first effort, and dyed it terracotta over scarlet, and the result was so beautiful I felt obliged to spend the next few days rather irritably hemming the thing to make a square to drape round somebody's throat.

The procedures I shall describe here are of the simplest; one tie method using string which is perfect for scarves or tablecloths or squares of fabric, one quick method using clothes pegs which will give an attractive broken stripe on odd lengths of fabric, and one slightly fussier process involving pebbles and string which makes a splendid rich pattern on velveteen. (One of the first things I shall do when I have finished this book is spend a whole day tying pebbles into velveteen for a pair of unique pants.) These few suggestions will almost certainly set you off thinking up variations of your own.

If you want large pieces of cheap cloth to glorify, try unbleached calico (Suppliers' Index). Boil it up before dyeing, to get rid of the dressing and whiten it. Tie-dyed calico is good for bedcovers, tablecloths, curtains and clothes, though it won't look as rich as silk or velvet of course. Other inexpensive materials to investigate are muslin, sheeting, cotton twill, lawn. Find odd lengths of glamorous fabric on remnant counters and in sales. By way of equipment you need an elderly saucepan or two, or an old metal bucket, for boiling things up in. Be prepared for your tie-dyed masterpieces gradually to fade with washing and exposure to light – they fade nicely, so that's no great drawback. And wash separately in case some colour runs.

Quick tie-dye method

You need a square of material (the finer the material the larger the area you can dye successfully), two dye colours and plenty of string.

Find the centre of the square, hold it in your left hand and pull the four corners out with the other till you have a bundle like a collapsed umbrella. Wind string tightly round the bundle (at intervals), starting at the centre point (figure 167). Leave gaps between these string bindings for a

Figure 167. *Quick method. Use roughly this arrangement, spacing the tightly tied strings as you fancy, for the first operation. For the second dyeing, add a second row of strings in the gaps to give fuzzy circles of a different colour*

second series of bindings later. The area under the string will remain largely undyed. Treat the four corners separately, folding each one into three and tying across twice. Dye as specified on the tin. Rinse the bundle in cold water till the water runs clear. Now tie a new, slightly narrower, set of bindings between the old ones, and re-dye in the second colour. Rinse as before. Remove the bindings and rinse again. It's a good idea to iron these tie-dyed articles dry to get rid of all the tiny creases. Iron them over sheets of newspaper to mop up any faint traces of dye.

Roll and peg method

This is good for a longish narrow strip of material like a muffler.

Concertina the material up into a narrow roll and peg – the old gipsy pegs give a dash-dash-dash sort of stripe while the usual spring ones give more of a dot-dot-dot – across the roll, first from one side then the other. If you want a two-colour pattern leave fairly wide gaps between for more pegs, otherwise space them as near as you want your stripes. Dye. Rinse well. Add more pegs for a second dyeing and re-dye. Rinse, remove pegs and rinse again.

Pebbles and string method

Tying the pebbles into your fabric at regular intervals will give you stripes made up of little, irregular circles. To keep your pebbles to the straight and narrow, either chalk a guide line on the back of the fabric or run a line of tacking. Tie a good twist of string beneath each pebble – the string equals the width of your undyed area, not the pebble. Dye. For a

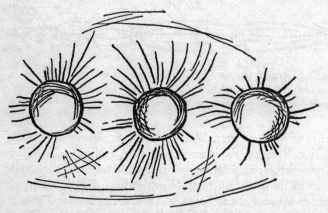

Figure 168. *A row of pebbles tied into cloth with string or elastic bands*

more elaborate effect, either tie in some more pebbles and re-dye a second colour, or tie a little polythene cap over each pebble before re-dyeing. If you used a pile fabric like velveteen try and stretch it out to dry. When dry, steam it flat with a steam-iron held just above the pile, or hold it over a boiling kettle till the creases vanish.

Candles

It's fascinating how crazes sweep through certain age-groups. After tie-and-dye it seems to be making candles; large, decorative ones, the sort that cost a lot. I put the word round that I was interested in candle-making for this book and soon afterwards a nice girl called Pebbles arrived to give me an expert account of the cheapest and easiest ways to go about it. With power strikes perpetually looming, a couple of candles like these would make quite a popular present. Or keep them for your own sultry candle-lit evenings.

To make them – a much easier process than one might imagine – you need wax, wicks, colourant (for fancy effects), moulds and an old sauce-pan. You can do all this on the cheap, using wax crayons for colour, and improvised moulds, or go the whole hog and get Dye Disks, paraffin wax in huge blocks, wick by the yard in different diameters, and ready-made moulds (Suppliers' Index). Personally, I should start small.

You need *either* a 2-pound block of paraffin wax (from chemists) and some wick (from artists' supply shop or craft shops), *or* a box of Price's wax candles which you melt down, re-using the wicks. Colour with ordinary kid's wax crayons; a quarter of a crayon is enough for one candle. A light aluminium saucepan is best, as it helps the wax melt speedily. Now moulds: Pebbles, who has a genius for improvisation, suggested such things as cardboard boxes, Sellotaped up for strength, plastic golden syrup containers from Sainsbury's, old solid deodorant containers in the sizes sold for men. To impress a pattern on your candle, stick flat buttons, or straws arranged in patterns, to the sides of your moulds with Evostick.

Making

Melt the wax in your saucepan and drop in the crayon or Dye Disk, shake it about for a few seconds but don't let it boil or stand as this will make your colour wishy-washy. Now, quickly dip the wick into the wax to coat it and make it stiff. Pour the wax into your mould and push the wick in just as it is beginning to go solid – the wax dips in the centre and gets a film on top. Hold the wick in place till the wax is solid. When quite cold gently push it out of the mould, or unwrap it if you were using a cardboard box. If the candle looks a little rough-hewn it can be polished with tissues. Should you want to make a multi-coloured, or tiered candle, it is important to leave the first colour to get really cold (in the fridge) before pouring on the next, otherwise colour two melts colour one and the result is messy. The wick must be set in place from the first, of course. For Leaning Tower of Pisa effects tip the tube or mould diagonally while the wax sets, then scrape a bit off the bottom to make a secure base. Scented candles can be made, so Pebbles assures me, by adding after-shave talc or crushed joss-sticks to the melted wax.

Child art for posterity

As every parent knows most children are capable of turning out the most spirited and colourful drawings and paintings in about five minutes flat. Their best efforts have a boldness of conception and execution as well as a highly original way of rendering familiar forms which adult artists must often envy, all spontaneous and effortless as it is. I really think parents should preserve their children's best efforts, for the sake of art (quite seriously) as much as to please the child. One way is to frame them properly (see Frames). Another attractive idea is to use the pictures as inspiration for fabric collages, as a friend of mine does, with very appealing results. At the risk of bringing the Embroidery Guild thundering down upon me, I would even go so far as to say that I only like fabric collages used to render the 'Douanier' Rousseau-ish imaginative world of child art. What might be called 'serious' fabric collages always look to me at once prissy and anaemic, like underdone paintings.

Choose a picture which has plenty of shapes and action, and not too many matchstick figures. Trace off the picture if you want to reproduce it faithfully. Cut shapes out of any fabrics you fancy, they can be as wildly patterned or as close to the original as you like. Glue down with Copydex or Bostik to a fabric backing. Flannel would look good and keep its shape well – the Victorians often used black flannel for embroidered pictures. Work any fine detail in embroidery stitches – chain, stem, herringbone would all keep the naïf look – and add beads, sequins, or any other sparkle you think the picture needs. Mount the picture by glueing it over a piece of thick cardboard or hardboard before framing.

A maple frame would be perfect for this sort of picture. They are expensive, though you might come across one in a sale or out-of-the-way junk shop. A plain wood frame dyed a bright colour (*see* wood finishing) would have a pleasantly primitive air about it too.

SOME TOYS

Decorating a doll's house

I bought a hideous modern doll's house in a jumble sale for 10p and enjoyed myself so much redecorating it I thought I would mention the possibilities to encourage some reader to follow suit. A real handyman would build his own, and get great pleasure from doing so, perhaps using the elegant proportions of an attractive period house as a guide. After all, a doll's house is not much more than a box divided into compartments, with a hinged front. All the rest is ingenuity and *trompe-l'oeil*. But you might well come across a secondhand doll's house cheaply. Mine was a suburban villa with glaring red roof, blue window frames and paper Bougainvillaea creeping across its cream walls. Now it looks like a neo-Georgian residence in one of the select parts of St John's Wood, very swanky and prosperous.

I concentrated first on the outside. Changing the cream walls to mellowed brick was first priority. I sanded the old finish down, removing the paper creepers, and gave it two coats of undercoat mixed with a little Polyfilla to give a slightly rough texture. Over this went two coats of brick red – Indian red oils mixed into flat white. When dry, I painted brick outlines in white on the front and sides, and tinted individual bricks in pink, ochre and blue to look like old brickwork. Quicker and easier to paper the house with special doll's house brick-paper, but the small town where I live doesn't run to such things. Anyway, this sort of patient elaboration is part of the pleasure of a conversion like this. Then the roof was repainted slate blue, to tone in with the bricks, the windowframes white, and the front door a cheerful yellow with a paper clip pushed through a slit to imitate a brass door knob. I made flagstones on the ledge outside the front door with Wallart and tinted them flagstone colours. Finally I glued two little trees – the kind sold for Christmas cakes – in tubs either side of the front door, and gave the exterior a coat of varnish.

The interior consisted of two large rooms, which seemed a bit dull, so I added wooden partitions with doors in them down the middle to make four rooms. The sitting-room I did out in great style with dull red walls and old greeny-blue tapestries (painted on bits of coarse calico and stuck down) hung round, and a black and white flagged floor – also painted on. I made a very simple mantelpiece of three bits of ply and painted them white and glued them to one wall to give the room a focus. A pocket mirror cut in half, with a bit of piping cord stuck round the outside, made a mirror over the fireplace. It's as well to strike a balance between fixtures and movable objects when doing out a doll's house or the place will look as if wreckers have been in within a few hours of turning children loose on it. Glue down as many of the carpets, mirrors and pictures as possible, and let the mites work out their power-drive moving the furniture about.

The dining-room is in tasteful country-gentleman style, with yellow and white panelled walls, a *trompe l'oeil* window painted on one wall, with chintzy curtains, and a piece of coarse hessian glued to the floor to look like rush matting. The panels I made by sticking bits of seating cane, cut to size, on the walls in rectangle shapes. I painted a view for the window – green grass, a tree and blue sky and, after sticking it down, glued a piece of plastic with white glazing bars painted on over the top. I fancied the idea of using a postcard reproduction of an early water-colourist like Cotman for the view, but I couldn't find anything on the right scale. Heads cut from postcard versions of Old Master paintings make excellent family portraits, glued round the walls. A real perfectionist could find Wallart immensely useful for simulating plasterwork, and elaborate door surrounds and fireplaces, as it sticks to anything, and can be modelled quite finely with something like the pointed end of a nail-file.

The bedrooms – a nursery, of course, and a bedroom for the parent dolls – are more cosy in feeling, with some scraps of Liberty-printed lawn, diminutively patterned, as wallpaper in the parental chamber, and spotted pink cotton in the nursery. Coloured felt, stuck down with Copydex, carpets both rooms. An odd piece of canvas-work I had left over from making a cushion made a needlework rug for the master bedroom, and the other half of the pocket mirror was glued on one wall lengthways as a dressing mirror. This is as far as I've got – no furniture as yet, though my brain teems with ideas. You can buy readymade sets of doll's house furniture, of course, but somehow the charm of these Lilliputian dwellings seems spoilt by introducing readymade stuff – the palatial Victorian doll's houses exhibited in places like the Bethnal Green Museum mostly have the look of a family enterprise – Papa making the furniture, while Mamma and the girls worked little needlework rugs and embroidered bed hangings, and painted tiny pictures to hang on the walls. They are mostly crammed with furniture, as the Victorians liked their homes to be, and one suspects the children were only allowed to play with the 'baby house' on special occasions, under their parents' watchful eyes. The trouble is, of course, as with model train sets, that the grown-ups get so passionately involved in the make-believe that they can scarcely bear to let their brutal children near, grabbing and despoiling and appallingly indifferent to the tasteful appointments and ingenious contrivances.

One modern convenience which casts magic over a doll's house for a child is electric light. This can be rigged up quite simply from a torch battery, and tiny torch bulbs set into the ceilings, with the help of a little soft solder. It is perfectly safe.

There are all sorts of ingenious ideas for furnishings. I won't suggest many because half the fun is thinking up your own. Postage stamps are a well known source of pictures and prints. Glue string or tiny strips of coloured Sellotape or even *passe-partout* round them for frames. Large shells – the cockleshell sort – can be set into Wallart to make a handsome Georgian-style decorative treatment over the front door. Thin bamboo can be used with plywood to make furniture like four-poster beds and tables. Glue the joins with Araldite. A small straw table-mat makes a splendid rush mat for the dining room. Iced lolly sticks, matchboxes, cotton reels – all the flotsam, and jetsam of one's daily life can be conscripted into the game.

Rocking toy

This endearing little rocking toy (*see* inset) is a copy of a traditional Bavarian wooden toy. It is much easier to make than might appear to those who have never done any whittling. My husband finished the carving and shaping in a few hours and says he enjoyed seeing the little figure emerge from the wood. 'Not exactly Michelangelo, but very satisfying.'

Standard deal is adequate. It is inclined to be brittle but if a small piece chips off it can be stuck back with Evostik wood adhesive. You will need a block 4×2 (inches), 16 inches long. Also a panel saw for roughly cutting the main shapes, and a Stanley saw-blade for finer cutting round the small figure's arms, horse's head, etc. Take the piece of wood and cut into three blocks as shown. A, B and C. Mark out the shapes with a felt pen, not worrying too much about perfect accuracy – no two toys are quite alike. Use a panel saw to rough out the shape on block A. Finish by planing with a Surform plane and then sanding with coarse, medium and fine sandpaper till smooth and shapely. Blocks B and C are roughly shaped with the Stanley saw-blade. Use this to cut between the rider's arms, finishing with a penknife or sharp knife. This is the most delicate part of the figure to shape.

Then, with a sharp penknife, start whittling away at the rough shapes. Soon you will have reached the exciting stage when you can reach for

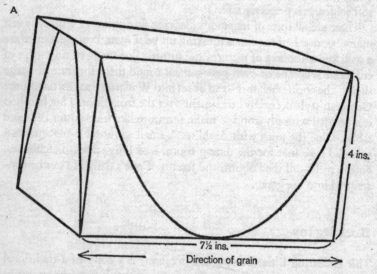

Figure 169 (a). *Base of rocking toy. Cut round line first, then cut along straight lines so that the base is wider than the top*

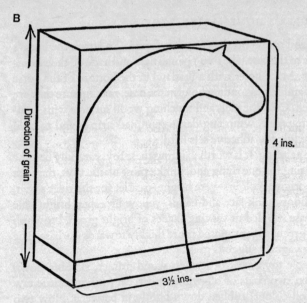

Figure 169 (b). *Guide for cutting horse's head. Use a Stanley saw blade*

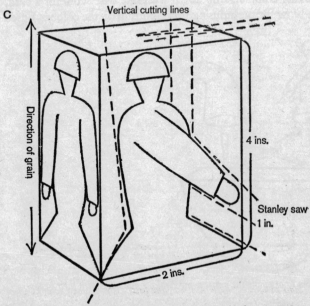

Figure 169 (c). *Guide for cutting figure, using saw blade*

the sandpaper and round off the complete figure. To attach the horse's head and figure to the base take two 1¼-inch nails and hack off their heads with a hacksaw. Make holes with a bradawl in the bottom of the horse head and rider, and corresponding holes in the base, making sure they are properly aligned. Coat the nails and touching wood surfaces with Araldite and press together, wrapping damp gummed strip round to hold them in place while the adhesive sets hard.

Now for the painting. It is worth painting these toys carefully because they take a beating for one thing and, unlike most plastic toys, they last for years. The original colours were bright – scarlet for the rider's coat, black hat and boots, pink face and hands, yellow breeches, bright blue saddle-cloth, base stippled in varying shades of bright green, brownish green, greyish green, superimposed more thickly towards the base. The green stippling vaguely suggests grass.

Give the whole toy a coat of leadless wood primer, rubbing down when dry. Then two coats of off-white undercoat (mix in a little raw umber artists' oil-colour) rubbed down lightly in between. Now two coats of eggshell, similarly tinted with raw umber (*see* painting wood for advice on mixing colours). Rub down with fine wire wool for a hard, satiny finish. Now for the amusing part – putting on the colours. I used

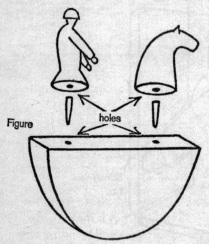

Figure

holes

Figure 170. *How to assemble the parts, using Araldite and nails with their heads sawn off*

artists' oils mixed into a little varnish to speed drying and give a harder finish. Acrylics (*see* decorative painting) are less suited to toys, I think, because they don't last so well under hard wear. Humbrol enamels – sold in tiny tins for model painting – are good for plain coloured areas, like the rider's coat, but I find them too thick to use for the stippled effects. I painted the toy in the original colours, but you could alter them if you preferred. Stippling looks effective and is easy to do, using a stiff bristled brush. First brush a thin, transparent coat of light green over the areas to be stippled. When this is dry, mix up some darker green, and a little brownish green. Stipple this over the pale green patches using the tips of the stiff bristles, varying the darker green with brownish green and going for an irregularly freckled look. I gave the horse and base a coat of glaze (raw umber mixed with linseed oil and turps – *see* classical decorative painting) to soften the colours a little. Finish with several coats of clear varnish, rubbing down in between for a very sleek surface which is pleasant to handle. Don't skip the varnishing. It doubles the life of the paintwork and gives a nice bright finish.

Dobbin

I found the instructions for the wooden horse on wheels (*see* inset) in one of those fascinating old home encyclopedias which cope with every conceivable contingency from food poisoning to building your own summerhouse. The encyclopedia was Edwardian but Dobbin's ancestry goes back considerably further. I have seen early Victorian editions of this traditional toy, clearly designed to help toddlers with their first steps, in museums, and I daresay older ones exist. Traditionally, the horse was left unpainted, but varnished, with coloured saddle and harness and a bristly fur mane and tail. This particular Dobbin might have looked better-proportioned with a slightly larger head I decided, after seeing him completed. Readers can suit themselves about that. My husband made the horse in four or five evenings, without an electric saw or drill, which would have speeded the job up. All the wood used was standard deal as sold by any timber merchant, which is cheap and fairly easy to work. As anyone who does much carpentry will know, standard deal is full of flaws. It's a good idea to inspect your pieces for cracks or warping. The hardest part of the making was shaping the body from a block of 4×4, a round 4 inches in diameter being unobtainable. He sawed the corners off to roughly the right size, planed off the surplus and sanded it smooth. It was the most complicated bit of carpentry he had attempted, but he says it was simple to make and the finished horse is remarkably solid – except for one weak spot. The original handle shafts were made of deal like the rest. My two-year-old daughter grabbed the toy for a trial run, bumped it down stairs and cracked one shaft clean through. Replacements were made from seasoned wood we happened to have lying around. I suggest you look out for something sturdy and seasoned for the shafts.

I decided to paint the horse, partly to hide the knots and flaws in the wood, partly to make it look more decorative. If you settle on a painted finish, remember that it is going to take endless wear and tear and banging about, and only a really perfectionist finish will stand up to that and still look shabbily distinguished a couple of generations hence. Several coats of plain varnish, rubbed down well when dry, would be an easier way of finishing the horse.

TIPS FOR AMATEUR CARPENTERS: let the weight of the saw blade do the cutting, don't waste energy bearing down on it; wrap sandpaper round a block of wood to distribute the pressure (progress from coarse to fine for finishing); the head can be cut out with saw-blade attachment to a Stanley knife.

Measurements and instructions

Dobbin's body is a 10-inch length of 4×4, shaped to a cylinder but flattened at the bottom; legs, 10 inches long cut from rounds 1 inch in diameter, tapered to $\frac{3}{4}$ inch at each end. Head, cut from piece $5\frac{1}{2} \times 4\frac{3}{4} \times \frac{1}{2}$ and set into the body to a depth of $\frac{1}{2}$ inch. Base is $12 \times 4 \times \frac{1}{2}$ with lengths of 1-inch section underneath to screw wheels to. If of wood, the latter are $2\frac{1}{4}$ inch diameter and $\frac{3}{4}$ inch thick. Handle shafts formed by two $18 \times 1 \times \frac{3}{8}$ lengths with a 4-inch length of $1\frac{1}{8}$-inch diameter round between.

The head is sunk and glued into a chiselled groove $\frac{1}{2}$ inch deep. Legs are tapered off at each end and sunk and glued into chiselled sockets in body and base. For extra strength run 1-inch screws up through base into legs. Sections for wheels are also glued and screwed to base. The wheels are screwed into the sections with small washers to help them

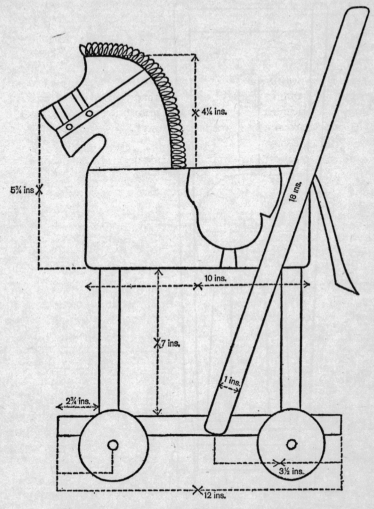

Figure 171. *Dobbin in profile showing overall measurements*

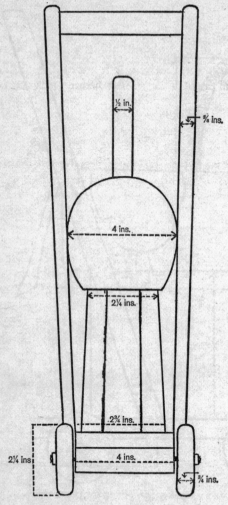

Figure 172. *Dobbin: rear view*

run freely. A stronger alternative would be to use metal bolts run right through the wheel blocks. The handle shafts are screwed to the base, into the horse's body and to the handle itself.

All visible screws should be countersunk, and the holes filled in with plastic wood. Finish any cracks where legs join body and base, and round neck in the same way. Sand plastic wood smooth before varnishing or painting.

Finishing

The whole horse should be sanded to satin smoothness. For a varnished finish, apply three to four coats of good varnish – spar varnish is a sturdy grade – rubbing down between each coat with fine wire wool or very fine sandpaper, brushing very carefully to remove particles each time. By rubbing down the first coat you force it into the pores of the wood and it acts as a grain filler.

If you are painting the toy give the whole thing a coat of leadless wood primer. Sand. Then two coats of ordinary undercoat, sanding in between. Then two coats of top coat, or one split coat and one top coat (*see* wood finishing). I used an off-white, made by mixing white egg-shell with a little raw umber, yellow ochre and a spot of black artists' oils. Dappling can be done by painting on irregular patches of darker grey, or brown, and these can be stippled with black. Don't overdo the dappling. Paint base, handles and wheels black or a cheerful contrasting colour. Finish with one or, better still, two coats of clear varnish, rubbed as above.

The mane is made from a strip of bristly fur (I used black-dyed fur trimming as sold in haberdashers) $\frac{1}{2}$ inch wide, glued in place. Secure with tiny tacks. Tail is a longer thin strip nailed onto horse's backside. (I was given some black horsehair so I used that instead). Make the saddle and harness from scraps of leather. These can be simply glued into place. I added the brass-headed nails for strength as well as decoration.

Pram toy

A French idea which makes a change from plastic ducks: a row of little stuffed dolls in bright cotton prints strung together on round elastic threaded with wooden beads, with a ring each end to fasten them to the

Figure 173. Pram toy made from small stuffed shapes threaded on to elastic with large wooden beads

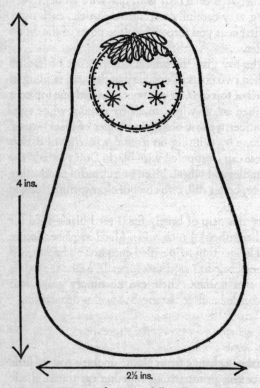

4 ins.

2½ ins.

Figure 174. Pattern for cutting dolls. Allow ½-inch seam allowance all round

pram or cot. Five dolls is about right for the average pram, made to the size shown here. Choose a different bright print for each one, machine round on the wrong side as for a cushion, and stuff with kapok or a special Terylene stuffing recommended for soft toys. Buttonhole white cotton circles on for faces, with buttonholed eyes, cheeks buttonholed in pink and pink stem-stitched mouths. Boy dolls have a shock of wool hair in yellow or red, as shown; girl dolls, two long plaits. Thread together with an upholstery needle threaded with round hat elastic, with a bright wooden bead between each doll. Thread one or two beads at either side, tie the end of the elastic over a small brass ring and push the ends of the elastic under the nearest bead.

I is for inkstand

Anyone with the patience to cut twenty-six perfect circles out of stiff cardboard could make a set of alphabet counters which would keep a young child – aged three to five, I would think – absorbed for hours. The original of this educational toy is Victorian (the Victorians believed in combining instruction with pleasure), hence the inkstand – now, alas, obsolete. The Victorian counters came in a little cylindrical box.

To make your own set, start with the box – a spill box, or one of those boxes peppermint chocs come in. Dress this up by covering with nice bright paper and a label saying ABC or something similar. Then make a thin cardboard template which will fit into the box neatly with a little to spare all round. Using this as a guide, trace off twenty-six (add a few more to be on the safe side) little circles on mounting board or stiff card-board. Cut round them with a Stanley knife (new sharp blade as always, and you may need to replace it half-way through). It's best to cut round a bit roughly, and neaten your shapes afterwards with a razor blade. Smooth the edges round with glasspaper or fine sandpaper.

The next part is fun. On one side of all the round counters ink in the letters of the alphabet with Indian ink, mapping pen (for the outlines), and watercolour brush. Get a book on type from the library and trace off the letters in a typeface that appeals to you. On the reverse side of each counter draw whatever symbol you think would appeal to a young child – apple, boat or button, cat and so forth. Choose things which can be drawn small and still be recognizable. Children don't give a hang for artistic skill but they like bright colours, so paint them all in – draw them

I IS FOR INKSTAND

Figure 175. *I is for Inkstand*

in pencil first, then Indian ink – with watercolours or gouache in nice bright colours. To drive home the point you can write A is for Apple and so forth under each little picture. Finish off the counters with a coat of watercolour varnish to protect them.

Home-made building blocks

A set of wooden building blocks is one of the best toys for a small child, and a cheap, easy one to make yourself. Use odd bits of wood, if you have any lying around, or buy lengths of deal section – 1×1 and 2×2 inches, plus odd pieces for making triangle or cylindrical shapes.

To make

Saw the section into cubes, marking these first with pencil or biro as a cutting guide. Then sandpaper all surfaces very thoroughly, starting with a coarse to medium grade – depending how rough the deal is – and working up to the finest glasspaper. It is essential to have the blocks perfectly smooth, without tiny splinters that will catch in a child's hands. Round the edges of the blocks a little, too; it makes them pleasanter to handle. You can finish them very simply by just rubbing in a little oil, which will bring up the grain and give a soft sheen. Or you could shellac them – shellac is ideal for this sort of job as it dries almost instantly – and then glasspaper or wire wool the surface till the natural wood texture shows through again. Or, if you like colour – and I suspect small children do – colour them by dyeing with one of the commercial wood dyes or ordinary Dylon, mixed very strong. Then shellac to protect the dyed finish, wire-wool lightly, and finish with a little oil.

If you want the gift to be as popular with the parents as with the child, make a container to put them in. A little canvas sack, closed with a drawstring, with the child's name painted or stencilled on it with Indian ink, would be ideal.

Jumping Jacks

These little toys – a sort of wall-puppet, I suppose – make attractive, cheap presents. They only cost a few pence to make if you own a pantograph (*see* silhouettes), and they are great fun to do. An extra large one (four times the size of the ones illustrated here) makes a pretty thing to hang on a wall, and not just in the nursery.

Jumping Jacks, or *pantins* as the French call them, were such a craze in late eighteenth-century France that the police finally banned them on the grounds that playing with the toy might cause pregnant women to give birth to children with twisted limbs. The ban must have been a relief to Boucher, the court painter, who was constantly pestered by grand ladies to paint them a *pantin* to eclipse all the rest. As a matter of fact it *is* a fascinating toy – no one, from babies upwards, can resist tugging the string to see the arms and legs fly up.

The two shown here are replicas of old French ones, nineteenth-century to judge by Columbine's tight lacing. Presumably the revolutionaries rescinded the ban. I made both of them up twice the size shown, using a pantograph to trace the main outlines in pencil onto mounting card, which is about the right weight. It comes in large sheets, white one side, cream the other. The cream side gives the toys an appropriately yellowed-with-age look. Go over the outlines and fill in the detail with a mapping pen and sepia ink. Paint the figures in watercolours

Figure 176. *Columbine*

Figure 177. *Pierrot*

or gouache, using clear, bright colours like crimson, ultramarine, sharp yellow. The toys look prettier if you vary their costumes with scraps of rich looking materials, velvet, lace or silk, and add lots of sparkle with sequins, beads and glitter dust. Use beads to keep sequins in place. Pierrot should have a white face, but no red nose as he was a figure of pathos rather than fun.

Cut the shapes out with a Stanley knife, using a new blade. Keep the blade as vertical as possible while cutting, and don't try to cut out the finicky bits like hands and feet too carefully. They can be shaped more easily afterwards with a razor blade. If your pressure was even the shapes may just lift out, but probably you will have to score over the faint ridges visible on the back. Ragged edges can be smoothed with fine sandpaper.

Stringing

Take a little trouble over the stringing to get the most movement from the toy. I used bifurcated rivets to hold the joints together. (Packets in various sizes from ironmongers.) Use the smallest size for the figures as shown here, larger ones if you are multiplying up. It is a good idea to start with ordinary paper clips as a temporary fastening while you experiment with the strings, because they are easily removed if you decide to alter something. First, punch holes in the torso and limbs as shown by the dots on the drawings. A leather punch is the ideal tool for this (from craft shops) but you can use something like an ice pick, or hammer a sharp nail through. If the rivets are very small a carpet needle would do.

The holes for the strings to pass through are made separately, and the positioning of these is important (see figure 178). Make them with a large darning needle almost above the rivet holes but just a fraction to one side. The main thing is to have the holes in line with each other, thus the two arm strings should be in line when the toy is suspended from the wall, and the two leg strings likewise. The position of these holes regulates the movement of the limbs, and unevenly placed ones will make one arm or leg fly up less satisfactorily than the other. It's not disastrous if this does happen. The toy will still be just as entertaining. It only means that it will be subjected to rather more wear and tear as people juggle about trying to get the movements symmetrical. For the actual stringing I used button

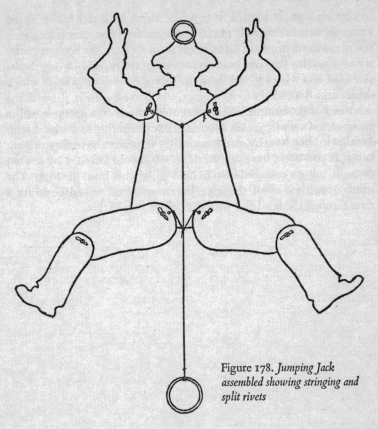

Figure 178. *Jumping Jack assembled showing stringing and split rivets*

thread for the small Jumping Jacks and ordinary string for the larger ones. Button thread is easier to control than ordinary cotton when tying fiddly knots. Use reef knots which don't slip. The neatest way to string is to have separate strings for each limb, knotting them together in the centre, and then taking a long string down from one pair to the next, knotting it to each (keep these knots central and one above the other as far as possible) and tying a small brass ring (a small curtain ring) to the end to pull by. People with a talent for this sort of thing may be able to work out a better system, but mine works quite satisfactorily. The Pierrot figure, incidentally, though less attractive to look at, is a more amusing toy in motion because his legs are jointed in two places and his lower limbs, as the Victorian writers delicately put it, fly around freely on their rivet joints. To fix the rivets firmly in place, insert them through the holes, turn the toy over and lay the rivet head on something really hard – a large hammer head was what I used – bang the forked ends slightly apart with a chisel or the flat end of a tack hammer, and then bang down flat with the other end of the hammer. This takes more knack than strength, unless the rivets are very large. Fix another brass curtain ring to the head with Araldite to hang it up by, making sure it is vertically above the stringing knots. If you don't have any Araldite, you could attach it by sewing through, using a coloured bead to hold the stitches from the front. The strongest method of all, though more conspicuous, would be to fix a rivet through the head and wire the curtain ring to that.

WHERE TO GET IT: SUPPLIERS' INDEX

Blind kits. In London these can be found at John Lewis, Oxford Street, W.1, the Army and Navy Stores, 105 Victoria Street, S.W.1, and Whiteleys, Queensway, W.2. These firms will deal with mail orders, but it might be quicker and cheaper to check whether the nearest big department store stocks the kits. Look in the local classified directory.

Brass strip. J. Smith & Sons, 50 St John's Square, Clerkenwell, London E.C.1, stock the half-round brass strip mentioned in the stair-rod table section. They normally deal with the trade but will supply to private customers.

Brass-headed nails, handles, etc. Beardmore & Co., 4 Percy Street, London W.1, is the Mecca for anyone in search of specialist brass fittings, nails, screws, etc. Worth making the trip because such things as brass-headed nails come considerably cheaper by the pound. Advisable to go on a weekday because the shop is packed with antique dealers, restorers and citizens on Saturday morning. Beardmore's have a wide selection of brass handles, knobs and castors, etc. in traditional styles, so it is a good place to go if you want to match up a missing period handle.

Calico, unbleached. Russell Trading Co., (*see* cambric). Also John Lewis, Oxford Street, London W.1, who have a good selection of basic stuffs like cotton sheeting, tailoring canvasses, 'doctor's flannel' in scarlet and cream, wadding for quilting.

Cambric, waxed. You can buy this or order it by post from the Russell Trading Co., 75 Paradise Street, Liverpool L1 3BP. They also supply materials for making your own duvets at 'keenest prices', and such useful items as unbleached calico, wadding, upholstery tools, curled hair, jute webbing in 18-yard rolls, piping cord in 16-ounce balls, lampshade tape in 36-yard rolls; cheaper than buying in small quantities. They will supply a catalogue on request. Mail orders are dealt with quickly in my experience. Postage comes extra.

Candles. For cheapest candle-making materials contact Candlemakers' Suppliers, 4 Beaconsfield Terrace, London W.14.

Cane. Split cane in all the various grades for recaning chairs can be ordered from Dryad Handicrafts (*see* marbling paper) plus any tools you might need. Or, if you live in London, get it at The Eaton Bag Co., 16 Manette Street, London W.1, who also deal with mail orders.

Cross-stitch rug. The Needlewoman Shop, 146 Regent Street, London W.1.

Danish carpet needle. Crafts Unlimited, 21 Macklin Street, London W.C.1. This is an excellent shop for slightly out-of-the-way craft tools and materials. They stock the bentwood boxes mentioned in the folk-art section at prices ranging from a few pence to £1, according to size. Also cotton balls (good for Christmas-tree decorations) and carpet adhesive in large tins. Try them too for bits and pieces to do with jewellery-making (clasps, shanks, etc.) and for special Deka paints for use on glass and ceramics which can be fired in a domestic oven. They will send a catalogue, and deal with mail orders.

Duvets. The Russell Trading Co. (*see* cambric) supply materials for the cover, also various grades of feather and down, or pure down, for the filling. They specialize in do-it-yourself duvets and will give useful advice on materials, sizes, etc.

Felt. The Felt & Hessian Shop, 34 Greville Street, London E.C.1, have a wide range of felts and hessians in different grades and excellent colours. They do a paper-backed hessian suitable for sticking on walls by the yard. They will deal with postal orders, and send a catalogue with samples on request.

Floorings, cheap. For coconut matting contact Jaymart Rubber and Plastics Ltd, one of the biggest importers, 39 Edgeworth Crescent, London N.W.4; telephone, 01–202 7531.

Printing felt – this *is* obtainable, with charm and persistence, from paper mills, where it is known as 'dry felt', off the rollers. Since it has to be collected in person, your best bet is to ring round local paper mills, for which see your Yellow Pages. London readers might start with Reed International.

Florentine papers. Paperchase, 216 Tottenham Court Road, London W.1, stock these, in beautiful small traditional designs and colourings: green, blue, red, brown on cream ground. Nice for replacing book endpapers. Also the most comprehensive range of decorative papers to be found anywhere.

Gilding. Transfer Gold Leaf and Dutch Metal, plus Writers' Gold Size for sticking it on with, can be found at George Rowney & Co. Ltd, 12 Percy

Street, London W.1, together with any other artists' materials mentioned in this book – oil and acrylic paints, gesso powder, Wallart, stencil board, picture varnish, etc. Outside London consult the Yellow Pages for the names of local artists' suppliers.

Leather. Many large department stores sell leather by the skin for making up into clothes. The Tannery Shop, Gomshall and Associated Tanneries, Queen Street, Gomshall, Surrey, will supply a wide range of skins – suedes, chamois, nappa leathers – direct from the tannery, which works out cheaper. Write for their price list and samples. J. Hewit & Sons, 89 St John Street, London E.C.1, stock decorative skins (e.g. watersnake) for trimmings. For whole or half hides for upholstery try Dryad's (*see* marbling paper) or Connolly Bros., 39 Chalton Street, London N.W.1. Dryad's stock all the tools you might need for leatherworking. Send for their catalogue.

Locker rug. Try Frank Herring Ltd, High Street, Dorchester, who still keep a stock of locker-rug requirements, as well as many other art and craft materials, tools and equipment. They will deal with postal inquiries.

Marbling paper. Dryad Handicrafts, Northgate, Leicester supply inks, ox gall, troughs, etc. This is the largest craft suppliers in the country, providing tools and materials for anything from bookbinding to woodcarving. Their excellent, copiously illustrated catalogue (supplied on request) is a good day's read in itself. The one snag with Dryad's is that most of their trade is with large institutions, and in bulk, so small private orders do sometimes take a while to come through. Try the beginning of the school holidays.

Perfecta paint remover. Buy this in large cans as sold to the trade from Gedge & Co. Ltd, French polish manufacturers, 88 John St, Clerkenwell, London E.C.1. Suppliers to the painting and decorating trade, they stock almost anything you can think of in this line, including emulsion glaze, wood fillers, bleaches, pumice powder, Scotch glue, brushes.

Universal Medium. Gedge & Co. Ltd, 88 John Street, London E.C.1; but any good decorators' merchants should stock it, or order it for you.

Upholstery suppliers. Tools and materials for upholstery can be difficult to track down. Dryad Handicrafts (*see* marbling paper) stock them, so does the Russell Trading Co. (*see* cambric), but if you live in or near London, or in Southern England, try Baxell Grant, 195a Upper Richmond Road, London S.W.15, who specialize in everything connected with do-it-yourself upholstery

– needles, twine, wadding, tools, etc. They will also cover buttons for a reasonable charge. Postal inquiries are dealt with very promptly, and the people there are helpful and informative.

Wallpaper trimmer. Write to the Ridgely Trimmer Co., 117 Clerkenwell Road, London E.C.1, for the names of the nearest stockist of the Ridgeley Champion. Alternatively, if you can make it to the Gray's Inn Road, James Parkin & Co., 188 Grays Inn Rd., will sell you one over the counter. Also suppliers to the painting and decorating trade, I found them very helpful and friendly over such questions as what brush to use for what, the proper grade of varnish, etc. They will order for you anything not in stock.

Some useful addresses:

ARTHUR BEALE LTD, 194 Shaftesbury Avenue, London W.C.2, stock glass mantles in various sizes for paraffin lamps. These can be difficult to track down, especially when there is a threat of power cuts. A yacht's chandlers, this is a fascinating shop to visit. A wide choice of oil and paraffin lamps, ropes, waterproof gear.

THE NEEDLEWOMAN SHOP, 146 Regent Street, London W.1, stock a wide range of items which you will find mentioned in the book, including rug and tapestry wools, canvas for embroidery, rug-making, etc., in a wide range of weights and widths, and 'crash' – a linen and cotton mixture used for making the adult's smock. The firm will supply a catalogue of their wares – useful if you do a lot of needlework and live outside the big cities. They have a mail order department but only deal with orders to the value of £3 and over.

J. PREEDY & SONS, 4A Ashland Place, London W.1 (off Marylebone High Street), sell special antiqued mirror-glass for replacing in valuable period frames. Handsome but very expensive. More usefully, perhaps, they will cut down a secondhand mirror to fit a period frame which would look wrong with bright new mirror-glass.

General Index

General Index

More about Penguins and Pelicans

Penguinews, which appears every month, contains
details of all the new books issued by Penguins as they
are published. From time to time it is supplemented by
Penguins in Print, which is our complete list of almost
5,000 titles.

A specimen copy of *Penguinews* will be sent to you
free on request. Please write to Dept EP, Penguin
Books Ltd, Harmondsworth, Middlesex, for your copy.

In the U.S.A.: For a complete list of books available
from Penguins in the United States write to Dept CS,
Penguin Books, 625 Madison Avenue, New York,
New York 10022.

In Canada: For a complete list of books available from
Penguins in Canada write to Penguin Books Canada
Ltd, 2801 John Street, Markham, Ontario L3R 1B4.

The Pauper's Cookbook

Jocasta Innes

Jocasta Innes dreamed of a cookery book planned for church mice. 'What greedy paupers needed above all, I felt, was a book where all the recipes were nice enough to be tempting but so cheap they would be painlessly trained to economize.' But no other indigent expert came forward to write it: so she has written it herself.

In *The Pauper's Cookbook* she has assembled a wealth (or should it be a poverty?) of recipes for meals costing between ten and twenty pence per head. Her collection of international, racially mixed and classless dishes promises good home cooking at 'Joe's Café' prices.

Some of the worst cooks waste hours on research: but *The Pauper's Cookbook* bypasses all that. You simply assess the 'cooking situation' and turn up the recommended treatment. The ffortescue-Smyths – or your parents – might call for Fancy Work; young Tomlinson and his dolly-bird, Fast Work; but the Joneses and all those children of theirs come in for Standards and Padding, including reconditioned leftovers. Thrifty tips on Programmed Eating (a week's meals at one session), on not eating (or dieting), and on Private Enterprise (or make-it-yourself) help to cut the costs; and Jocasta Innes starts right where the trouble begins – in the shops.

So leave it to the affluent to court indigestion at the Waldorf-Ritz: here's how to live it up in your own squalid tenement without recourse to poaching, rustling, guddling, scrumping or shop-lifting.

Self Help House Repairs Manual

Andrew Ingham

Given sufficient practical information, almost anyone can do their own house repairs, cheaply and efficiently.

This book covers all basic repairs: electricity – repairing existing installations, putting in a new circuit; water – hot and cold pipework, sinks, baths, lavatories; gas – water heaters, cookers, fires; general repairs – glazing, roofing, flooring, dry rot, plastering.